Punishment and Prisons

Power and the Carceral State

Steal a little and they throw you in jail;
Steal a lot and they make you king.

— Bob Dylan

I think we have to rescue the past. It's the old much-quoted saying, 'The struggle of people against power is the struggle of memory against forgetting'. We have to rescue the past, and we have to know the 'why' of things, because otherwise you can't combat it.

— Ken Loach

Show me a prison,
Show me a jail,
Show me a prison man,
Whose face is growing pale,
And I'll show you a young man,
With many reasons why,
And there but for fortune,
May go you or I,

— Phil Ochs

Punishment and Prisons

Power and the Carceral State

Joe Sim

Los Angeles | London | New Delhi
Singapore | Washington DC

First published 2009

SAGE Publications Ltd
1 Oliver's Yard
55 City Road
London EC1Y 1SP

SAGE Publications Inc.
2455 Teller Road
Thousand Oaks, California 91320

SAGE Publications India Pvt Ltd
B 1/I 1 Mohan Cooperative Industrial Area
Mathura Road
New Delhi 110 044

SAGE Publications Asia-Pacific Pte Ltd
33 Pekin Street #02-01
Far East Square
Singapore 048763

Library of Congress Control Number: 200893417

British Library Cataloguing in Publication data

A catalogue record for this book is available from the British Library

ISBN 978-0-7619-6003-4
ISBN 978-0-7619-6004-1 (pbk)

Typeset by CEPHA Imaging Pvt. Ltd., Bangalore, India
Printed in India at Replika Press Pvt Ltd
Printed on paper from sustainable resources

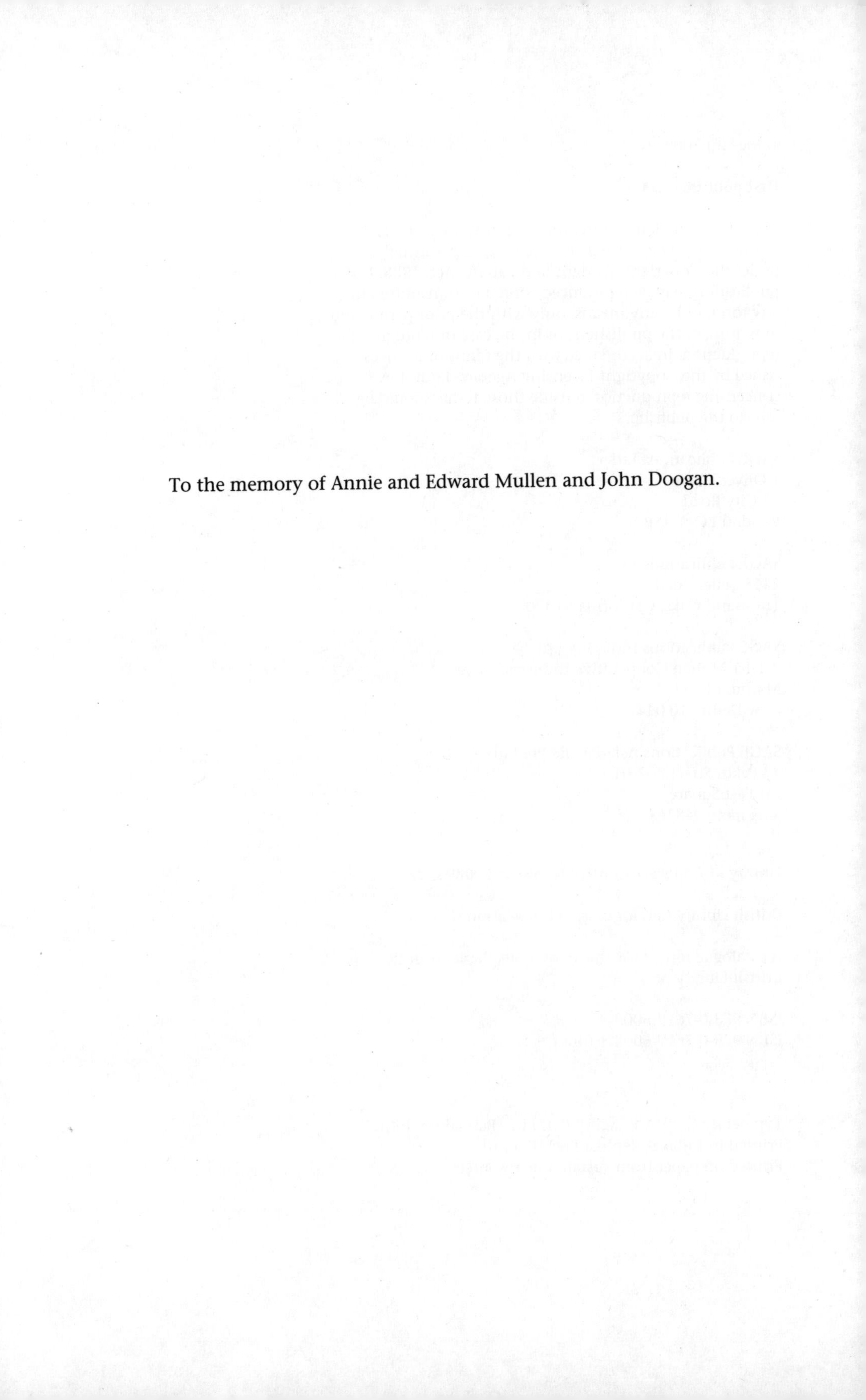

To the memory of Annie and Edward Mullen and John Doogan.

CONTENTS

ACKNOWLEDGEMENTS

In time-honoured fashion, I remain responsible for any errors in this book. At the same time, the following people contributed to the book more than they will ever know or, indeed, might want to know:

Eric Allison, Ove Andersen, Alana Barton, the late Ernie Buck, Tony Bunyan, Pat Carlen, Deborah Coles, Gerry Condon, Mary Corcoran, Karen Corteen, Mike Fitzgerald, Richard Fontenroy, Pete Giu, Paul Gilroy, Barry Goldson, Danielle Griffiths, Stuart Hall, Jeremy Hawthorne, Trevor Hemmings, Barbara Hudson, Jeff Hughes, the staff at INQUEST, Janet Jamieson, Niki Lacey, Barbara and Pieter Lawman, Dave Llewellyn (for the trips on the 'magic, swirling ship'), Bethan Loftus, Dave MacDonald, Gill McIvor, John Moore, Dave Morran, Martyn Nightingale, Teresa, Daniel, Paul and Paul O'Brien, Susan, Grace and James O'Malley, Tina Patel, Simon Pemberton, Hans Pedersen, David Scott, Helen Shaw, Gerry and Karen Sim, Tillie and Joe Sim, David Tyrer, Reece Walters, Tony Ward, Anne-Marie, Ricky, Jamie and Richie Webster, Joe Yates.

Special thanks to Kristi Ballinger for her technical skills and for reminding me of the Flintstones; and to Tia Ballinger for her radically different interpretation of the meaning of the 'archaeology of knowledge'.

I am particularly indebted to Roy Coleman, Paddy Hillyard, Mick Ryan, Steve Tombs and Dave Whyte for their personal and intellectual support over the years.

During the time it took to write this book, Chris Cain made me (semi) respectable; staff at The Elms and The Priory in Liverpool made me healthy; S.L. Jakubovic made me appreciate Colgate Total; and Ian Davis helped me quite literally to see better.

Julie Callaghan, Rhona McSporran, Sara Newton, Maria Ng, Kate Simmons and Mandy Vere from News from Nowhere bookshop in Liverpool provided an independent and critical space for buying and ordering books. It embodies everything a bookshop should be in challenging the desperate influence of, and shadow cast by, multinational bookstore chains.

Michael Simmonds in Conservative Central Office was extremely helpful in facilitating my access to the Conservative Party's library in Smith Square.

Catherine Fell at the Prison Service College Library provided excellent service and expedited any requests I had for books and articles. The staff in the libraries at Liverpool University and Liverpool John Moores University, especially Joan Shaw, also provided a first class and helpful service.

Acknowledgements

Thanks to the Research Committee in the School of Social Science, Liverpool John Moores University, for funding some teaching relief between January and May 2004.

Over the years, a number of institutions and organizations invited me to speak to their staff and students. This allowed me to think through some of the ideas in this book in environments which were challenging and critical. In particular, thanks to staff and students at the University of Central Lancashire (and to Keith Soothill for his attendance and comments), the University of Stirling and the University of Lincoln. Thanks also to those who attended lectures I gave to the Howard League for Penal Reform in Scotland and to the Rehabilitation and Research Centre for Torture Victims in Copenhagen for their critical input.

Antonio Gramsci said that football was 'the open-air kingdom of human loyalty'. The following people shared the great highs (the road to Seville in 2003; Tannadice, 22 May 2008) and the desperate lows (Fir Park, 22 May 2005) following Celtic: Danny Anderson, Brian Crommie, Jim, Bryan and Claire Crossan, Andy Gallagher, Monica Gallagher, Joe Gormley, Paddy Jackson, Ritchie Kelly, Martin Maxwell, Calum MacDougall, Robert McAbe, Alfie and James McAllister, Paul McCartan, Martin McFadden, Fran McStay, Chris Mullen, Tony Quail and Brian Toolan.

Bob Dylan's music, and different concerts on his 'never-ending tour', provided the perfect soundtrack during the seemingly never-ending years that it took to complete this book. John Bohanna's recordings of many of these concerts, as well as Dylan's XM Radio shows, helped me to get up in the 'jingle, jangle mornings' to keep writing.

Thanks to Gillian Stern and Miranda Nunhofer for supporting the initial proposal to SAGE.

Particular thanks to Caroline Porter at SAGE, who not only exhibited extraordinary patience and good humour in waiting for the finished text, but also made a number of very supportive and insightful comments as the manuscript took shape.

Finally, as ever, Anette Ballinger has been an intellectual and personal inspiration.

PREFACE

In the first decade of the new millennium, the production of criminology books and the pursuit of criminological knowledge have become fetishised commodities to be bought and sold in the marketplace of higher education. In the UK, the rabid and often unscrupulous search by universities for funding in response to the seemingly endless problems with resourcing their activities, the demand that knowledge be relevant to 'what works' in social policy terms and the rampant, psychologically withering managerialism embedded across higher education institutions, have increasingly compromised the role of academics as social and moral critics. What counts as knowledge (and its political converse, what does *not* count as knowledge) and, crucially, the uses to which knowledge is put (or indeed not put) have become the objects of a hybridized, often state-inspired system of surveillance and regulation to which many of the new breed of university managers have given their overt, and often brutal, support. At the same time, the academic producers of this knowledge have increasingly subjected themselves to a self-surveilling, self-censoring gaze in response to the iron grip of commodification that has swept through higher education (and other) public service institutions. Capitalist modernity has meant subsuming the social and the human to the dictates of a higher education, free market ideology that valorises conformity, individualism and objectification.

In making this point, it is not my intention to construct a reductive, conspiratorial position where *every* decision made, and *every* action taken by state servants and university managers, is determined by the invisible workings of a ruthless, capitalist political economy. As theorists such as Bob Jessop and Stuart Hall have long recognized, the state is a much more contingent and contradictory set of institutions than early Marxist writers argued. At the same time, it would be naïve to think about the relationship between criminological knowledge, universities and the state without considering the question of power and thus the material, political and ideological processes which have shaped and governed (and continue to shape and govern) criminology's development and application. It is also not my intention to present an idealistic vision of a previous era in which every publication in criminology, and every action undertaken by criminologists, were mobilized to challenge the state or the powerful. Indeed, historically, criminology as a discipline, as is now being increasingly recognized, has been yoked to the state with respect to the restricted ideological definitions of crime within which the majority of its practitioners have operated, which, in turn, have underpinned the reformist policies that they have pursued (Hillyard and Tombs, 2004). Additionally, state servants have often used criminological research to inform their often philistine policies and practices.

It is also clear that the regulation of research and individual self-censorship have long preceded the rise of neoliberal managerialism as a governing discourse in criminology. My point is that these processes have been intensified and compounded in the last three decades as the politics and practices of neoliberalism have become consolidated in the hearts and minds of the governing class in the UK, of whatever political persuasion. They have also been intensified by intellectually and spiritually corrosive developments such as the Research Assessment Exercise (RAE), which have become so institutionalized in higher education that for younger scholars in particular, it often appears less career-threatening to challenge the scientific claim that the earth revolves around the sun than to confront the often vapid claims made by defenders of the exercise that this is an objective test of academic worth, esteem and scholarship.

At the same time, as with any social process, the current bleak situation is contradictory. The fact that this book has been produced at all indicates that however unrelenting neoliberal policies might be, there are spaces and gaps that nurture and sustain critical, academic work. Indeed, one of the great paradoxes of the last three decades has been the rich and stimulating research that has been produced by critical thinkers and scholars, from a range of diverse backgrounds and persuasions, who have challenged the theoretical and methodological supremacy of administrative and conventional criminology.

This book is designed to contribute to that critical tradition and follows Foucault's observation that books should be seen as 'instrument[s] ... in a real struggle' (Foucault, cited in de Folter, 1987: 44) It seeks to chart the continuities in penal policy, and the role and place of the prison as an arena of often unrelenting punishment and pain, from the mid-1970s to the first decade of the new millennium in a land that has had to contend with the psychological immiseration and social detritus generated by the brutal exigencies of neoliberalism. The book also suggests that the 'real struggle' around prisons should be conducted from an abolitionist perspective if the institution's nefarious influence on the confined, on those staff trying to provide humane and decent care and on the debates around law and order more generally, is to be contested, undermined and replaced by an alternative vision of penality that both heals the individual offender and protects the wider society.

I finally finished writing the text at a time of intensive media coverage of the 40th anniversary of the 'year of the barricades' – 1968. That year was also hugely significant for criminology with the formation of the radical National Deviancy Conference (NDC), which sought to provide a forum for a more critically engaged, politically interventionist criminology. It is therefore fitting to close this preface with a quote from Stan Cohen's Introduction to the first collection of papers, published by the NDC in 1971 under the title, *Images of Deviance.* In his usual perceptive and prescient manner, Cohen noted that, 'Sociologists are increasingly becoming traders in definitions: they hawk their versions of reality around to whoever will buy them. There is a responsibility to make such definitions not only intelligible, consistent and aesthetically satisfactory, *but also human*' (Cohen, 1971: 24, emphasis added). Forty years on, Cohen's words remain utterly relevant to a world that is still devoid of the human and the humane. According to some, usually politicians, it is a world which has changed beyond recognition, even redemption. However, as this book illustrates, with respect to the prison, the justifications mobilized to defend its continuing existence, and the population the institution incapacitates for often-brutal interventions, it is a world that has hardly changed at all.

Joe Sim
Liverpool
June 2008

1

CONTINUITY AND CONTESTATION IN PENAL POLITICS

> History ... can help to pierce through the rhetoric that ceaselessly presents the further consolidation of carceral power as a 'reform'. As much as anything else, it is this suffocating vision of the past that legitimizes the abuses of the present and seeks to adjust us to the cruelties of the future (Ignatieff, 1978: 220).

In 1979, in a typically elliptical and tantalising remark, Michel Foucault cautioned against becoming nostalgic about the criminal justice system. For Foucault:

> ... twenty years ago, or even a century ago, criminal justice was neither better organised nor more respectful ... The transformations that are taking place before our eyes, and which sometimes leave us baffled, ought not to make us nostalgic. It is enough to take them seriously: we need to know where we are heading and to take note of that which we refuse to accept for the future (Foucault, 1988: 159–160).

Foucault's scepticism towards viewing the criminal justice system through the lens of nostalgia provides the starting point for this book. It is concerned with contesting the histories of punishment that have become prominent in criminology with respect to developments in penal policy since the mid-1970s. Central to these histories has been the emphasis on shifts and discontinuities in the apparatus of punishment, underpinned and legitimated by a political and populist hostility to offenders. Punishment, it is argued, has shifted towards managing the dangers and risks posed by feral collectivities rather than integrating malfunctioning individuals back into the welfare comfort blanket of rehabilitative social democracy. This well-known and influential analysis was developed initially in Malcolm Feeley and Jonathan Simon's seminal article, published in 1992 (Feeley and Simon, 1992), and was further refined by David Garland in 2001 in his influential book *The Culture of Control* (Garland, 2001). However, while this work has contributed significantly to the sociological understanding of contemporary punitive trends through detailing their individual impact and wider social ramifications (Pratt et al., 2005), the analysis developed in this book follows a different theoretical and methodological trajectory. There are four dimensions to this trajectory that I want to explore in this introductory chapter: continuity and discontinuity in penal policy and practices; the role of reform, rehabilitation and social welfare discourses in prison; contestations and challenges to penal power; and finally the question of abolitionism as an organizing, conceptual framework for analysing the social problem of modern penal arrangements.

Continuity and discontinuity

As noted above, the analysis developed by new penologists concerning epochal discontinuity and the forward march of a more retributive, denunciatory and mortifying discourse of punishment, fuelled by the new right's economic, social and cultural ascendancy in Western Europe and North America in the 1970s, has been theoretically significant with respect to recent academic debates around the modern prison. In John Pratt's evocative phrase, neoliberal social arrangements have ushered in the 'return of the wheelbarrow men' (Pratt, 2000). However, as Ian Loader and Richard Sparks have pointed out, the emphasis on shift and discontinuity not only 'frequently betrays a tendency to construct a straw version of the past' through establishing 'some rather unhelpful binary oppositions' but also this explanatory model:

> ... run[s] the risk of doing violence to the past, of underplaying its tensions and conflicts, of inadvertently re/producing one-dimensional – implicitly rose-tinted – accounts of both the history and politics of penal modernism, and the reasons for its (apparent) demise (Loader and Sparks, 2004: 14–15)[1].

As they suggest:

> ... we need to revisit the terrain ... Garland maps with a more quizzical *historical* sensibility. Such a sensibility would be minded to think seriously about the past. It would be actively oriented towards historical investigation and interpretation. It would,

> in short, seek to grapple with the contours and conflicts of crime control in the latter half of the twentieth century *in their own terms*, while at the same time remaining attuned to the trajectories of competing practices, ideologies and ideas and the legacy particular signal events and conflicts bequeath to us today (2004: 15, emphasis in the original).

In addition, the theoretical and political orientation of the discontinuity thesis is built on a reductive periodization with respect to developments in modern penal policy.[2] It conceptualizes these developments as a long march which originated in the reforming 1890s, consolidated in the rehabilitative 1950s and 1960s and culminated in the 1970s with the punitive turn alluded to above (Garland, 2001). According to Mark Brown, this account is problematic in that it is based on the supposition that 'there is something distinctly late-modern about the recent rise in penal excess'. For Brown, the theoretical and empirical focus should be on 'the existence of cyclical or recursive trends within penal modernity'. Thus, 'a more satisfactory explanation of recent trends may ... be one which emphasizes various tools in the armoury of modern government, tools that are general features of this form of government rather than particular responses to specific events' (Brown, 2002: 415). Similarly, Yvonne Jewkes and Helen Johnston have pointed out that the punitive policies pursued in the late twentieth century, 'bear remarkable similarities to the conditions of the mid nineteenth century'. These policies included prolonged periods of solitary confinement, military interventions to suppress prisoner demonstrations and the use of photographic surveillance 'to trace repeat offenders, all of which beg the question: just how "new" *is* the "new punitiveness?"' (Jewkes and Johnston, 2006: 287, emphasis in the original).[3]

A further problem with the discontinuity thesis lies in its tendency to read the social history of the prison as an account from above. As such, it relies on official documents, papers and statements, which construct a narrative account of this history from the perspective of the powerful individuals who were responsible for developing penal policy and ensuring, at least in theory, its implementation. Consequently, accounts from below – prisoners' autobiographies and letters, as well as documents and publications from prisoners' rights organizations – are either missing or marginalized in this narrative. Prisoners' autobiographies, which began to appear in the late 1860s, and which have continued into the twenty-first century, articulate a very different version of penal 'truth' to the reality depicted in official prison documents. As Alyson Brown and Emma Clare have noted, the subjective accounts of prisoners concentrate on the deeply embedded rationalities of punishment that govern their everyday lives. Consequently:

> ... in the context of net–widening penal policy and overcrowded penal institutions of the early twenty-first century it seems appropriate to re-emphasize the extent to which the experience of the prison can be psychologically and physically damaging. *Such an analysis also highlights that through all the changes in policy and practice during*

the nineteenth and twentieth centuries, the experience is one more marked by continuity than change (Brown and Clare, 2005: 50, emphasis added).

These accounts also challenge the idea that rehabilitative discourses have *ever* been an institutionalized presence in the everyday, working lives of prison officers or the landing culture that legitimates and sustains their often-regressive ideologies and punitive practices. They indicate that prisons remained invisible places of physical hardship and psychological shredding throughout the twentieth century. It was a system of punishment and pain underpinned by the nonaccountable power of prison officer discretion. Thus, even when the privilege of talking was introduced into the prison system:

> Prisoner autobiographies suggest that the formal, and crucially discretionary, introduction of the privilege to talk had altered little in practice – the use of discretion whether to punish talking continued to be used as a control mechanism whatever the regulations formally stated (2005: 57).

Reform and rehabilitation: rhetoric and reality

For those who managed the criminal justice system in the immediate post-war period – 'the platonic guardians' – there was a deeply held belief in the process of rehabilitation which 'came ... to be contingently attached during the mid-twentieth century to what one civil servant called "the project of being civilized ..."' (Loader, 2006: 561 and 565). There are three points to be made about this 'civilizing' project. First, implicit within this project is a vision of a society built on consensual, communitarian integration, which was regulated magically by informal mechanisms of social control that, in turn, were orientated towards the benevolent reintegration of the deviant. However, in post-war Britain, for subordinate groups such as women, newly arrived immigrants, gay men and lesbian women, this sepia-tinted nostalgia bore little relation to the often violent reality of their everyday lives. For victims of domestic violence, for example:

> Those who can remember the 1940s and 1950s will probably be able to recall the moral censure, the embarrassment, the shame and the cultural 'disguising' that often accompanied the issue. During this period, women suffering domestic violence had no one to turn to, except perhaps themselves, nowhere to go, no agencies, no safe havens, few housing, medical and social services, no counselling centres, no publicity or media coverage, not much in the way of legal remedies and very little help from the police who, until recent improvements which have so far had mixed and uneven effects, traditionally regarded a man's home indisputably as his castle (Hague and Wilson, 1996: 7–8).

More specifically, behind the project lurked a deeply punitive array of policies and practices that were carried out in the name of rehabilitation and reform across different institutions. They ranged from using drugs such as crystal methamphetamine through to experimenting with LSD (lysergic acid diethylamide) on women suffering with post natal depression or postrape trauma (Mortimer, 2006) and onto electroconvulsive therapy, leucotomies and outright physical brutality (Sim, 1990).[4]

Second, believing in a project built on civilizing the social detritus is clearly not the same as either seeing this belief being put into practice or indeed having the power to ensure that this belief *is* put into practice. As Frances Fox Piven has pointed out, not only is policy decision-making a complex business but also crucially 'the importance of informal and discretionary processes of implementation' (Piven, 2004: 83) should be considered, and their consequences analysed, if a fully comprehensive analysis of social policy implementation is to be undertaken. Furthermore, as noted above, it was those who staffed penal and other institutions who had the discretion, and therefore, the power to choose whether or not to mobilize and implement supportive and inclusive policies of rehabilitation and reform. In practice, the majority of prison officers chose not to do so. Instead, they inhabited and supported a landing culture that was (and is) central to maintaining the often-vulpine and mortifying order of their respective institutions (Sim, 2008a).

Lucia Zedner has also indicated that even at the historical moment when the discourse of welfare was at its most intense 'it is questionable whether it dominated practice in the way that [David] Garland suggests ... the fine remained the most frequently used penal sanction'. Zedner continues:

> This points to an interesting disjuncture between the promotion of welfarism as a political ideal and a continuing commitment by the courts to classical legalism. The criminal law has always been retributivist in its orientation, resting on the presumption of the responsible subject and geared towards the attribution of culpability. To focus on the prevailing rhetoric of welfarism, as opposed to its law and practice, overlooks the persistent commitment to classical legalism that might partly explain the later "revival" of retributivism (Zedner, 2002: 344–345).

Finally, if the discourse of social welfare was so important to prison regimes up to the 1970s, as official accounts and new penologists claim, why was this discourse not institutionalized in the everyday practices of the prison system? Or to put the question another way, why have those programmes which have had a positive impact on offending behaviour (in other words they have 'worked'), been drastically subverted by the discourses of pain and punishment which underpin and give meaning to the everyday experiences of many of the confined? Raising this question casts serious doubts on Martinson's much cited and hugely influential phrase, 'nothing works' (Martinson, 1974). According to accepted criminological wisdom, for the new right, Martinson's research legitimated their demand for a more retributive penal policy; for liberal and critical prison scholars this research signalled the death of the rehabilitative ideal. However, this misses a fundamental point. Rehabilitation policies never worked because, in the majority of penal institutions, they were *never* actually put into practice. Those institutions that did work – the Barlinnie Special Unit – or which continue to work – Grendon Underwood – places whose working practices did not, and do not subscribe to the dominant retributive penal discourses, were either closed down or have remained marginal to the 'real' business of the prison system which is the delivery of pain and punishment. I shall return to this point in Chapter 7.

Contesting the power to punish

David Brown has argued that while the accounts which have emphasized discontinuity and shift, 'have enriched and revitalized penology, reconnecting it with broader social theory ...' he has also noted that 'there are tendencies in some of them which result in minimizing the extent of contestation in penal and criminal justice struggles ...'(Brown, 2005: 28 and 42). In highlighting the contestability of penal power, Brown is pointing to an important issue which again is missing in the various analyses that emphasise convulsive, epochal ruptures in the punitive mentality. This has resulted in an 'over-reading [of] the return of cultures and practices of cruelty and the pervasiveness of punitiveness; and in [an] underplaying [of] the resilience of penal welfarism and its social democratic heritage' (2005: 42). For Brown, welfare ideologies have *not* been obliterated by the punitive turn engendered by the emergence of a new right-led social and penal authoritarianism. Rather, they have retained their place as subjugated discourses within modern penal arrangements.

Prison medical care provides a paradigmatic example of this contradictory and conflictual process in the sense that while prisoners have historically and contemporaneously been subjected to the full punitive gaze of a medical profession that has treated them as less eligible subjects in need of control and restraint, *some* medical staff have resisted the dominant punitive discourse and attempted to implement policies and practices which provided support and empathy for the confined, even in the mid-1990s, when the punitive turn, theoretically, was at its most intense in England and Wales (Sim, 2002).[5] Thus, the survival of welfare ideologies, and their restraining impact on the prison's 'punitive obsession' (Playfair, 1971) should be considered if the complexity of contemporary penal arrangements are to be fully understood. Lucia Zedner has made a similar point with respect to the ongoing, reforming role of groups such as probation officers, who, in the 1980s and 1990s, continued to work towards the goal of rehabilitation, 'albeit in a markedly less benign political environment' (Zedner, 2002: 346).

Furthermore, the punitive power of the prison has also been contested by the interventions and hegemonic impact of radical prisoners' rights organizations in England and Wales, which emerged in the early 1970s and which have continued to campaign and organize into the twenty-first century. These groups – *The National Prisoners' Movement (PROP), Radical Alternatives to Prison (RAP), Women in Prison (WIP), INQUEST* and most recently *No More Prison* – have provided a focal point for resisting the encroachment of penal power into the lives of the confined while impacting hegemonically on traditional, liberal prison reform groups by pulling them onto a more critical and radical terrain (Sim, 1994a). In the case of *INQUEST*, the organization's challenge to the negative ideological construction of those who have died in the custody of the state, *as well as* the policy changes it has helped to instigate, provides a paradigmatic example of hegemonic contestability in action. The challenges posed by these groups, and their capacity for exploiting the contradictions and contingencies in the operationalization of state power, are a recurring theme in this book, for they raise significant theoretical and political questions, not only about how current penal arrangements can be radically transformed but also about the limitations of state power, despite the intensification in its authoritarian tendencies over the last three decades.

Developing an abolitionist position[6]

The final strand that underpins this book is the use of an abolitionist perspective in order to frame and develop its central arguments. In particular, the book illustrates not only how theories and concepts articulated by different writers in the abolitionist tradition can help to explain the role of the modern prison more analytically, but also how abolitionism can offer radical policy solutions, which both critique and transcend what currently passes for penal policy in England and Wales. What are the distinguishing features of this position? There are three of them that I want to highlight here.

First, there is the issue (or rather the problem) of liberal reform and the role played by liberal prison reform groups in buttressing the ideological and material power of penal institutions. As Foucault has pointedly made clear, since its emergence at the end of the eighteenth century, the modern prison has not only been tirelessly critiqued but also has been subjected to endless reforms which have attempted to alleviate the failure of the institution to achieve its stated, overt goals of crime prevention, individual and collective deterrence and the reform or rehabilitation of the offender. Despite these critiques, the institution has always been offered as the solution to its own problems: '... word for word, from one century to the other, the same fundamental propositions are repeated ... So successful has the prison been that, after a century and a half of "failures", the prison still exists, producing the same results *and there is the greatest reluctance to dispense with it*' (Foucault, 1979: 270 and 277, emphasis added).

Therefore, in analysing developments in penal policy since 1974, this book challenges much of the accepted liberal (and indeed criminological) wisdom that there are distinct differences between those at the centre of penal policy making, for example, between 'liberal' Home Secretaries such as William Whitelaw and 'reactionary' populists such as Michael Howard. From an abolitionist perspective, both stand on the same ideological terrain in that they support the continuing presence of the prison as a bulwark against the criminality and disorderly behaviour of the powerless. The gap between these individuals, and between the Conservative and (Old and New) Labour parties more generally, is miniscule, their political position on prisons being dominated by what Freud called 'the narcissism of minor differences' (cited in Gray, 2005: 36).

Thus, the liberal obsession with *which* individuals hold *what* positions within the government and the state, and the concomitant need to continually lobby these individuals and their officials in order to generate changes in the system, inevitably leads to omitting detailed consideration of broader structural configurations which transcend the ideologies and idiosyncrasies of individuals and whichever office they hold. Central to these structural configurations is the material role of the modern prison, as a *state* institution, intimately connected with the reproduction of an unequal and unjust social order divided by the social lacerations of class, gender, 'race', age and sexuality.

For abolitionists, the prison is involved in the complex process of defending and reproducing these social divisions. Like the other coercive arms of the state – the police, courts and the military – it is concerned with what has been called 'the materialization of order' (Mitchell, cited in Coleman and Sim, 2005: 103). The fact that abolitionists recognize the complex interrelationship between the prison, the state and the wider social order, clearly distinguishes their position from liberal reformists, whose theoretical, political and policy emphasis is focussed on the plurality of power relationships, the progressive nature of benevolent reform and the magnanimity of the majority of state servants whose everyday work with prisoners is, it is wrongly contended, besmirched by the recalcitrant activities of a few, maladjusted prison officers.

Importantly, taking an abolitionist position does not mean conceptualizing the state in instrumental terms. As Bob Jessop has noted, the state is not: 'a unified, unitary, coherent ensemble or agency ... the state does not exercise power: its powers ... are activated through the agency of definite political forces in specific conjunctures. It is not the state, which acts: it is always specific sets of politicians and state officials located in specific parts of the state system. It is they who activate specific powers and state capacities inscribed in particular institutions and agencies' (Jessop, 1990: 366–367). Jessop's model of state power captures the essence of abolitionist thinking with respect to recognizing that the state's sphere of action, and its influence, is often contingent, contradictory and unpredictable. I shall return to this point in Chapter 8.

Second, for abolitionists, the prison is a place of soul-crunching punishment and pain for the economically and politically powerless, many of whom are confined in the acrid stagnation of local prisons. This has specific relevance for thinking about the sociology of punishment, the continuities between different historical epochs with respect to what groups and which behaviour has *always* been punished and the central role of the prison in the delivery and distribution of that punishment, a point I return to throughout this book, particularly with respect to the construction of prisoners as less eligible subjects who *deserve* punishment. Allied to this is the modern prison's ideological role in the assertion and reassertion of the dominant discourses around crime, what Thomas Mathiesen called 'the diverting function of imprisonment' (Mathiesen, 1974: 77). As different chapters indicate, since the mid-1970s (and indeed long before that time period), politicians and policy makers have focussed on the disorderly and depraved world of sub-groups of the poor and powerless whose depredations, it is argued, need to be controlled through criminal justice interventions, one of which is the prison. For those who have ruthlessly (and, in many ways, hopelessly) governed the society in the last three decades, the iconic and symbolic status of the prison is paramount. It is an institution which retains a deeply embedded ideological presence in the interpellated, individual subjectivity and collective consciousness of the governing class and a professional elite who, as Hywel Williams has argued, utilize and tolerate 'methods ... to enforce both discipline and distance behind prison walls which involves complacency and cruelty – complacency about the consequences of imprisonment and a cruelly class-based understanding of what makes a criminal' (Williams, 2006: 154).

Conversely, the massive and systemic social harms and collective depredations engendered by the activities of the powerful – individuals, organizations, institutions and states – have remained, and still remain, virtually ignored, not only within the world view of liberal reform groups but also within mainstream criminology and, not surprisingly, within the state itself. Therefore, while a powerful figure will occasionally be imprisoned, and while there are limitations placed on the corrosive activities of the powerful by criminal and civil law, and even by the often-insipid interventions of state servants, these interventions are socially and politically constrained, usually to the point of invisibility. As Steven Box argued over twenty five years ago: 'not only does the state with the help and reinforcement of its control agencies, criminologists, and the media conceptualize a particular and partial ideological version of serious crime and who commits it, but it does so by concealing and hence mystifying its own propensity for violence and serious crimes on a much larger scale' (Box, 1983: 14). Paddy Hillyard and Steve Tombs have developed this argument further:

> Many events and incidents which cause serious harm are either not part of the criminal law or, if they could be dealt with by it, are either ignored or handled without resort to it ... corporate crime, domestic violence and sexual assault and police crimes [are] all largely marginal to dominant legal, policy enforcement, and indeed academic agendas, yet at the same time [they create] widespread harm, not least among already disadvantaged and powerless peoples. There is little doubt, then, that the undue attention given to events, which are defined as crimes, distracts attention away from

more serious harm. But it is not simply that a focus on crime *deflects* attention from other more socially pressing harms – in many respects it positively *excludes* them (Hillyard and Tombs, 2004: 13, emphasis in the original).

Both Conservative and New Labour governments have had everything to say about the crimes of the powerless and the punishment that powerless individuals should receive. In contrast, they have had very little to say about crimes of the powerful and what should be done about them, despite the huge social costs that their depredations inflict. In 2002, the annual cost of crime was £35 billion. Embezzlement accounted for 40 per cent of this figure. Recorded white collar crime increased by 500 per cent during the year, while there was a 7 per cent drop in burglary and robbery. Additionally, despite the fierce political assertions that law and order needed to prevail against the encroachment of the depraved, deprived and dangerous, judges were not extending this rhetoric towards middle class offenders. Those with jobs and reputations, it was argued, had more to lose than those with little economic or political status (Riddell, 2003).

In terms of the tax system, in the 20 years up to May 1996, a period which covered both Labour and Conservative administrations, 'the accountants Deloitte & Touche ... calculated that taxes out of which the Crown had been swindled ... totalled £2 trillion, or £2,000 billion at current [1998] prices. This colossal figure counts in tax evasion only, and takes no account of tax avoidance, practised on a huge scale by corporations' (Elliott and Atkinson, 1998: 99).[7] In the three months up to March 2007, '67 new types of tax avoidance scheme[s] were notified under "disclosure" rules introduced three years ago, most of them pushed by the big accountancy and law firms' (*Private Eye*, 14–27 September 2007).[8]

By the end of 2005, corporate fraud and corruption was costing UK businesses 6 per cent of their annual revenue: 'put in terms of the UK's GDP, that is equivalent to undetected and unreported fraud costing businesses over £72 billion every year' (de Reya, 2005: 1).[9] The figures concerning money laundering were equally compelling. Of the $1trillion laundered through Western banks and companies in 2001:

> Approximately half of that sum is generated by violent criminal activity, such as organized trafficking in drugs, weapons, or people. The other half is illegal flight capital – tax-evading money derived from kickbacks, bribes, falsified invoices, and sham transactions by overseas nationals who place that money into outside secure accounts, mostly in U.S. institutions. Whether the individual behind these ill-gotten gains is a murderous "godfather," a corrupt government official, or a tax-evading but respectable executive, it's important to understand that they all use the same process to launder their money (Harvard Business School, 2001: no page number).

At the same time, individuals and institutions in Britain accounted for over £300 billion of the $2,500 billion laundered internationally each year (Sikka, 2006: 32).

Additionally, middle class crime was (and remains) widespread. The middle class not only engaged in a range of serious illegalities but they also refused to recognize the rule of law, and indeed, were often contemptuous of the law and its application:

> Citizens discuss justifications and techniques for committing crimes of everyday life with considerable ease in pubs, with friends and with neighbours. This creates a moral climate that encourages such types of behaviour right in the centre of society ... ongoing encouragement of entrepreneurial comportment and pursuit of self-interest has its price in terms of market anomie, which shows itself in the centre of society, not at its margins. The 'law-abiding majority', which politicians like to address, is a chimera. The crimes of everyday life that they commit are perhaps less worrying than the contempt for laws and rules and the accompanying cynical attitudes that are spreading among those who think of themselves as respectable citizens (Karstedt and Farrall, 2007: 7–8).

How have successive governments responded to crimes committed by the powerful? In 2001, the UK was the only member of the *Organisation for Economic Cooperation and Development (OECD)*, which had failed to pass legislation making it illegal to bribe officials of a foreign country.[10] This offence was created under the *Antiterrorism, Crime and Security Act* of 2001. By March 2007, no prosecutions had taken place. In contrast to the legislation that targeted and focussed on crimes of the powerless, the introduction to a government consultation paper, published in 2005, indicated that 'change in the law represented a positive step forward – our aim always was to change attitudes and behaviour, not fill the courts' (cited in Pallister, 2007: 38). This theme is developed in subsequent chapters through an exploration of the 'anti-statist strategy' (Hall, 1988: 152) pursued by both Conservative and New Labour governments since the mid-1970s with respect to the powerful and their activities.

The third dimension in abolitionist thought highlighted here concerns the issue of resistance and contestation. Critics have long accused abolitionists of being idealistic utopians with respect to crime and punishment. For Roger Matthews, abolitionists have adopted an 'anarcho-communist position' and have been 'preoccupied with abolishing or minimizing state intervention rather than attempting to make it more effective, responsive and accountable' (Matthews, cited in Sim, 1994a: 265). However, since the 1970s, and contrary to Matthews' argument, abolitionists *have* been deeply involved in activist interventions across the penal spectrum, which attempted to make the prison 'more effective, responsive and accountable'. These interventions can be seen in the various successful campaigns in which abolitionists have been directly involved or which have been underpinned by an abolitionist theoretical position and political strategy. They have included: the closure of the secretly established, mind-wrecking Control Units in the mid 1970s; the abolition of the prison medical service in the early 1990s; and the ongoing legal changes instigated to support the families of those who have died in state custody, primarily instigated by *INQUEST*, with the support of many of those who had been involved in the first British abolitionist group, *Radical Alternatives to Prison* (Ryan, 1996). The theoretical starting point, and political finishing point, for these campaigns are quite distinct from more liberal, reformist strategies in these areas, with the concomitant danger of state incorporation that taking a liberal position entails. Therefore, central to this book's argument is an understanding of abolitionism as a hegemonic force, which is generated by, and responds to, the 'contingent, fundamentally open-ended' nature of politics (Hall, 1988: 169). Abolitionist praxis can be seen as part of the struggle to develop a radical discourse around law, order, crime and punishment; in Gramscian terms, as an attempt to replace 'common sense' with 'good sense' (1988: 142 and 169). It is also a praxis, which has impacted hegemonically on more traditional penal reform groups, leading them onto a more critical terrain with respect to penal policy. These themes are explored more fully in Chapter 7.

This chapter began with a quotation from Foucault and concludes with another taken from an interview that was published in June 1984, the month of his death. Here Foucault talked about the role of the *Groupe d'Information sur les Prisons* (GIP), the radical prisoners' rights group formed in France in 1971. He argued that the GIP was a '"problematizing" venture, an effort to make problematic, to call into question, presumptions, practices, rules, institutions, and habits that had lain undisturbed for many decades. This effort targeted the prison itself, but through it, also penal justice, the law, and punishment in general' (Foucault, 1984/2002: 394). Over two decades later, Foucault's words remain entirely and poignantly relevant to thinking about prisons in the early twenty-first century. By 'problematizing' contemporary structures of punishment, scholars and activists conversely can make them unproblematic for the confined and thereby make a difference both with respect to the political complacency that surrounds them and the individual pain and collective misery that inhabits them.

Notes

1 Thanks to Mick Ryan for pointing out this reference to me. George Rigakos and Richard Hadden have also argued that while there might be evidence of an emerging 'new times', which includes the rise of the service sector, significant changes in the means of communication and in the processing of information 'and even the continued refinement of risk technology …' there are significant areas within the capitalist economic system which, in their view, shows signs of 'far more continuity than change …' (Rigakos and Hadden, 2001: 79–80).

2 In political science, similar critiques have been made, particularly with respect to the methodological problems surrounding reductive comparisons between different historical epochs. See Mackie and Marsh (1995).

3 Roger Matthews has also argued that the key terms in this debate such as '"punitiveness" and "populism" remain largely undefined'. Additionally, 'since the deployment of punitive sanctions has historically been an endemic feature of the criminal justice system we are faced with the question of "what is new?"' (Matthews, 2005: 175).
4 In Canada, prisoners were also used 'in a number of ... experiments, including clinical trials for pharmaceutical companies' (Osborne, 2006: 284). Thanks to Kathy Kendall for pointing out this reference to me. It is also worth remembering the brutal, physical methods mobilized by the British state in their 'colonies' during this time. See, for example, Anderson (2005) and Elkins (2005) on the use of punishment in Kenya and Hillyard (1987) for an analysis of the British state's coercive strategies in Northern Ireland.
5 Steven Hutchinson also cautions against seeing 'the current state of affairs as completely new, and as catastrophically different from "modern" rehabilitation. Rather, punishment and reform can be seen as always braiding together variously in modern liberal penality. Marked punitiveness during rehabilitation's heyday, as well as the recent emergence of important (transformed) correctional projects demonstrates this characteristic braiding. Even if there seems to be an overall expansion of punitivenss and a retraction of correctionalism in some jurisdictions, it is important not to confuse jurisdictional trends with global (or western) ones, or to ignore counter-currents to what is (mis)perceived as an unstoppable wave of control' (Hutchinson, 2006: 459–460).
6 This section draws on arguments developed elsewhere in Sim (1994a, 2004a, 2006a) and in Ryan and Sim (2007). As I have argued elsewhere, it is important to recognize that abolitionism 'is not a homogenous theoretical and political movement but varies across cultures'. Thus, there are a number of distinct differences between the abolitionist movement in England and Wales and the abolitionist movement in Europe. In particular, British abolitionists have 'advocated engaging in more interventionist work to develop a "criminology from below"' (Sim, 2006a: 3).
7 In March 2005, the Tax Justice Network estimated that globally 'there was an annual tax loss of approximately $255 billion resulting from wealthy individuals holding their assets offshore'. The Network's research suggested that. 'approximately US$11.5 trillion of assets are held offshore by high-net-worth individuals; the annual income that these assets might earn amounts to US$860 billion annually [and that] the tax not paid as a result of these funds being held offshore might exceed US$255 billion each year' (Tax Justice Network, 2005: 2 and 1). *The Observer* called this document 'the most authoritative study of the wealth held in offshore accounts ever conducted'. The newspaper quoted a member of the Network who argued that, 'This is one of the defining crises of our times. One of the most fundamental changes in our society in recent years is how money and the rich have become more mobile. This has resulted in the wealthy becoming less inclined to associate with normal society and feeling no obligation to pay taxes' (*The Observer*, 27 March 2005). The common view that tax evasion is a 'victimless' crime has been challenged in a report by Christian Aid, which noted that the 'illegal trade-related tax evasion will be responsible for *5.6 million deaths* of young children in the developing world between 2000 and 2015. That is almost 1,000 a day. Half are already dead' (Christian Aid, 2008: 2, emphasis in the original).
8 In taking this position, it is important to recognize that abolitionists, at least in the UK, have not condoned conventional criminal activity or underestimated its

impact on the powerless. The sterile debate around crime, which dominated critical criminology in the 1980s was based on a 'straw man' version of the work of both critical criminologists and abolitionists (Sim et al., 1987). The key point here is recognizing the indisputable sociological fact that the prison remains the big house for the poor and the powerless no matter what illegal activities the powerful may or may not engage in.

9 Given New Labour's obsession with evaluation studies, and the management of risk with respect to the crimes of the powerless, the comments made Gary Miller, a partner in Mischon de Reya, provide an ironic comment on this obsession: 'Corporate Britain is failing to accurately evaluate and effectively manage the risk of fraud' (cited in *The Observer*, 20 November 2005).

10 In terms of violence more generally, Wayne Morrison, has pointed out that in the twentieth century the number of people killed by state-sponsored massacres or 'other forms of deliberate death' was between 167 and 175 million. This figure excluded *'military personnel and civilian casualties of war* ...' Importantly, '... the vast majority of the people who caused the deaths of the 167–175 million persons ... were not subjected to criminal justice processes or penality ...' (Morrison, 2005: 294, emphasis in the original).

2

LAW, ORDER AND THE PENAL SYSTEM 1974–83

> Many of the things we hold dear are threatened as never before, but none has yet been lost. So stay here, stay and help us defeat Socialism, so that the Britain you have known may be the Britain your children will know. These are the two great challenges of our time – the moral and political challenge, and the economic challenge. They have to be faced together and we have to master them both (Margaret Thatcher, speaking at the Conservative Party Conference, Blackpool, 1975).

The previous chapter noted that one of the central themes of this book is the continuity in punishment across different historical epochs. It also noted that it has become a matter of criminological commonsense to identify the mid-1970s as a moment of profound rupture and epochal change when the state shifted its ideological and material gear and moved onto a new penological terrain in terms of crime and punishment. As the chapter noted, such developments are more complex and nuanced than the 'new penology' thesis implies, rich and stimulating though that argument is. What transpired is perhaps better understood as an *intensification* in law and order processes which were already deeply embedded in the political and cultural institutions of the state and civil society, processes which had a much longer history with respect to which groups and what behaviour, were targeted for state intervention.

Before considering the issue of the prison system from the mid-1970s to the early 1980s, particularly the crisis confronting the system, this chapter will establish the political and cultural context in which the crisis took place and within which it should be understood. It was a context increasingly dominated by events in the Conservative Party, and the emergence of the Thatcherite bloc in the party. Although in opposition, and indeed in a minority in the Party itself, this bloc was to play a key hegemonic role, not only in the social construction of how the wider crisis in the society was perceived, but also, more crucially, in setting the ideological parameters for establishing where responsibility lay and what should be done about it. It is the profound social impact of this bloc which provides the starting point for this chapter.

'Britain: a decadent new Utopia'

The two defeats suffered by the Conservative party in the General Elections of February and October 1974 had a seismic effect on its members and fellow travellers. Galvanized by these defeats, and traumatized by the organic crisis that gripped the wider society, a number of intellectuals, journalists and politicians engaged in what Stuart Hall has called 'formative efforts', which were aimed at generating:

> ... a new balance of forces. ... the attempt to put together a new 'historic bloc', new political configurations and 'philosophies', a profound restructuring of the state and the ideological discourses which construct the crisis and represent it as it is 'lived' as a practical reality: new programmes and policies, pointing to a new result, a new sort of 'settlement' – 'within certain limits' (Hall, 1988: 43).

The key figure in the ideological and strategic restructuring of the Conservatives was Sir Keith Joseph. Joseph had joined the Conservative Party in 1944 and initially established a reputation as a keen interventionist and as a liberal on a number of social issues. In the late 1940s, he joined the liberal Howard League for Penal Reform (Halcrow, 1989: 10). By 1974, a profound shift had taken place in his thinking. Thirty years after joining the Party, he was finally 'converted to Conservatism ... I had thought that I was a Conservative but now I see I was not really one at all' (cited in Young, 1989: 79). In a series of speeches during the year, Joseph delivered a cauterising critique of, and offered an alternative vision to, the post-war settlement which had left the Conservatives and the country 'stranded on the middle ground' (Joseph, 1976). Ten days after the Party's second election defeat, he spoke to Birmingham Conservatives in Edgbaston. It was a speech that was to generate enormous controversy for its eugenic undertones but, as significantly, it was also a speech that articulated a new strategy in which the battle for ideas was as important, and sometimes more important, than struggles around economic policy. Joseph's fervid conversion was to strike a chord with those in the Conservative hierarchy who were profoundly antagonistic to the politics of Edward Heath and by extension the politics of the post-war settlement. For free-marketeers such as Nicholas Ridley, between February 1974 and February 1975, 'Keith Joseph was the undisputed leader of the rebel group' (Ridley, 1991: 6).[1]

Britain: A Decadent New Utopia was the banner headline in *The Guardian* on Monday 21 October 1974, which accompanied the full text of Joseph's speech. At the time he was the Shadow Home Secretary, prospective leader of the Party and personal friend and political ally of Margaret Thatcher. According to Thatcher, Joseph 'had emerged from the wreckage of the Heath Government determined on the need to rethink our policies from first principles' (Thatcher, 1995: 250). His speech highlighted what he saw as the threat to 'the balance of our population, our human stock'. The threat came from the illegitimate pregnancies of single, divorced or deserted mothers in Social Classes 4 and 5, 'some ... of low intelligence' who produced 'problem children, the future unmarried mothers, delinquents, denizens of our borstals, subnormal educational establishments, prisons, hostels for drifters'. Policy interventions through contraception would reduce the opportunities for this detritus to bear children and thus eliminate their capacity to reproduce both their depraved offspring and deprived social circumstances. However, for the lachrymose Joseph, this was the thin end of a positivist wedge in that contraception was likely to encourage immorality among the very classes who were subject to 'already weak restraints on strong instincts' (Joseph, 1974: 7).

The policy implications of the speech in terms of eugenic interventions into the lives of what were regarded as working class, moral degenerates, particularly, fecund, working class women, were hardly new. Strident calls for such interventions have long been a significant discourse in the social policy pronouncements of the educated middle and upper class of whatever political persuasion (Sim, 1990). Despite this history, however, it was agreed by most commentators that the speech effectively destroyed his chance of succeeding the increasingly vulnerable Edward Heath as leader of the Conservative party. In turn, it created the space for Margaret Thatcher to challenge what she called the 'directionless expediency of the previous few years' (Thatcher, 1995: 274). It also presented Thatcher with the opportunity to excoriate the philosophical, moral and political values on which Heath's economic and social policy had been based and which, in her view, had profoundly corroded the power and influence of the Party and the country, which were linked together by the mystical, umbilical cord of nationhood.

The concern with what a fellow Conservative quaintly described as 'the feckless breeding habits of the lower orders' (Bruce-Gardyne, 1984: 2)[2] was to become the template in the politics of demonization over the next two decades. At the same time, the speech was also about the politics of Tory revaluation, a re-evaluation that Joseph had been demanding since imbibing the free market ideas of the *Institute of Economic Affairs* the previous spring. In terms of the philosophical underpinnings of Conservatism, he maintained that 'real' Tory politics should shift away from an 'exclusive concern with economics'. The Party had 'to get economics into proportion as one aspect of politics, but never really the main thing'. He argued that the Party's economic policies would be undermined, and would eventually fail, if wider political values were not in place. He told his audience:

> The aspect of the Tory approach I wish to discuss here tonight relates to the family and to civilized values. They are the foundation on which the nation is built: they are being undermined. If we cannot restore them to health, our nation will be utterly ruined, whatever economic policies we might try to follow. For economics is deeply shaped by values, by the attitude towards work, thrift, ethics, public spirit (Joseph, 1974: 7).

Despite the rise in real incomes, as well as in the education and social welfare budgets, he contended that there had been a concomitant surge in deviant behaviour including:

> ... delinquency, truancy, vandalism, decline in educational standards. Some secondary schools in our cities are dominated by gangs operating extortion rackets against small children. Teenage pregnancies are rising; so are drunkenness, sexual offences and crimes of sadism. For the first time in a century and a half, since the great Tory reformer Robert Peel set up the Metropolitan Police, areas of our cities are becoming unsafe for peaceful citizens by night, and some even by day (1974: 7).

In terms of political strategy, Joseph maintained that the construction of ideologies, and the dissemination of ideas, meant that the institutions of civil society had to be harnessed to the Conservative's governing moral and political project. He argued that:

> We must do more as Tories to make our voices heard and our influence felt, as a party, as people in public life, high or lowly, in religious life, on councils, voluntary bodies, educational institutions. The arguments are on our side and *we have good friends among the teachers, the sociologists, the psychologists, if only we will call on them and give the lead for them to follow*. We must fight the battle of ideas in every school, university publication, committee, T.V. studio, even if we have to struggle for our toehold there; we have the truth, if we fail to make it shine clear, we shall be to blame no less than the exploiters, the casuists, the commercializers (1974: 7, emphasis added).

He concluded that the next political period 'could be a watershed' in the life of the country and once again linked the moral and the economic:

> Are we to move towards moral decline reflected and intensified by economic decline, by the corrosive effects of inflation? Or can we remoralise our national life, of which the economy is an integral part? It is up to us, to people like you and me (1974: 7).

Reacting to the speech, Mary Whitehouse indicated that she was 'tremendously grateful' to Joseph. She noted that, until he spoke, 'the people of Britain have been like sheep without a shepherd. But now they have found one'. He received 7,000 letters supporting his speech. One correspondent 'felt compelled to inform [him] that "too many Irish are breeding" ', while another argued that he deserved praise for 'having spoken out against the high birth rate among those of "low intelligence" ' and maintained that 'the same lesson ... could apply on a global scale at a time when the birth-rates in "advanced" nations were shrinking' (Denham and Garnett, 2001: 267–268).[3]

The following month, Joseph spoke about law and order. In the wake of the Birmingham pub bombings, he indicated that he was in favour of prison sentences that were both short and 'bleak', a word that was to become synonymous with prison regimes in the 1990s under Michael Howard. He maintained that while the death penalty for murder was 'probably not a deterrent in a general way, and while it would not be useful in Northern Ireland, there was a case for executing those convicted of acts of terrorism committed on the mainland' (cited in Halcrow, 1989: 93).

The restoration of law and order was not just a concern for Joseph. Three years earlier, in 1971, Peregrine Worsthorne had already voiced his demand for a return to an earlier retributive age in his book *The Socialist Myth*. In the book, he articulated a number of themes, which were to become central to Conservative Party discourse over the following two decades. For Worsthorne:

> ... a "civilized" Britain means a country which the reigning minority approves of, finds congenial to its predispositions – a country made in their image. It is a Britain with a guilt complex about her imperial past, and therefore disposed to believe in her duty to open up her shores to coloured immigration, and to romanticize the underdeveloped world. It is a Britain with little concern for preserving the national identity, nationalism being deemed old-fashioned and primitive, and therefore, disposed to romanticize the potentialities of federal Europe. It is a Britain which, because she is fascinated with moral permissiveness – authoritarian regulation being regarded as unnecessary if not harmful – is peculiarly susceptible and sympathetic to student agitation. It is a Britain soft on law and order, because the retribution side of punishment is seen as a hangover from barbarism. It is a Britain with a contempt for tradition and continuity, since the need for both is ignored. In a word, it is a Britain fit for intellectuals to live in (Worsthorne, 1971: 215–216).

At the Oxford Union in December 1975, Joseph berated his fellow Conservatives for 'ceasing to fight the battle of ideas' and for seeking and supporting the middle ground of the post-war settlement, which 'is a guarantee these days of a left-wing ratchet'.[4] Again, he mapped out a series of intertwined issues and events, which were taking the country to an apocalyptic reckoning:

> The economy is in crisis, a deeper crisis than most people realise. The unspoken consensus, which makes society work is severely eroded. The rule of law is seriously attenuated from both ends by vested interests, which use force and intimidation to gain their purposes: and by an ever more powerful and insolent executive. Crime and vandalism have increased to an alarming extent. We spend more than ever on education and health, but with results which can please only the most blinkered. We spend more on welfare without achieving well-being, while creating dangerous levels of dependency (Joseph, 1976: 19).

In Gramscian terms, Joseph's intellectual interventions, his demand for moral reform and his disburdenment of traditional Conservative beliefs, can be understood as an attempt to create 'a new conception of the world with its consequent ethics, which must show itself to be both viable and superior to the prevailing one' (Morera, 1990: 167). Significantly, his goal was not simply 'to radicalise the Tories but also to make Labour safe for capitalism by forcing it to love free markets' (Lawson, 2005: 33), a point that I return to in Chapter 5.

Thatcher's moment

For Margaret Thatcher, the viability and superiority of Joseph's ethico-political discourse was self-evident. His economic, political and strategic apostasy was crucial in galvanising her putative, but unfocussed and unsophisticated ideas, about the nature and direction of policy, party and country (Gamble, 1988: 85).[5] The link between ill discipline and crime, which he espoused, struck a pragmatic and punitive chord with an individual who, in thirty-two years in Parliament, had voted against the Party line on only one occasion. In 1961, concerned about the 'creative potential of free enterprise and social discipline', Thatcher and other Conservative MPs supported a new clause which they wished to see added to that year's Criminal Justice Bill. The clause 'would have introduced birching and caning for violent young offenders'. Although defeated, 69 Tory backbenchers voted for it in 'the biggest Party revolt since it came to power in 1951' (Thatcher, 1995: 116–117).

Joseph's prescience with respect to economic policy and social discipline became particularly important in the strategic influence that he exerted when Mrs Thatcher was elected Conservative leader in February 1975 (the same year Tony Blair joined the Labour Party). Those in the Thatcherite bloc were clear that the mobilization of a cadre of organic intellectuals to fight the 'battle of ideas' was the key to constructing a hegemonic consensus around crime, punishment and the maintenance and reproduction of social order. Joseph, together with the Centre for Policy Studies (CPS),[6] targeted 'the fairly small number of people who influence the thinking of a nation' and then wined and dined 'people in powerful or influential walks of life: eating our way to victory, as Sherman put it' (Halcrow, 1989: 66 and 108). For Thatcher:

> It was Keith who really began to turn the intellectual tide against socialism. He got our fundamental intellectual message across, to students, professors, journalists, the 'intelligentsia' generally ... If Keith hadn't been doing all that work with the intellectuals, all the rest of our work would probably never have resulted in success (cited in 1989: 97).

The CPS was regarded as 'Mrs Thatcher's intellectual home' while the intellectual cadre who worked there 'saw themselves as outsiders in the "stupid party" and prepared an intellectual and political assault on it'. It was also one of a number of key think tanks, including the *Mont Pelerin Society* and the *Institute of Economic Affairs*, which were:

> ... central to the Thatcherite project. They provided it with a critique of the welfare-state consensus, which seemed coherent and intellectually respectable. It was indispensable to the emergence of the Thatcherite ideological realignment from the crumbling of the consensus. Their philosophy also contained a vision of the future Britain, which, despite its philistine simplicities, did inspire a critical if small, group of key people. Moreover the think-tanks did crucial spade-work in preparing numerous well-worked out proposals for reform which the more committed among the Thatcherite ministers could implement (Desai, 1994: 29 and 59).

As she consolidated her position as leader, Thatcher's speeches increasingly used metaphors, imagery and even phrases which had their origins in Joseph's apocalyptic vision and vocabulary. In October 1976, she wrote the foreword to a pamphlet by the Conservative historian Lord Blake. Blake argued that the Conservatives should campaign on the slogan of 'getting the government off our backs' and that law and order should be a 'rallying cry, with a party commitment to restore the death penalty' (*The Times*, 4 October 1976). In March 1977, drawing on what was to become a favourite metaphor of invasion and repulsion (particularly during the year-long coal dispute seven years later) she told the *Zurich Economic Society* that the ills of the body politic were 'creating their own antibodies' (Thatcher, 1977: 98). Addressing the Conservative Local Government Conference in February 1978, she drew directly on Joseph's metaphorical language.

> The coming Election is a watershed Election. Every General Election is important. But next time the vote could decide what sort of country we are going to live in for the rest of this century .... I am profoundly convinced that what we are saying today is

> more in line with the hopes, the anxieties and the ambitions of the people than it has been for years. They are Tory at heart – the Wilson and Callaghan years have seen to that. Those years of the Labour locust are coming to an end. Let us hasten that end with all our energy, all our will (Thatcher, 1978: 11–17).

Thatcher's doom-laden perception of impending social collapse was also influenced by a number of other advisors, such as Brian Crozier and Robert Moss, 'who believed that Britain was descending into chaos and required exceptional measures to reassert the authority of the state and the sanctity of private property'. Crozier, whose activities were funded at different times by the CIA, had established the *Institute for the Study of Conflict* in 1970. He 'provided Thatcher with regular briefings on subversion that she appears to have taken entirely seriously' (Anderson and Mann, 1997: 237 and 423). It is no surprise that Thatcher took these briefings seriously as she also felt that the country was witnessing 'a deliberate attack on our values, a deliberate attack on those who wish to promote merit and excellence, a deliberate attack on our heritage and our great past' (Thatcher, 1977: 32).

The attack on British values was to be confronted through engaging in a hegemonic 'battle of ideas', which was taken into the heart of the mass media. Again, Joseph was central to this process. In 1988, reflecting back on his role, Thatcher indicated that he had made 'faith in what could be done ... into something that intelligent people were willing to share. And their acceptance spread the message through the press and other media to everybody' (cited in Halcrow, 1989: 97). The appointment of former TV producer, Gordon Reece, to Thatcher's full-time staff, facilitated Joseph's work. It allowed the Conservatives to focus on their traditional supporters who read *The Times* as well as the *Daily Telegraph* and its Sunday equivalent while simultaneously targeting those middle-England readers who bought the *Daily Mail* and the *Daily Express*. For Thatcher, the 'real revolution' lay in targeting *The Sun* and the *News of the World*.[7] These newspapers 'were crucial in communicating Conservative values to non-Conservative voters'. Despite the pressure of work as Leader of the Opposition 'when Gordon said we must have lunch with such-and-such an editor that was the priority' (Thatcher, 1995: 294). As Margaret Scammell has argued, Reece, along with the Saatchi brothers and Harvey Thomas, 'set out to change the face of political presentation'. Their strategy:

> ... set the parameters for her political programme, identified the target voters and supplied the appeals and slogans tailored to win them over. The marketers' task was assisted by the adoration of Maggie in the pro-Tory tabloid press, especially *The Sun* with its high proportion of skilled working class readers (Scammell, 1994: 36–42).

Sir Ian Gilmour observed his Party's developing relationship with *The Sun* from his place at the Cabinet table. Rupert Murdoch was central to this relationship. He was 'as far right as Mrs Thatcher' and regarded the Cabinet 'wets' as 'hypocrites and "pissing liberals"'. For Gilmour, the Thatcherite bloc found that controlling most of the Conservative press was as easy as controlling Conservative backbenchers: 'their attempts to control the rest of the media were the most conspicuous demonstration of Thatcherism's urge for power, not unmixed with paranoia' (Gilmour, 1993: 44 and 236).

Thatcher's law and Whitelaw's order

On the morning after her election as Conservative leader, Margaret Thatcher asked William Whitelaw, one of her co-challengers for the Party leadership, to serve as her Deputy. According to Whitelaw, this was the start of a relationship, which he 'enormously appreciated'. It enabled him to feel that he had 'played some part in [Mrs. Thatcher's] remarkable achievements as Prime Minister and Leader of our Conservative Party' (Whitelaw, 1989: 143).

On assuming this post he immediately 'set about a systematic revision of the Party's policies in the main areas of Home Office concern – police, prisons, crime, broadcasting, race relations and immigration' (1989: 149–150). By 1977, he had developed a set of policies for the criminal justice system designed to become 'key features of our policy in Government'. They included short, sharp detention centres for young offenders, ending the policy of closing attendance centres and developing 'more imaginative alternatives to custody'. In terms of the prison service, he proposed that it should have greater independence from the Home Office, which 'would give a better corporate identity and more pride to the service'. Whitelaw also called for a 'significant programme of prison building in order to reverse the cumulative neglect of decades' (1989: 152).

A number of the suggestions were generated by a small study group established by Whitelaw, which was staffed by MPs and outside advisors who had experience of the courts, prisons, probation and the Parole Board. Its Chair was Edward Gardner, the Conservative lawyer, MP and later knight of the realm. Gardner, who as Chair of the *Select Committee on Home Affairs*, was to play a significant and influential role in instituting the debate around the privatization of the prisons in the 1980s (Ryan and Ward, 1989), was also Chair of the *Executive Committee of the Society of Conservative Lawyers* from 1969 to 1975 and its actual Chair from 1975 to 1985. The Society had published *Crisis in Crime and Punishment* as early as 1971 and followed this with *The Proper Use of Prisons*, published in 1978.[8] In late 1977, Whitelaw indicated the thinking behind the Conservative strategy:

> Whatever the government do, we Conservatives are determined that after the next election, the Conservative Government will be ready to meet the challenge of rising crime, lawlessness and violence which threatens the whole basis of our democratic society (*Hansard*, 7 November 1977: col. 344).

Whitelaw's views on crime and punishment were complex and nuanced. In early 1982, in a speech to the Conservative Association at Cambridge University, he was clear about the priority the government should give to law and order: 'fighting crime has been among the first priorities of this Government'. For him, it was:

> ... idle to pretend that crime could ever be eliminated. To argue thus would be to deny the obvious truth that there *are* imperfections in the human character. What we can do is to deny opportunities to commit crime, to deter potential criminals and to make certain that their crimes will be detected, and proper punishment and proper treatment given to them after sentence in the courts (Conservative Central Office, 1982: 1, emphasis in the original).

Because of these views, sociologically and popularly, Whitelaw has been constructed as a liberal within a Cabinet of new right authoritarians. Yet, he did not stand outside or above the intensification and extension in the power of the state that came with Thatcher's first election victory. Despite his 'wet' credentials, and what Hugo Young calls his 'social distaste' for Mrs Thatcher, 'professionally, he bound himself completely to her' (Young, 1989: 235).

The prisons

Joseph's concern about the rising tide of crime and social anarchy, and Whitelaw's attempt to develop a law and order strategy while in opposition, took place against a background of a prison system in crisis. From the perspective of both the Labour government and their Conservative opponents, the institution was abjectly failing to deter the criminal, reform the offender and protect and defend the wider society from their forbidding ravages. Central to the sense of crisis was the apparent unwillingness of a group of state servants – prison officers – to act reasonably and responsibly with respect to managing offenders, ensuring order and maintaining security. From the mid-1970s, prison officers began a series of campaigns that undermined the basis of hierarchical authority which a militarized service such as the prison system relied on to function efficiently and effectively. The militancy of prison staff was one element in a series of interlocking crises that gripped the system during this period (Fitzgerald and Sim, 1982). The crisis generated by this militancy was so severe that, in November 1978, prison governors forebodingly warned that there could 'be a serious loss of control', which might have to be 'quelled by armed interventions with the probability of both staff and prisoners being killed' (1982: 3).

The crisis also cut across several other dimensions over and above the militancy of the prison officers which, taken together, undermined the legitimacy of the institution in the eyes of politicians, public and prisoners themselves (1982: 23–24). Appalling conditions and severe overcrowding in local prisons were the most obvious manifestations of the deeply embedded problems confronting the institution. Additionally, the challenges to penal 'truth' mounted by radical prisoners' rights organizations to the hegemony of official accounts of life inside (Fitzgerald, 1977; Ryan 1978) – what Foucault termed 'the insurrection of subjugated knowledges' (Foucault, 2004: 7) – were crucial in highlighting the fact that for all the 'state talk' (Corrigan and Sayer, 1985) (and indeed much of criminology's 'talk') about rehabilitation, reform and progress since the end of the nineteenth century, prison life for many of the confined remained bleak, brutal and bewildering.

The state's attempt to maintain the fragile order of the prison brought these issues into sharp focus as a number of strategies and policies were pursued which, paradoxically, often generated further, negative, unintended consequences for the system. These strategies included: the introduction, in secret, of psychologically withering Control Units, which were used against those labelled as recalcitrant; the militarization of the state's response to disorder through training every prison officer in techniques of riot control, which was allied with the use of special squads such as the Minimum Use of Force Tactical Intervention Squad (MUFTI); the use of segregation within, and the 'ghosting' of prisoners between, different institutions; the mobilization of brutal violence against demonstrating prisoners at Hull in 1976 (especially towards Irish and black prisoners) and at Wormwood Scrubs in 1979 (the inquiry into which was described as 'Whitelaw's Whitewash' by the radical prisoners' rights group, PROP (Coggan, 1982: 3);[9] and the use of drugs to control those labelled as 'difficult' (Warren, 1982) or against those deemed 'unable to cope', especially women (Sim, 1990). These strategies provided a clear, unambiguous indication that the state's unnerving capacity for drastic interventions into the lives of the confined had not been eliminated in the ideological drive to construct the prison as a place of munificent and benevolent reform.

The Labour government's response to the crisis was predictable: the establishment of an inquiry under Mr Justice May. May's findings and recommendations were also predictable given the baleful and nefarious control exerted by the Home Office over the terms of reference and the final report. They were built on a poorly conceived managerial explanation for the crisis while propounding an equally naive managerial solution to the same crisis (Fitzgerald and Sim, 1980). Crucially, the inquiry failed to confront one of the key issues and dimensions underpinning the crisis, namely the discretionary and nonaccountable use of prison officer power, a failure which was to reverberate through the coming decades. As was noted at the time:

> The May Report was an opportunity not simply to review but to change fundamentally the 100-year-old recipe of more prisons and more prisoners. In the event, it passed up that opportunity, preferring, like so many Inquiries before it, to represent the recipe for prison crisis as a recipe for prison salvation. It simply won't work (1980: 84).

The crisis in the prisons, particularly the 'crisis of legitimacy' (Fitzgerald and Sim, 1982: 23), symbolized the broader social crisis of legitimacy and hegemony in the wider society (Hall et al., 1978). Again, as was noted at the time, 'the crisis of the British prison system thus reflects not simply a concern about the state of the prisons, but a more widespread belief that the prisons of the State are not making a contribution to the maintenance of social order' (Fitzgerald and Sim, 1982: 23–24).

The Labour government's tired, and indeed shambolic, response to the prison crisis, appeared to perfectly symbolize the fact that ministers had little to offer by way of political solutions, either to this crisis or to the crisis gripping the wider society. With Labour defeated at the General Election in May 1979, and the government of Margaret Thatcher in power, the apocalyptic concerns articulated by Joseph over the previous five years, while not achieving complete hegemony (as no ideas ever do), nonetheless began to work their way into her government's programme for law and order. Ominously, for a range of already economically and politically powerless groups, it was a programme increasingly based on the principles of the free market and the strong state (Gamble, 1988).

The strong state

> Make no mistake about it: under this regime, the market is to be Free; the People are to be Disciplined (Hall, 1980: 5).

Stuart Hall and his colleagues have made the point that the consolidation of the Thacherite bloc, and their subsequent elevation to power in May 1979, was built on the wider crisis of hegemony that gripped British society from the mid-1970s (Hall et al., 1978; Hall, 1988). It was a crisis fuelled by a series of racialized moral panics, which plugged into the sense of apocalyptic disaster that Joseph had articulated during the same period. The sense of crisis was not unique to the Conservatives but cut across party boundaries. Indeed, the previous Labour government under James Callaghan had:

> ... provided the overture for Thatcherism, pioneering many of her themes – aggressive policing (the use of riot shields on the mainland for the first time at the Ladywood by-election in 1977), the bussing in of strike-breaking workers at Grunwick, a national debate on standards in education – and a lot of her social conservatism, including surprise that any decent citizen would not be in bed by eleven (when responding to a question about a late-night TV blackout caused by industrial action) (Elliott and Atkinson, 1998: 53).

Crucially, for Hall, the strong state that began to take shape during Thatcher's first government was underpinned and legitimated by an 'authoritarian populism', which he defined as a series of ideological interventions by the new right designed to 'harness to its support some popular discontents, neutralize the opposing forces, disaggregate the opposition and really incorporate some strategic elements of popular opinion into its own hegemonic project' (Hall, 1988: 152). Crime was central to this project:

> ... when crime is mapped into the wider scenarios of 'moral degeneration' and the crisis of authority and social values, there is no mystery as to why some ordinary people should be actively recruited into crusades for the restoration of 'normal times' – if necessary through a more-than-normal imposition of moral-legal force (1988: 143–144).

The intensification in state power could be seen across a range of different social areas: significant increases in the number and powers of the police and on expenditure on the force; the technological and operational militarization of the force; the passing of anti trade union legislation; restrictions on the reporting of court trials; the extension of the Prevention of Terrorism Act; reviews of the laws governing public order designed to restrict the right to demonstrate and for the state to impose conditions on marches; the normalization of special powers in Britain derived from the war in Northern Ireland and the passing of a series of immigration laws which gave the police greater discretion to engage in 'fishing expeditions' in minority ethnic communities (Sim, 1983). This programme was underpinned by attempts from within the state to widen the definition of subversion to include:

> Anyone who shows *affinity* towards communism, that's common sense, the IRA, the PLO and I would say anyone who's decrying marriage, family life, trying to break that up, pushing drugs, homosexuality, indiscipline in schools, weak penalties for anti-social crimes ... a whole gamut of things that could be pecking away at the foundation of society and weakening it (Former Chief Constable, Harold Salisbury, cited in Sim and Thomas, 1983: 80, emphasis added).

At the same time, it was also evident that the new government's concern was to police the morals and behaviour of the powerless. As Stuart Hall has noted, the Conservatives came to power not only on the back of an authoritarian, interventionist agenda but also on the back of an 'anti-statist strategy' which he defined as a strategy which was:

> ... not one which refuses to operate through the state; it is one which conceives a more limited state role, and which advances through the attempt, ideologically, to *represent itself* as anti-statist, for the purposes of populist mobilisation ... (Hall, 1988: 152, emphasis in the original).

The strategy of authoritarian state intervention into the lives of the powerless, coupled with institutionalized state circumspection with respect to the policing of the powerful, was encapsulated in the spring of 1978, the year *before*

Thatcher came to power, by John Nott, the future Secretary of State for Defence:

> It is the function of Parliament to be ever-vigilant about the over-zealous tax inspector, local official or any other public servant. If tax inspectors, in pursuance of suspected tax evaders, are to inquire into the lifestyles and expenditure of individual citizens, their inquiries should be clear, sensible and in no way oppressive (Conservative Central Office, 1979: 1).

In 1980, the year *after* she came to power, the Howard League for Penal Reform described the implications of this 'anti-statist' strategy for the policing of the powerful:

> Expenditure in other public services is being curtailed and this is beginning to affect agencies other than the police which bring prosecutions. For example, it was announced that the frequency of site visits by the Factory Inspectorate would decline from an average of one every five years per plant to one in every seven years; and the Companies Registration Office at Cardiff will, due to shortage of staff, bring less prosecutions for non-registration of essential company details (Howard League for Penal Reform, cited in Sim, 1983: 17).

As subsequent chapters indicate, the contrast between the policing of the powerless, and the policing of the powerful, as well as the continuity between Conservative and New Labour governments in these key areas, was to be a redolent, and indeed, hypocritical theme in the development of criminal justice policy over the next three decades. The immediate question, however, is what impact was the intensification in social authoritarianism having on the prisons?

Prisons of the state

In a number of ways, the prison system reflected the drive towards the social authoritarianism articulated by the first Thatcher government. For Steven Box, the rise in the prison population between 1971 and 1981 was tied to the 'deepening economic crisis' that gripped the country which, in turn, had 'affected the way governments and the judiciary have "criminalized" subordinate groups'. Presciently, in 1983, he wrote that:

> Prisons are being used to punish more and more offenders and particularly the young. They are also being used to serve as a warning to those not deserving imprisonment this time round. Given the usefulness of prisons both for incapacitating offenders and deterring some potential offenders, there can be no doubt that the number of prisoners will rise to fill the capacity made available by the government's prison building programme (Box, 1983: 207).

Box concluded that 'prisons are getting younger ... and blacker' (1983: 218).[10] This process was related to the changes in the political economy of the society as well as the ideological and cultural perception of the powerful regarding the nature of the problems confronting the UK and what should be done about them:

> ... the growth in unemployment, which is itself a reflection of deepening economic crisis, has been accompanied by an increase in the range and severity of state coercion, including the rate and length of imprisonment. This increased use of imprisonment was not a direct response to any rise in crime, but was rather an ideologically motivated response to the *perceived* threat of crime posed by the swelling population of economically marginalized persons ... The judiciary being an integral part of the state control apparatus, makes its contribution to this increased level of coercion by imprisoning more, particularly those typifying the actually, or potentially, disruptive problem populations ... Whilst the powerful are getting away with crimes whose enormity appears to sanctify them, the powerless are getting prison (1983: 212, 217 and 219, emphasis in the original).

Consequently, expenditure increased on prison building and refurbishment schemes, as did the number of prison officers. In October 1982, Andrew Rutherford captured the nature of penal expansionism, a process that had begun, as he noted, in the decades before the mid-1970s:

> For some years, expenditure on the prison system has risen at a faster rate than public expenditure generally. Since 1950, the number of prison officers has been increased at a rate three times that of the prison population. Over the same period 18,000 cells have been added to the prison system, an increase of 85 per cent, with a further 5,000 planned by the end of the decade (Rutherford, 1982: 3).

The number of prisoners, and the length of the sentences handed down by the courts, also rose. Official reports from the time reflect official concerns about the increase in the prison population and the repercussions for the system. In the prison department's report for 1980, officials bemoaned the fact that the population rose sharply from 42,000 in 1979, to 44,626 in March [1980] (Home Office, 1981). The report for 1981 indicated that in July of that year the prison population climbed to 45,500, 'the first time this century it had exceeded 45,000' (cited in *The Guardian*, 9 September 1982). In the report for 1982, officials again noted that the population rose from 'about 40,800 in early January until late March when the total was just over 44,000' (Home Office, 1983: 6). In the same report, the Director General of the Prison Service commented that, 'what was noticeable during 1982 was that the enlarged building programme initiated in 1979, but delayed by the industrial action of 1980–81, was producing practical results in many establishments' (1983: 3).

At the same time, as in the 1970s, the public, media and political debate about prisons was centred on the 'crisis' inside and what should be done about it. The toxic mix generated by the self-reproducing menace of appalling conditions and overcrowding remained the lens through which the crisis was seen and explored. Conditions were so bad that, by the early 1980s, two prison governors wrote to the press in damning terms. The governor of Wormwood Scrubs described himself as the 'manager of a large penal dustbin' while the governor of Strangeways described conditions in the prison as 'an affront to a civilized society' (cited in State Research, 1982: 100). In June 1982, over 16,000 prisoners were sharing cells, while in Wandsworth, 200 men were sharing four lavatory cubicles and one hot water tap (New Law Journal, 1983: 314). For those who sat on the *Expenditure Committee of the House of Commons* (Home Office et al., 1980) or who were involved in the *Tory Reform Group* (Tory Reform Group, 1983), alternatives to custody, shorter sentences and changes in sentencing policy were among a series of policy recommendations they felt were necessary to generate, in the words of the Expenditure Committee's authors, 'the reduction of pressure on the prison service' (Home Office et al., 1980: front cover). Whitelaw initially articulated a similar strategy in terms of considering legislation that would reduce the prison population by 7,000. However, according to Andrew Rutherford, that strategy was abandoned by late 1981 when:

> Whitelaw had changed course. The inner-city disturbances, the defeat of the official law and order motion at the Conservative Party Conference and rumblings of judicial discontent led to jettisoning notions of automatic parole. In March this year [1982] Mr Whitelaw told the House of Commons: 'We are determined to ensure that there will be room in the prison system for every person whom the judges and magistrates decide should go there, and we will continue to do whatever is necessary for that purpose'. This declaration, which may signal the abandonment of the bipartisan standstill policy on the prison system, was repeated at the Conservative Party Conference earlier this month (Rutherford, 1982: 3).

As ever, the impact of the crisis was felt most acutely by the prisoners and, more specifically, by some of the most vulnerable in the prison population. For some commentators, the question of deaths in custody was a central issue. Between 1969 and 1980, 696 prisoners died in prison custody: 'in the last two of these years, the percentage of deaths[s] from unnatural causes or suicide increased alarmingly to 41.1 (30 out of 73) in 1979 and 49.2 per cent (33 out of 65) in 1980' (Coggan and Walker, 1982: 11). For Coggan and Walker, prisoners were dying disproportionately compared with those outside. In 1980, the prison suicide rate was 'nearly eleven times the national rate'. As they also pointedly noted, neither Roy Jenkins nor Merlyn Rees, the Labour Home Secretaries between March 1974 and May 1979, nor their Conservative successor, William Whitelaw had 'done anything but talk' (1982: 13–14). Furthermore, under Whitelaw's stewardship at the Home Office, one of the most notorious deaths in prison custody occurred, that of Barry Prosser. Thirty-two year old Prosser, who was on remand for causing criminal damage to a door handle, was described by a doctor giving evidence at his inquest, as being covered in bruises 'from head to toe' (Coroner's Court,

Birmingham, 1981: 18). The doctor noted that he had 'died of Shock (sic), due to rupture of the stomach and oesophagus caused by a crushing injury' (1981: 14). Among the prisoner's 'head to toe' injuries were injuries to his feet, anus and private parts. In the case of the latter two, the doctor commented that:

> I think the probability is that the injuries to the private parts and the anus came before the [fatal] blow. It is not impossible to visualise the situation where he got a kick or a stamp in the groin and in the back passage after having received his severe injury to the abdomen. That would have been a perfectly ghastly and wholly unnecessary thing to have done. It would have been a sadistic act.
>
> Assuming that the injuries to the feet at least precipitated the fatal blow, I would expect a man of the deceased's physique to show some retaliation, if he had been free to do so.
>
> During my examination, I found no injuries that could be described as defensive injuries. That indicates to me that as well as his feet being stamped on, that it raises the possibility that others were holding him. If one is retaliating, one is not necessarily going to show signs of retaliation with one[']s fists.
>
> The knee in his private parts would cause him pain and incapacity. It is an incapacitating type of injury. It would put him out of action and I am not able to say if that preceeded (sic) or succeeded the fatal blow.
>
> Taken as a whole, the picture is of a powerful man being restrained and held down while other men kick him. Once he is down, there is no need to hold him down. The injuries to the feet, the groins and the private parts could well have been caused without him being held down, but once he is down, I postulate the dropping of a heavy weight on his abdomen as being the cause of the fatal blow to the abdomen. If he anticipated that someone was going to fall or drop heavily on his abdomen, he was tough enough to prevent the fatal injury if he had been able to do so at that time.
>
> There were two bursts, one to the gullett (sic) or the oesophagus and one to the stomach. These two ruptures are very close to each other and in my view there were two ruptures of the stomach and the oesophagus as well as ruptures to the back of the lungs and they were all caused by one and the same blow (1981: 18–19).[11]

As the following chapters indicate, the issue of deaths in custody was to reverberate throughout the following decades. In their own way, these deaths contributed to the ongoing, long-term crisis of legitimacy that prisons experienced as they galvanized a new generation of radical prisoners' rights organizations such as *INQUEST* and *Women in Prison*, who continued to challenge the social construction of official 'truth' articulated by the state, both in relation to deaths inside and crucially the conditions and circumstances in which prisoners were dying.

Removing Thatcher's Willie

In the short term, Whitelaw's time at the Home Office was coming to an end as a new wave of Thatcherite politicians were moved into the offices of state in the attempt to construct a criminal justice system fit for an iron lady living in 'Iron Times' (Hall, 1988: vii). Despite being professionally bound to Margaret Thatcher, his tenure was dominated by the Tory right's attempts to portray him as a weak and ineffectual procrastinator in the fight against crime. In March 1982, this hostility reached its peak with a moral panic around law and order. The *Daily Mail* led the attack with a full-page article entitled 'Why the Public Should not Trust this Man'. The release of the annual crime figures by the Metropolitan police appeared to confirm the right's view that a tide of crime in general and 'black' crime in particular, was overwhelming the law-abiding majority. Despite the spurious methodological basis of the statistics, the newspaper supported the decision by Scotland Yard to release the figures and used them to call for Whitelaw to be removed from his post and to be sent to the House of Lords (cited in Sim 1982: 63). The Prime Minister, it was reported, was expected to take personal charge of the government's 'promised war against crime' (*The Guardian*, 16 March 1982). Whitelaw responded by meeting over 100 Conservative MPs where he listed a series of changes that the Conservatives had made to the criminal justice system including: increasing police numbers by 8,000; more than doubling expenditure on the force to the point where 'pay was at an all-time high'; promising further expenditure of £500 million on prison building and repairs; building another eight prisons over the next four years; and making 'short, sharp shock' detention for young offenders 'shorter and sharper'. He told the assembled MPs that he would sanction a tough law and order response through the police 'go[ing] in hard' to deal with outbreaks of street disorder. Officers would utilize 'Snatch Squad' techniques imported from Northern Ireland. Finally, he indicated that he accepted the case made by the *Royal Commission on Criminal Procedure* for the extension of police powers. This was 'an important success for the police. They were now to add significant new powers to the extensive [powers] which they already had available' (Sim, 1982: 69 and 71). However, the Conservative right's call for more intensive coercion was not entirely successful; their position in some areas remained highly contested. In early 1982, the Police Federation demanded the restoration of capital punishment for certain crimes. Eighty Conservative MPs backed the Federation who, in their magazine, claimed to have the support of over 150,000 people (*Police*, 1982: 4). Despite this mobilization, and a £30,000 newspaper campaign, when the vote was held, the House of Commons, as in 1979, rejected the demand for restoration, this time by 357 votes to 195 (*The Times*, 13 May 1982).

By the summer of 1983, Whitelaw's ties to the Prime Minister were increasingly brittle and fragile and were eventually broken when he was removed from his post as Home Secretary and replaced by Leon Brittan. For Thatcher, the issue was straightforward. While she recognized that Home Secretaries 'never do have an easy time', with Whitelaw:

> There was more to it than that. Willie and I knew that we did not share the same instincts on Home Office matters. I believe that capital punishment for the worst murderers is

morally right as retribution and practically necessary as a deterrent: Willie does not. My views on sentencing in general and on immigration are a good deal tougher than his. And, flatteringly but often awkwardly, the great majority of the Conservative Party and the British public agreed with me and showed it regularly at our Party Conferences (Thatcher, 1993: 307).

According to Thatcher, Brittan was someone who 'would have no time for the false sentimentality, which surrounds so much discussion of the causes of crime' (1993: 308). He was, therefore, given the chance to construct a criminal justice and penal system the leader wanted, the Party needed and, from Thatcher's perspective, the country demanded. Brittan's time at the Home Office, his impact on penal policy and the subsequent debates around the prison system in the 1980s is the subject of the next chapter.

Notes

1 Ridley was linked to other 'economic Powellites' such as Enoch Powell himself and John Biffen, as well as to those Tory Treasury ministers who had resigned from Harold Macmillan's government in 1957 in protest at the government's failure to cut public expenditure. Importantly, this group was linked with traditional Conservative thought, which involved 'cutting public expenditure and distancing government from the economy'. In this respect, Edward Heath's 'corporatist period' from 1972–4 and 'Harold Macmillan's interventionism from 1961–3 appears as an aberration in the twentieth-century history of the Conservative Party ...' (Bognador, 1996: 377).

2 In fact, Joseph had begun to articulate these concerns as early as 1959 (Denham and Garnett, 2001: 221).

3 He also received a supportive telegram from Sir Laurence Olivier, which he 'proudly displayed to friends' (Denham and Garnett, 2001: 268).

4 Joseph particularly targeted higher education to discuss his ideas. Between 1975 and 1979 he spoke at over 150 institutions (Desai, 1994: 55).

5 Thatcher was not known for having policies developed in advance. In 1970, she arrived in the Education Department as Secretary of State with 'no great printed document, but with a page from an exercise book with fourteen points she had made up herself' (Sir William Pile, cited in Ball and Seldon, 1996: 26).

6 The Centre was established by Joseph in August 1974 with Margaret Thatcher as its President (Kavanagh, 1987: 89).

7 Thatcher's love for the *News of the World* continued into the late 1980s. In his journals, Woodrow Wyatt describes a conversation he had with the then Home Office minister John Patten in March 1988. Patten asked Wyatt to write 'something in the *News of the World* about what they were trying to do about crime'. According to Wyatt, Patten went on to say that he was a ' "bit like Margaret. She always says, "I read dear Woodrow's column in the *News of the World* and carefully avoid letting my eyes fall on anything else" ' (Wyatt, 1998: 522).

8 Gardner was also a pivotal figure in the passing of the British Nationality Act 1981. In 1980, the study group he chaired published *Who Do We Think*

We Are? The threefold definition of nationality the group developed, underpinned the government's 1981 legislation (*The Independent*, 28 August 2001).

9 PROP took this position as the person appointed by Whitelaw to carry out the inquiry into the injuries sustained by prisoners at the hands of the notorious Minimum Use of Force Tactical Intervention Squad (MUFTI) had sent a 'congratulatory message to Wandsworth prison officers for the part they played in the riot squad – a "disciplined body of men" who "obeyed their every command" – scarcely a position of impartiality from which to conduct an investigation' (Coggan, 1982: 3).

10 At the time, Ashford Remand Centre had 'a black population of about 50 per cent', in Rochester and Dover borstals, 15 per cent of the prisoners were black while 'even in the three dispersal prisons in the South East the proportion of black prisoners [was] about 15 per cent' (*The Howard Journal*, 1982: 179).

11 The inquest jury returned a verdict of 'unlawful killing'. In March 1982, three prison officers were subsequently tried for Prosser's murder. They were found not guilty. In the same month, the Home Office announced that they would not face disciplinary action, because there were 'no grounds to justify the officers' dismissal or proceedings under the code of discipline for prison officers' (*The Times*, 25 March 1982).

3

HARD REIGN: THATCHERISM AND THE CONSOLIDATION OF PENAL AUTHORITARIANISM 1983–90

There was a revolution still to be made, and too few revolutionaries. The appointment of the first Cabinet in the new Parliament [in 1983] ... seemed a chance to recruit some (Thatcher, 1993: 306).

In the 60 years up to 1985 there were just six criminal justice acts, but in the following decade there were six – one every 18 months instead of one every decade (Dean, 2006: 4).

Convicts and conviction politicians

Just before she became Prime Minister, Margaret Thatcher indicated that she was neither a consensual nor a pragmatic politician. Rather she described herself as a 'conviction politician' who needed a 'conviction Cabinet' (cited in Gilmour, 1993: 4). When she reshuffled the Cabinet after the Conservative's devastating victory in the 1983 General Election, her 'conviction Cabinet' began to take formidable shape. Her supporters and allies were moved into key positions of power: Geoffrey Howe was moved to the Foreign Office, Nigel Lawson was made

Chancellor of the Exchequer, and Cecil Parkinson was installed at the newly created Department of Trade and Industry (DTI) while Norman Tebbit continued as Secretary of State for Employment. Other supporters such as Peter Rees and Michael Jopling were brought into the Cabinet 'and when Cecil Parkinson resigned in October 1983, the newcomer to the Cabinet was Nicholas Ridley, an economic Thatcherite from the early 1970s, even before the Prime Minister herself' (Riddell, 1985: 52). Tebbit was moved to the DTI while Tom King took his place at the Department of Employment. There was one other significant promotion. Leon Brittan, former Minister of State at the Home Office and Chief Secretary to the Treasury for the previous two years, became Home Secretary, replacing William Whitelaw, who became Lord President and Leader of the House of Lords. In Hugo Young's view, Brittan was 'the prime example, after [Cecil] Parkinson, of a complete Thatcher creation .... [he] looked like the right sort of Home Secretary for an administration intended to mark the rise to power of Mrs Thatcher's friends' (Young, 1989: 335).

According to Thatcher, Brittan had been 'the best Chief Secretary to the Treasury' during her time as Prime Minister (Thatcher, 1993: 308). He had also been a major ally in 1981 when the meltdown effects of three successive, neoliberal, 'prudent' Budgets manifested themselves inside the Cabinet in terms of bitter dissent and outside Whitehall in terms of unemployment, inflation and urban disorder. During the summer of that year: 'the Prime Minister found herself virtually alone in a laager with Keith Joseph and the two Treasury Ministers, Geoffrey Howe and Leon Brittan' (Gilmour, 1993: 46).

Brittan, who had voted for Joseph against Thatcher in the 1975 leadership election (Denham and Garnett, 2001: 284), wasted little time in building on what David Mellor was to call 'the work of his noble predecessor' (*Hansard*, 12 December 1983: col. 807). In his first speech as Home Secretary to the Conservative Party Conference in October 1983, he paid particular tribute to the work that Whitelaw had initiated, 'especially in relation to police and prisons ... I am proud to build on that foundation' (Conservative Party News Service, 1983: 1). From the outset his intentions were unambiguous. He announced the biggest prison-building programme of the twentieth century, which meant constructing 14 new prisons, refurbishing other institutions and employing over 5,500 new prison staff. He also announced a number of major changes to sentencing and to the working of the parole system.

For Brittan, sentencing was of 'vital importance'. Sentences which failed 'to reflect society's deep abhorrence of violent crime undermine[d] ... confidence and so weaken[ed] the whole criminal justice system'. Lifers would remain in prison until the Home Secretary sanctioned their release, while minimum sentences of 20 years were to be given to those who murdered police and prison officers or who carried firearms in the course of a robbery and used them. He also proposed to introduce legislation that would allow what were seem as over-lenient sentences to be referred back to the Court of Appeal by the

Attorney General. In what he regarded as his most important announcement, the parole system was to be changed so that violent offenders sentenced to over five years would not be released except in the last few months of their time inside. Additionally, drug traffickers were to 'be treated with regard to parole in exactly the same way as serious violent offenders – they should not get it' (cited in Ryan and Sim, 1984: 6).

These changes were linked into a broader agenda: first, confronting the fundamental tasks facing the government and, second, building a hegemonic bridge with the wider society:

> There is today a great wave of anger against the wanton violence which disfigures our society. That anger is not confined to this Conference and this Party. It is real, it is genuine. I share it to the full. Where we Conservatives *are* unique is not in our anger, nor in our concern, but in the fact that we are seen by millions of people as the only Party willing to stand up to the men of violence, the terrorist, the thug, the child molester. The public have shown their confidence in us. I am determined that that confidence will not be betrayed (Conservative Party News Service, 1983: 2, emphasis in the original).

Two weeks later, he outlined three elements in his law and order strategy. First, he argued that in dealing with crime 'government has a necessarily limited role because the potential for effective action by government alone is itself necessarily limited'. In highlighting this issue, Brittan was focussing on a key strategy in criminal justice policy in the 1980s and 1990s, namely crime prevention, which, (at least in theory), was to become the responsibility of a range of different agencies, including the police, the local authority, the school and the community itself whose vigilance 'can achieve far more than the police alone can ever hope to do' (Brittan, 1983: 1 and 3). Second, he pointed to the strategy of bifurcation and argued that this should be a central plank in penal policy involving long periods of imprisonment for the 'most serious violent offenders' while 'developing a more flexible range of alternative remedies' for those outside of this category (1983: 4–5). Again, he highlighted an issue which was to reverberate through the following decades, namely the need to ensure that 'probation orders are firmly supervized and to make community service orders really demanding on those who serve them'. (1983: 13). Finally, he returned to a theme that he had articulated in his conference speech, the relationship between the government and the wider public:

> ... the great majority of people do require that their own values should be mirrored in the broad run of decisions applied by the courts. Nothing has done more to undermine confidence in our criminal justice system among people who are themselves entirely committed to the institutions of justice than a deeply ingrained feeling that we – politicians, professionals and commentators – just do not understand, care about or share their values and fears. It is my aim, and not the least of my responsibilities, to ensure that this gap in confidence is bridged (1983:16).

Brittan also pointed to another theme that was to be central to the politics of criminal justice in the coming decades. It was a theme which was to be labelled by New Labour as 'joined-up government' over ten years later. In September 1983, he argued that the government needed to construct 'an overall strategy for dealing with crime', including: developing crime prevention measures, ensuring the 'effective use of police resources', thinking about sentencing policy and confronting the question of 'how to deal with those committed to prison'. He told his audience that 'all of these issues inter-relate ... we shall make no serious headway in tackling crime if we concentrate on any one aspect to the exclusion of others' (Conservative Party Research Department, 1983: 395). He repeated the same message in January 1984: 'On taking office I decided that we needed a strategy which would enable us to pursue our priorities and objectives in a deliberate and coherent way' (cited in Sim, 1987: 206).

For Foucault, this strategy, which began in the late 1970s, was related to the ancient principle of the defence of society which was 'starting – and this is what is new about it – to become an effective principle of operation'. Thus the different constituent parts and actors in the criminal justice system – police, prosecutors and judges – as well as the differences between them, were becoming 'blurred in favour of a continuity which is accepted, even demanded'. This blurring, and the continuity that flowed from it, was legitimated by the discourse of danger and a 'catch-all strategy', which 'instils fear, makes examples of people and advocates action against a "target population" ... an unstable, friable and unsettled population which might one day become restless: unemployed youths, students, secondary school pupils, etc'. (Foucault, 1988: 161).

State authoritarianism

Brittan's plans for the prison were formulated in the context of a series of more general policy developments, which saw an intensification of the power of the state's capacity for the interventionist targeting of the behaviour of the poor and the powerless with respect to law and order and social welfare. This was evident in a number of different areas: the extension of police powers; the ongoing centralization and militarization of the police; the widening definition of subversion to include the 'enemy within';[1] the intensification and extension of surveillance technologies and the passing of a number of Acts and Bills culminating in the Public Order Act 1986, which consolidated and extended the capacity of state servants to intervene in, and regulate and control, public protest and demonstrations. There were also major increases in the financing of criminal justice institutions and the security services. However, it was the police who were:

> ... the greatest beneficiaries of the priorities of Thatcherite policies. Police pay, police clothing, police weaponry, police vehicles and police numbers have all received the

> Home Office's most faithful attention. Police manpower is larger by 10,400 than it was six years ago [in 1979] (Young, 1985: 19).

As with the prison system, the strategies of intervention mobilized in the wider society were underpinned and undercut by the use, or threat of violence, especially towards those groups regarded as politically and socially problematic, as 'forces of chaos and anarchy' made up of 'the obscene, lawless, hideous, dangerous, dirty, violent and young'.[2] In the mid-1980s, particularly during, and after the miners' strike, a range of 'folk devils', including 'soccer hooligans, race rioters, black muggers, Greenham women, animal rights protestors, Scargill's army and Irish terrorists' were:

> ... summoned and conflated ... and used as evidence that the 'Kingdom's unity' is threatened by a broad alliance of 'enemies within' ... It has been as part of this process – the criminalisation of economically and politically marginalised neighbourhoods and identifiable groups – that the police have responded selectively and differentially. The process of criminalisation also justifies the regulation, containment and use of unreasonable force, thus emphasising the structural relations of marginalisation and invoking popular approval and legitimacy – the manufacture of consent – in support of the state (Scraton, 1987: 182).

Vituperative, regulatory processes were also evident in the ongoing, disciplinary management of social policy and the criminalization of welfare claimants, a process, which, as Chapter 5 illustrates, was to continue through to New Labour's time in office (Jones and Novak, 1999). In 1980, an extra 1,050 staff were employed by the Department of Health and Social Security:

> ... at a time when [the government] was otherwise cutting back on civil servants, not to ensure that claimants received the money to which they were legally entitled, not to pursue tax dodgers, but solely for the purpose of fraud control in the DHSS (Andrews and Jacobs, 1990: 165).

This development was supported by a number of other strategies. Specifically, the government established specialist squads both nationally and regionally to investigate benefit fraud (1990: 165). More generally, in the context of Margaret Thatcher's obsessive desire to revolutionize government, and by extension the state itself, thereby creating an administration based on the politics of conviction, those who disagreed with her policies were shunted aside and replaced. By 1988, of the twenty-seven Permanent Secretaries in the Civil Service who were in post at the time of Thatcher's first election victory, only three remained, while twenty-four had retired or resigned (Jones and Novak, 1999: 146). She had 'replaced them with men who tend to do things the Thatcher way' (*The Observer*, 21 February 1988, cited in 1999: 146).

However, there are two issues which should be considered before developing the analysis further through focussing on the prison system itself. First, it is important to recognize that the drive towards the strong state model of Conservative governance was not absolute. In 1983, there was a renewed effort to bring back hanging. As Chapter 2 noted, demands for its restoration had been defeated in July 1979 and again in May 1982. In July 1983, before yet another vote, the Police Federation wrote to MPs arguing for the reintroduction of capital punishment for those found guilty of murder. Despite its coruscating law and order editorial line, *The Sun* opposed its reintroduction. Writing in the *Sunday Telegraph*, Peregrine Worsthorne supported its reintroductions on the grounds that:

> No penal policy can work if prisons contain a growing numbers (sic) of undeterrable brutes, whose company constitutes an altogether inhuman extra punishment – over and above the deprivation of freedom – which ordinary offenders in no way deserve. That is the uncovenanted consequence of showing mercy to monsters – the worsening of conditions for all other prisoners (*Sunday Telegraph*, 26 June 1983).

The motion supporting the death penalty was defeated by over one hundred votes (*The Standard*, 4 July 1983; *The Sun*, 13 July 1983; *The Sun*, 14 July 1983). The vote was carried in spite of Brittan's support for restoring the death penalty for terrorist offences while opposing its restoration for other forms of murder. Importantly, therefore, there were still social democratic constraints on the popular and political capabilities of those who articulated authoritarian ideologies and demanded coercive policies in the attempt to achieve hegemony around law and order, however brittle, fragmented and defensive these constraints appeared to be.

Second, invariably, social and penal policies do not always achieve the outcomes intended by those who develop and articulate these policies. There are contradictions and contingencies inherent in, as well as unintended consequences that flow from, developments in social and penal policy. In that sense, there was no easy and inevitable link between Brittan's vision of a coherent criminal justice strategy and its seamless appearance, fully formed and working with rational effectiveness on the ground. Theoretically and politically, it would be wrong to conceptualize the world of politics working in such an untrammelled and unproblematic manner. However, Brittan *did* lay down the parameters for the debate that was to follow, particularly with regard to the use of the prison as a material and ideological bulwark against the criminality and deviance of those at the bottom of a society, where the distribution of wealth and power was increasingly becoming more uneven and, inevitably, more unjust.

The expanding prison complex

By the mid-1980s, the prison service was part of this expansionist, authoritarian process. In 1985–6, the budget for the service was £638 million. This was a rise of 36 per cent in real terms and 156 per cent in cash terms compared with the financial year 1978–9. The number of uniformed and nonuniformed officers also rose significantly while 16 new prisons were in the planning stage. Major developments were taking place at over 100 prisons. Taken together, these plans were designed to add 11,700 places to the system by the early 1990s. In August 1985, the average daily population had reached the then record level of 48,165, which gave England and Wales a rate of imprisonment of 96 per 100,000 of the population. At the annual conference of the Prison Officers' Association, held the previous May, Brittan noted that their numbers had increased by a fifth since 1979, that the prison budget had risen by 85 per cent while yearly expenditure on prison building, repairs and development had risen by nearly 400 per cent. Overtime pay had also increased by 137 per cent, rising from £34.3 million in 1979 to £76.7 million in 1985. Despite these impressive figures, he was barracked and booed by conference delegates (Sim, 1987: 190–192; *The Guardian*, 21 May 1985; Ballantyne, 1985).

Brittan's proposals, announced in October 1983, were also impacting on the system. By 1984 the number of adult male prisoners serving sentences of five years or more was approximately 4,000, while in the first six months of the year 13 violent offenders and drug traffickers were granted parole compared with 113 in the same period a year earlier (Sim, 1987: 196). The very human consequences of his strategy were evident in the suicide of Tony Taylor, a life sentence prisoner who was told in November 1984 that he would have to wait for 17 years before his case went before a local parole review committee (*The Guardian*, 24 January 1985). As Peter Jenkins noted, 'by denying to some even the hope or dream of early release, Mr Brittan has offended against humanity and natural justice in order to win the plaudits of his party' (Jenkins, 1984: 19).

However, this major expansion in places and personnel failed to alleviate the crisis inside and outside the prison walls. Outside, recorded crime continued to rise. Inside, prison numbers also rose. By August 1985, the average daily population was over 48,000, while 'the population at the end of the year was about 3,000 higher than a year earlier' (Home Office, 1986a: 1). During the year 1985–6, over 18,500 prisoners at one point were sleeping 2 or 3 to a cell (NACRO, 1986). At the same time, both the average daily prison population and the numbers being moved, often desperately, through the system, indicated that the UK in general, and England and Wales in particular, headed the European league tables for prison use. In 1986, just under 150,000 people were processed in England and Wales, giving the country an imprisonment rate of 229.9 per 100,000 of the population.[3] With an average daily population of 95.8 prisoners per 100,000, the UK had a 'higher prison population, both in terms of absolute numbers and relative to its population, than any other EC country'. The equivalent figure for England and Wales was 94.1 per 100,000 of the population (NACRO, cited in Haringey Police Research Unit, no date: 46 and 47).

Overcrowding, appalling conditions, the ongoing militancy of prison officers, their hostility towards management (which resulted in the removal of a liberal prison governor from Styal in early 1986), and the ongoing conflict between prisoners and staff meant that the good order and discipline of the system, and its wider legitimacy, remained under serious threat. Between January 1984 and March 1985, there were, what the Prison Service euphemistically called, 37 acts of 'concerted indiscipline', including refusing to work and refusing to take food. The number of prisoners involved ranged from 7 to 420 while the indiscipline lasted from under an hour to ten days (Sim, 1986: 8). Between April and June 1985, 135 prisoners and over 300 staff were injured in confrontations. In the same period, probation officers complained that young offenders were punched in Aldington prison 'for forgetting to say "Sir", for not knowing their number even though they had not been given [one] and for not running quickly enough'. Furthermore:

> ... there was a large demonstration by 43 women in Holloway ... protesting about brutality inflicted upon a fellow prisoner who was said to have been dragged into a cell by 8 prison officers, forcibly stripped and was later refused permission to see a doctor (Sim, 1987: 192).

As in the previous decades, the prison authorities pursued a number of strategies as a result of these confrontations, to ensure that good order and discipline was maintained, particularly regarding those prisoners who were labelled as difficult and subversive. Psychotropic drugs, the mobilization of the Minimum Use of Force Tactical Intervention Squad (MUFTI), solitary confinement, segregation units and special cells, particularly for women prisoners, were mobilized to maintain or restore order. Violence, and the threat of violence, also remained central to the state's repertoire of responses:

> In Wandsworth, prisoners were treated little better than cattle, and anyone who complained or tried to fight back was quickly stamped on by the screws ... the screws would openly flaunt racist tattoos and wear NF [National Front] badges on their ties. They classed all prisoners as "scum" and treated them as such. The punishment block was a dark, evil place where men were beaten until they cried out for mercy, and beyond ... When it came to instilling fear and dishing out brutality, the screws at Wandsworth were experts (Smith, 2004: 294 and 325).

The 'anti-statist' Tories

The often-brutal interventions by the state into the lives of the powerless, both within and without penal institutions, stood in marked contrast to criminal justice interventions into the lives of the powerful. Thatcher herself was clear about the role the state should play in socially organizing the society:

> There was a case for the state to intervene in specific instances – for example to protect children in real danger from malign parents. The state must uphold law

and order and ensure that criminals were punished – an area in which I was deeply uneasy, for our streets were becoming more not less violent, in spite of the large increases in police numbers and prison places. But the root cause of our contemporary social problems – to the extent that these did not reflect the timeless influence and bottomless resources of old-fashioned human wickedness – was that the state had been doing too much (Thatcher, 1993: 626).

'Doing too much' was a potent and powerful euphemism for cutting back and retrenching those institutions whose role and function arose out of the post-war settlement between capital and labour with respect to providing a material, social democratic comfort blanket for the powerless. In early 1983, a Public Spending White Paper, published by the Treasury (whose Chief Secretary was Leon Brittan) indicated that, compared with public expenditure in 1978–9, the defence budget in 1984–5 was projected to rise by 24 per cent, law and order by 30 per cent and farming by 25 per cent. At the same time, while there was a slight increase in the budget for health, the housing budget was cut by 55 per cent, education by over 6 per cent and arts and libraries by over 4 per cent (*The Guardian*, 2 February 1983).

The significant increase in the law and order budget was reinforced by the plethora of new bills and Acts, referred to above, which focused relentlessly on the world of the public with respect to disorder and criminality. In the case of public order, this legislation was designed to enhance and intensify the power of the state to respond quickly, efficiently and ruthlessly to challenges to its authority, particularly after the inner city disturbances in 1985. Similarly, in directing its gaze towards criminality in the public sphere, state agencies and institutions inevitably and invariably neglected and effectively ignored the violent depredations experienced by women in the world of the private. In October 1983 (ironically, the very month when Brittan spoke at the Conservative Party conference), Sir Kenneth Newman, the Metropolitan Police Commissioner, categorized domestic disputes alongside 'stranded people, lost property and stray animals' and not as 'real crime work' (cited in Greater London Council, 1985: 6). For Susan Edwards, the major Acts passed during the 1980s – the Police and Criminal Evidence Act 1984 and the Public Order Act 1986 – which extended the powers of the police both inside and outside the police station, made it 'self-evident' that the state was attempting to increase 'control of public order as opposed to private family order situations ...'. As she pointedly made clear:

It is no accident that the man who beats his wife on the street is more likely to be prosecuted than the man who behaves in exactly the same way in his own home. The visibility of their behaviour is one of the reasons police regularly arrest and prosecute prostitutes for street soliciting, while the organizer, producer and controller of prostitution, who organizes behind closed doors in saunas, clubs and massage parlours goes unseen and relatively untouched (Edwards, 1989: 20 and 32).

The 'anti-statist' strategy was also evident in policing the powerful outside the home. The number of wage inspectors was halved between 1979 and 1988.

This had a precipitous impact on the prosecution of those firms who were illegally underpaying their workers. Between 1979 and 1991, over 4,000 workplaces underpaid their workers, which resulted in nine prosecutions: 'overall, between 1979 and 1991, 100,000 companies were caught underpaying their workers. Sixty-seven, or 0.067 per cent, were prosecuted' (*The Independent*, cited in Sim, 2000a: 325). Furthermore, between 1979 and 1983, the number of Factory Inspectors declined from 978 to 833 while the number of workplaces inspected fell in the same period from 22.5 per cent to 15.5 per cent. Prosecutions for contraventions of the Health and Safety at Work Act fell from 2,127 to 2,022. For those companies prosecuted under the Act, the average fine was £205 (Gilroy and Sim, 1987: 73). Furthermore, 'in the mining industry there were 1.03 people killed or seriously injured per 100,000 shifts in 1979 and 'by 1983 it had gone up to 1.97 ... in other words there has been a 12 per cent increase in the number of people killed or seriously injured in the mines even in the last year' (*Hansard*, cited in 1987: 73).

In 1987, a draft document complied by the *General and Municipal, Boiler-makers and Allied Trades Unions* criticized the government's strategy of deregulation and pointed out that there had been a 24 per cent increase in workplace deaths and serious accidents since 1981. In 1985 alone, more than 400 people had been killed in accidents at work while there had been almost 20,000 major accidents and over 500,000 minor accidents (*The Guardian*, 23 February 1987).[4]

Hurd's moment: liberalising Tory authoritarianism?

Leon Brittan was Home Secretary until September 1985. Between March 1984 and March 1985, during the year-long coal dispute, he had been responsible for 'Britain's largest and longest running police mobilization ever' (Milne, 1995: 26).[5] It was a mobilization built around a number of significant changes in the organization of the police in the light of public order failures three years before during the inner city disturbances in London and Liverpool (Young, 1989: 368). However, despite his role in defeating the miners, he had failed Margaret Thatcher in one crucial, hegemonic respect: 'he just did not carry conviction with the public' (Thatcher, 1993: 419). As ever, she was concerned with the presentation of policy and, by extension, taking the public with the government on the key issue of crime and punishment:

> I replaced Leon at the Home Office with Douglas Hurd, who looked more the part, was immensely reassuring to the police, and, though no one could call him a natural media performer, inspired a good deal of confidence in the Parliamentary Party. He had become a harder and wiser man through serving as Secretary of State for Northern Ireland. He also knew the department, having earlier been Leon's number two there. By and large, it was a successful appointment (1993: 419).

According to Hurd, his 'marked promotion' from his post in Northern Ireland came as a complete surprise. He was 'amazed; there had been no hint, no gossip'. Thatcher told him 'an unlikely tale that she was moving Leon Brittan to Trade and Industry because she wanted more attention paid to these subjects' (Hurd, 2004: 346). Although commentators described him as a 'liberal home secretary', Hurd doubted that this label was:

> ... accurate, at least during the early years of my tenure. Rather, I looked on the penal system as just one part of the wall of protection of the citizen against crime. Wherever the wall was shown to be crumbling, it was my job to repair it, without much time considering the philosophy of the repair work (2004: 387).

In a lecture to the Prison Reform Trust in 1986, Hurd was clear about the continuities with his predecessors. Utilizing prison sentences 'coincides with that of my predecessor and the Court of Appeal'. In particular, he supported Brittan's policies regarding long prison sentences for serious offenders and the restrictions on parole for those who engaged in violence and drug trafficking. He had also been persuaded that for less serious offenders prisons should be used 'sparingly, and that non-custodial penalties should be used whenever possible ...' (Hurd, 1986: 41–42). He concluded:

> William Whitelaw began the work by focussing public attention on prisons, opening the system up to a much greater extent than before and winning support for the necessary expenditure. In the years since then and guided later by Leon Brittan, a broad programme of work has been developed. It has already made an impact. My task is to carry it steadily forward, coping with short-term difficulties if they arise, but not allowing the programme to be diverted from its long-term objectives (1986: 50).

Despite this optimism, Hurd was faced with the same prison crisis that had confronted Brittan. Report after report, official and unofficial, pointed to the desperate conditions endured by prisoners, especially in remand centres and local prisons, where the stench of urine and excrement pervaded their everyday life to the point where the Chief Inspector of Prisons noted that in one institution, 'so awful is this procedure [of slopping out] that many prisoners become constipated. Others prefer to use their pants, hurling them and their contents out of the window when morning comes' (cited in Aitken, 1987: 19). As the numbers inside continued to rise, the government responded by drawing up plans for the early release of 6,000 prisoners (*The Guardian*, 12 March 1987). (It was also a strategy, which their New Labour successors were to pursue exactly 20 years later to deal with yet another prison crisis).[6]

A report by the European Society of Friends pointed out that British prisons had 'virtually the worst record for insanitary conditions and overcrowding in Western Europe' (cited in *The Guardian*, 11 February 1987). Despite this criticism, Hurd rejected a code of minimum standards which Brittan had supported

(*The Guardian*, 6 February 1987). At the same time, the prison continued to be a place for warehousing the poor, powerless and, increasingly, members of minority ethnic groups, particularly women. In 1985, 24,000 people were jailed for nonpayment of fines. One third of women jailed were imprisoned for the same crime after originally being convicted of drunkenness and prostitution. As Frances Crook noted, '70 per cent of these men and women are unemployed' (Letter to *The Guardian*, 4 March 1987). Furthermore, minority ethnic group men constituted 8 per cent, and women 12 per cent, of the prison population. In comparison, they made up 1 and 2 per cent of the general population, respectively (Home Office, 1986b: 2). The remand system was also part of this process. The proportion of remand prisoners had tripled since the 1950s and doubled since the enactment of the 1976 Bail Act, ironically an Act that was designed to increase the number of offenders on bail as opposed to remanding them in custody (*The Guardian*, 3 February 1987).

Allegations of violence towards prisoners also continued to be made, particularly by young offenders in 'short, sharp, shock' detention centres such as Haslar and Blantyre House. In the case of the latter, one prisoner complained that:

> ... prison officers asked him his name, which he gave them. "I got a punch from each side and one of them said 'That was for not saying sir'. My face went numb afterwards and a couple of days later it started aching". Later the same day ... he was punched by another prison officer who brought him and a group of other boys tea. "He said, 'What do you say?' I said 'Thank you'. Then he punched me in the stomach for not saying 'Sir"' (cited in *The Guardian*, 24 November 1986).

It has become accepted (and acceptable wisdom) that, as Home Secretary, Hurd was a pragmatic politician who was different in personality and politics from his predecessor, Brittan, and from his most famous successor, Howard, whose time and impact as Home Secretary is discussed in the next chapter. This is a dominant theme in the work of many of those who have commented on this era (Cavadino et al., 1999; Faulkner, 2001).[7] This argument is then used to underpin the contention that the 1991 *Criminal Justice Act* was a liberal measure that had a direct impact on the numbers inside. At one level, there is some support for this argument, not least in terms of the actual fall in the average daily population. However, there are a number of dimensions to Hurd's tenure at the Home Office which deserve closer scrutiny, as they provide a different perspective to his time there.

First, as Barbara Hudson has noted, the 1991 Criminal Justice Act was not a radical break with the past but was 'a culmination of tendencies becoming more and more apparent during the 1980s'. Second, as she also noted:

> Such clarification as has been achieved in sentencing policy has not been matched by equal attention to other criminal justice processes. Focusing on problems like disparity in sentencing and achieving a politically adequate response to crime has not been accompanied by equal concern with *the nature of regimes*, or by concern with the

fate of offenders after sentences, still less by concern for the relationship of penal policy to social justice: the 1991 Act, for example, contains merely ... [an] 'oblique recognition' of a duty not to discriminate on the ground of race, sex or other 'improper' characteristic (Hudson, 1993: 53–54, emphasis added).

Third, following Hudson's point about the nature of the regimes, it is important to recognize that, like many liberals, politicians or otherwise, Hurd's understanding of the dynamics of prisons stopped at the level of policy documents or at the prison gates after a fleeting, overwhelmingly sanitized, visit to a particular institution. Consequently, the everyday dynamics of power on the ground, the discretion afforded to, and centrality of, prison officers in the operationalization of this power, and the often negative impact on prisoners, psychologically and physically, is missing not only from Hurd's world but also in the analysis that constructs him as a liberal. The events at Risley in May 1989 illustrate this point.

On 1 May, a year before the Strangeways disturbance, which is discussed in the next chapter, 120 prisoners occupied a landing inside Risley.[8] There had been a demonstration the previous evening, which had been put down by the MUFTI squad. According to one of those involved:

> The now infamous observation by Judge Tumin that Risley was "barbarous and squalid" assumes terrifying substance when it is noted that six of the suicides in the last decade occurred in the last year, and that in a five-week period in 1988, there were three suicides. This "squalor and barbarism" was not limited purely to the carnage of inmate corpses but manifested itself in the filthy, inhuman squalor and putrid conditions which drove a great many of us to the fringes of suicide, when, that is, it did not drive us out of our minds completely. It was the institutional callousness and environmental brutality, which defined the nature of "Gris Ris" and it is our collective refusal to tolerate this celebration of brutality and challenge and resist the culture and politics of "barbarism and squalor", which define the events of 1–3 May 1989 (cited in Jameson and Allison, 1995: 176–7).[9]

The brutality and callousness of the regime was symbolized by the use of strip cells as to punish prisoners:

> I don't know the official use of the strip cell, I believe they are to prevent suicides, but they are used as a punishment. Anyone being "disruptive" is stripped and thrown into this cell. I have seen prisoners beaten and have recorded these events. In fact, the Senior Medical Officer has told me that if I get cheeky or familiar with him, I will be thrown into one of these cells ... Some three months ago I was sick due to losing blood from my back passage. I thought I had seen a Doctor, but it was a Nurse. As I walked into the "Surgery", the Officer had his feet up at the table, smoking a cigarette and said, "What's up?" I informed him that I was losing blood and he went to a cupboard, pulled something out, threw it on to the table and told me to "shove it up my arse". I told him I was disgusted by his manner, he laughed, I left ... Tonight, at 8.30 pm., a prisoner [who] had been put into a strip cell No. 11, about one hour earlier, was "buzzing" and asking for water and to be removed from the cell due to

cockroaches crawling about in there. The Officer told him to "Train them and more will come". This was Officer B, the lad went mad smashing his light, then, the S/O called for the Riot Gear. Eight Riot Officers rushed in to help him, injected him and put him in Strip Cell No. 13.[10]

Furthermore, for many prisoners, the system in general still remained a place of punish-ment and pain. In September 1986, a report from the *Home Office Working Group on Suicide Prevention* indicated that prisoners were four times more likely to commit suicide compared with those outside. Suicide was particularly acute amongst prisoners on remand; thirteen out of the 23 prisoners who committed suicide in 1984 were on remand. This compared with nine out of 23 the previous year (*The Guardian*, 6 September 1986). Between January 1987 and December 1988, there were 159 deaths in prison. Furthermore, between April 1987 and March 1988, there were 429 incidents of self-harm amongst women prisoners and 107 amongst young offenders (*Hansard*, 24 February 1989: col. 840). The pressure group, *INQUEST*, was clear about the causes of the deaths in custody that occurred during 1989–90. The group highlighted, the 'scandalous number of prison suicides', which had risen from 48 in 1989 to 51 in 1990. *INQUEST* also pointed to 'deaths due to the lack of medical care and treatment. Many of these deaths highlight the inhumanity and brutality of the prison regimes' (*INQUEST*, 1990: 2).

Fourth, Hurd's relationship to prison officers was built on his attempt to reform their working practices through the proposals contained in the document, *A Fresh Start* (Home Office, 1986c). This meant confronting their union, the Prison Officers' Association. It is not the intention here to explore the complex nuances in the proposals contained in *Fresh Start*, this has been done elsewhere (King and McDermott, 1995: 29–36). The important point is that even on their own terms, not only did the proposals fail to defuse the conflict between rank and file prison officers and prison managers, but, crucially, the discretionary power base of prison officers, and the lack of democratic accountability that flowed from this power base, also remained untouched. In short, the power of prison officers remained undiminished. This failure was to resonate over the next two decades as research continued to show the often nefarious and insidious impact of the landing culture of prison staff on the lives of prisoners, as well as on those officers who were concerned with offering empathic support to the confined (Scott, 2006; Sim, 2008a). I will return to this question in Chapter 7, as it raises some profound issues regarding the development of an abolitionist position on prisons.

Fifth, in the three years up to May 1989, there were 11 disturbances in prisons and remand centres where 'a substantial number of inmates' acted 'in concert', which lead 'to significant damage' (*Hansard*, 12 May 1989: cols. 561–562). Consequently, Hurd was concerned with the maintenance of good order and discipline and developing strategies to deal with disorder as well as the threat of disorder. Like his predecessors, these strategies were based on a militarized response to the grievances of the confined. In November 1988, an internal prison service circular revealed that the Home Office was preparing to improve the 'state of preparedness to deal with inmate violence' as well as changing the 'techniques to deal with violence on a large scale'. Consequently, the Minimum Use of Force Tactical Intervention Squad (the squad, known as MUFTI, which had been involved in repressing the demonstration at Wormwood Scrubs discussed in the previous chapter) was to be replaced with Control and Restraint (C and R) 3 techniques based on:

> ... teams of 36 (three teams of twelve) who will have "newer style helmets, flame-retardant suits", "shields", "protective gloves, shin/knee guards" and "specialist protective boots". Male officers will have new "side-arm batons" and female officers will have "kubotans". Kubotans are the type of batons used by US and Canadian police with a handle projecting at right angles. All officers will be trained in C & R 1 and C & R 2 self-defence. "A body of officers" in each prison will be trained in C & R 2 teams of 12 and C & R 3. Over 4000 officers will be trained in C & R 3. This is far more than the numbers involved in MUFTI. ... In short MUFTI is to be replaced by a bigger, better-trained, better-equipped riot squad with a unit in every prison. As is always the case with Home Office doublespeak, phase out means crackdown (O'Halloran, 1995: 180–181).

In contrast, he rejected a recommendation from the Prior Committee to establish an independent appeals system for prisoners found guilty of disciplinary offences, a decision described by the Prison Reform Trust as 'paltry and ill-judged' (cited in *The Guardian*, 22 December 1986). He also endorsed a Cabinet Office report to restrict the automatic right of remand prisoners to appear in court every eight days to argue that they should be bailed rather than remanded in custody (*The Guardian*, 29 November 1986).

Sixth, whatever liberalizing tendencies Hurd had, it is important to note that he also remained committed to the prison as a totemic bulwark against crime.[11] In May 1989, his Under Secretary of State at the Home Office pointed out that eight new prisons had been opened since 1985, a further seven were under construction and another institution was being converted from buildings already in existence. By the end of 1989, he noted, nearly 2,000 new places would have been added to existing prisons while 'by the mid-1990s we will have added 25,000 places to the system' (*Hansard*, 11 May 1989: col. 985). At the same time, according to the Prison Reform Trust, this commitment was built on ensuring that capital expenditure on the new prisons was protected and supported by cutbacks in the running costs in other areas of regime delivery. Thus, closing workshops, restricting the privileges of remand prisoners and:

> ... reducing the overtime budget ... seem to have been designed to protect the massive capital programme of new institutions. This has resulted in a deterioration in the prison regime, while at the same time sending an unmistakable signal to the courts endorsing current sentencing practice. The rhetoric of 'law and order' combined with the building

programme have swamped the contrary message (which it is fair to say has also been present in Government statements) that many non-violent offenders can be adequately punished without being sent to prison (Prison Reform Trust, 1986: 8).[12]

Seventh, and more generally, Hurd's attitude towards a range of other areas in the criminal justice system chimed with the broader authoritarian orientation of the government and the Prime Minister. As Ian Aitken noted at the time, 'Mrs Thatcher's hyperactive Home Secretary' was:

> ... in charge of a cascade of bills and white papers dealing with a whole range of civil rights issues, which have excited widespread hostility. These include the future funding (and therefore survival) of the BBC; the duties of television reporters dealing with the IRA; the right of accused persons to remain silent; the period during which suspects in terrorist cases can be held without charge; the imposition of an absolute and life-long duty of silence on everyone connected with security; and the removal of a "public interest" defence for people accused of unauthorizsed leaks of government secrets (Aitken, 1989: 19).

Aitken pointedly concluded that, as there was to be a vote on Hurd's bill reforming the Official Secrets Act after only two days of debate, this was:

> ... not much of an achievement for a great reforming Home Secretary bearing the torch of liberty. But then, the other argument Mr Hurd now uses to justify his behaviour is that people have always got him wrong. He never was much of a wet or a liberal, just an old-fashioned Conservative (1989: 19).[13]

Finally, the issue of privatization, which had been raised as early as 1983 by one of Thatcher's ministers, had, by 1987, 'become one of the most distinctive policies and themes of the Thatcher government' (Gamble, 1988: 7). Hurd indicated that he was interested in private prisons and that he was also considering privatizing parts of the probation service (*The Guardian*, 23 March 1987; *The Guardian*, 23 October 1987). It is not the intention here to explore the nuanced issues and debates around the privatization of the prison system or aspects of the criminal justice system more generally. This has been done elsewhere (Ryan and Ward, 1989). The important point, with which this chapter concludes, is that the debates around privatization under Hurd's stewardship at the Home Office did not lead to the wholesale privatization of the prison system in England and Wales. Indeed, in 2007, twenty years after the initial debates, the vast majority of institutions were still run and managed by the state. In that sense, it was the prison as a *state* institution which remained central to the Conservative's law and order strategy and to the vision of social order that underpinned that strategy. Therefore, whether privatized or not, the targets of the prison system, and the criminal justice system more generally, remained the same. If anything, the emergence of more privatized elements within the criminal justice system merely reinforced the ideologies and discourses which dominated popular and political consciousness as to who criminals were (and are) and what should be done to them once they were caught and punished. As David Coates has noted in 1991, Margaret Thatcher left behind a state which:

> ... may present itself as a limited one; but it is a state of considerable power. For even where state functions are now privatized, it is still the state, which sets the boundary links between the public and the private (Coates, 1991: 159).

The next chapter addresses the issue of penal policy in the years between 1990 and 1997. It was a period when the Conservative government was confronted by the political and ideological force of a New Labour opposition whose position not only embraced the punitive orientation of the government's law and order and penal policies, but also was proactive in intensifying them still further. As identifiable, separate political entities, the impact of the strategies pursued by both parties was toxic. In the 1990s, as they became more politically aligned and ideologically intertwined, their collective impact was deadly.

Notes

1 This phrase was first used by Margaret Thatcher in a speech to the 1992 Conservative Backbench Committee on 19 July 1984, during the miners' strike. It came on the back of the definition of subversion articulated by Harold Salisbury, the former Chief Constable of York, referred to in the previous chapter.
2 This phrase is taken from the song 'We Can Be Together' by Jefferson Airplane which although released in 1969, and focussing on the political and social situation in America, precisely captures those groups who, from the perspective of those in power, had come to be regarded as socially and politically deviant. It was therefore a perspective that both preceded the 1970s and 1980s and, as subsequent chapters illustrate, resonated beyond those decades.
3 The total figure for the UK was 197,044 or 347.9 per 100,000 of the population. For Scotland and Northern Ireland, the equivalent figures were 41,327 (807.3 per 100,000) and 5,944 (383.1 per 100,000) (NACRO, cited in Haringey Police Research Unit, no date: 47).
4 These figures undoubtedly underestimate the number of deaths and injuries at work. See (Tombs and Whyte 2007: Chapter 2) for an analysis of the problems around the statistics concerning health and safety at work.
5 Fourteen million police hours were spent policing the strike at a cost of £200 million. Approximately 10,000 miners, and their supporters, were arrested (*The Guardian*, 3 January 2006).
6 The impact of the crisis manifested itself in other ways, including: delaying the processing of parole applications; failing to produce remand prisoners in court; shuffling prisoners around the system and keeping untried prisoners in appalling conditions in prison and police cells.
7 Thanks to Roy Coleman and Barry Goldson for discussing this point with me.

8 In September/October 1986, there had also been a demonstration against overcrowding that had lasted for six days.

9 A year after the demonstration, 21 prisoners were tried in Liverpool Crown Court accused of criminal damage and riot. They were found not guilty after a five-month trial (Hawthorne, 1995).

10 This account is taken from a letter sent by a prisoner to Judge Stephen Tumin, the Chief Inspector of Prisons, in September 1988, eight months before the demonstration. It was one of a number of documents used by the defence in the trial of the demonstrators referred to in footnote 9 above.

11 He also used the phrase 'punishment in the community' in yet another speech dealing with the prison crisis in March 1988, which provides some indication of how he saw the direction of alternatives to custody (*The Guardian*, 31 March 1988).

12 In February 1987, it was also reported that 10,000 community jobs for ex-prisoners were to be cut during the year due to the fact that government funding for different job schemes did not meet the cost of the 255,000 places, which had been promised in the previous year's budget (*The Guardian*, 23 February 1987).

13 When he left government, Hurd, now Lord Hurd, became chairman of the Prison Reform Trust. Other commentators noted that 'the media's very fascination with character over context, with anecdote rather than record' had 'enabled Hurd to pass himself off, since he retired from politics, as a genial cove – a lovely old liberal *really* – quite unconnected with the more distasteful aspects of the Tory administration, such as the Pergau Dam aid-for-arms deal, the Matrix Churchill trial, or, for that matter, the disgraceful and pretty successful, attempt to deny the public an informed debate on the Scott Report. Hurd ... was one of those appointed to rubbish the report before it came out .... Thanks to the "decay" of the press, thanks to all that missing context, Hurd's political past already seems remote: it's been left to a few dogged commentators to keep reminding us that mad hair and beautiful manners are perfectly compatible with the chilliest kind of fixing – or whatever realpolitik's called when you do it for a bank, for £250,000 a year ... Francis Wheen has repeatedly pointed out that Hurd's labours for NatWest have included a "working breakfast" and lucrative privatization deal with the genocidal Slobodan Milosevic' (Bennett, 1998: 21, emphasis in the original).

4

FROM BIG HOUSE TO BLEAK HOUSE: PRISONS IN THE 'IRON TIMES' 1990–97[1]

In truth there has never been a 'golden age' of freedom from which to mark the current state of our 'decline' ... Kenneth Baker, David Waddington and Michael Howard were at least as controversial in their day as John Reid, Charles Clarke and David Blunkett have been in theirs (Gearty, 2007: 49).

Between 1992 and 1997 the [prison] population increased by 33 per cent, which was similar to the increase in South Africa, America and Russia. The population was heavily racialised with 19 per cent of prisoners drawn from minority ethnic backgrounds when they constituted only 4 per cent of the general population. The incarceration of women was also accelerating compared with men. (Home Office, 1999, Digest 4, cited in Sim, 2000b: 175).

In May 1990, the Centre for Policy Studies (CPS) held a conference on 'crime culture'. Among those in attendance were Kenneth Baker, who was soon to become Home Secretary, Lord Thomas, an advisor to Mrs Thatcher, Lord (formerly, Sir Keith) Joseph, and a Deputy Under Secretary from the Home Office who apologized for the non-attendance of David Waddington, the current Home Secretary. David Walters, the Director of the Centre, told the audience that British social research was 'at worst Marxist, at best state Fabian'. He rejected sociological and environmental views on crime and instead pointed to the work of the American geneticist Richard Hernstein, the co-author with James Q. Wilson of *Crime and Human Nature*, who had indicated that he could not believe that 'our ability to anticipate crime from a person's parents early in life or even before their life had begun will be ignored. Somewhere down the road this knowledge ... will be applied'. Kenneth Baker told Charles Murray, the populizer of the underclass thesis, that he was 'just at the moment reading your brilliant latest book with the greatest of interest' (cited in James, 1990: 21).

This conference epitomized the discourses surrounding crime and punishment which were to underpin the political rhetoric of the Conservative government and its New Labour challengers in the first years of the 1990s and beyond. Indeed, in February 2001, a decade after the CPS conference, at which Wilson, along with Jonathan Sacks, the then Chief Rabbi, Irwin Stelzer, a consultant close to Rupert Murdoch, the former Conservative government minister, Lord Young and David Miliband, the future Foreign Secretary addressed a breakfast seminar attended by Gordon Brown at which Wilson 'made repeated references to the way moral decline is related to the growth of single parenthood – a direct cause of crime, he said' (*The Guardian*, 1 February 2001). The images of, and the dangers posed by, a revitalized and morally dangerous underclass, which transfixed both Conservative and New Labour politicians, were underpinned by the reassertion of a positivist emphasis on causation and prediction, which was then overlaid by an emphasis on the rationality and responsibility of offenders for their actions. At the same time, causation, prediction, rationality and responsibility were themselves underpinned by the reassertion of the discourse of the community in general and the nuclear family in particular, as the praetorian guards in the fight against crime.

This worked in two ways. First, the idea that the community could strategically come together to fight crime became increasingly important in Conservative (and crucially in New Labour) thinking. The Home Office document, *Tackling Crime*, published in August 1990, summed up the trajectory of this approach. In his foreword, David Waddington talked of the 'welcome upsurge in the number of citizens who in different ways are active against crime'. The document went on to note that crime prevention was 'not just a matter for the individual – there is potential for whole communities to get involved. Information, responsibility and expertise are scattered between different groups in society. Their fusion could make a powerful force in deterring crime' (Home Office, 1990: 3 and 24). Thus, the emphasis on the community as a crime prevention strategy was mobilized by the government in order to underline:

> ... the responsibility of private citizens for personal and public safety ... [They] managed to integrate the community-based approach into their ideological framework while retaining a commitment to "hard" policing and retributive prison regimes (Benyon and Edwards, cited in Sim, 2000b: 170).

Second, the discourse of community as an ideological buttress and cement resonated in Conservative thinking as the party, now led by John Major, looked backwards to a mystical past in order to construct a mythical present built around a free economy, responsible subjects and a sense of homogenized unity, which cut across the old, and from the perspective of the government, redundant social divisions of class, 'race' and gender that paralyzed the society and suffocated its entrepreneurial progress. It was a sepia-tinted vision designed to unite the society against those who would threaten and subvert a way of life whose roots lay in a hazy, Arthurian past and whose present tranquillity, and future prosperity, could not be compromised by the amoral lifestyle and parasitical presence of an 'enemy within'. It was an enemy who ranged from conventional criminals to illegal immigrants and from drug takers to single parents who were increasingly 'elided into one apocalyptic vision of chaos and breakdown, an unmanageable detritus out of control' (Ryan and Sim, 1995: 124).

The Conservative government, and what was evolving into New Labour, were ideologically cojoined with respect to these discourses as each vied to outflank and outdo the other in the remorseless battle to win the hearts and minds of a wider public, which itself was manifesting a sense of fragmented dislocation in an increasingly globalized world. As in the 1970s, crime was a key metaphor for that sense of individual dislocation and collective feeling of desolation. The relationship between criminal behaviour and a broader sense of impending doom was central to the political and moral vision of Tony Blair when he became Shadow Home Secretary in July 1992. In his two years in the post, Blair repositioned the Labour Party towards what he regarded as a more realistic perspective on crime and punishment. In January 1993, in an interview with the BBC's *The World This Weekend,* Blair argued that New Labour had to be 'tough on crime and tough on the causes of crime'. The following month, James Bulger was murdered in Liverpool. In a speech in Wellingborough, he described the child's brutal murder in apocalyptic terms:

> The news bulletins of the last week have been like hammer blows struck against the sleeping conscience of the country. ... A solution to this disintegration doesn't simply lie in legislation. It must come from the rediscovery of a sense of direction as a country ... not just as individuals but as a community. ... We cannot exist in a moral vacuum. If we do not learn and then teach the value of what is right and wrong, then the result is simply moral chaos that engulfs us all (Blair, cited in Seldon, 2004: 150–151).

Blair directly attacked 'the liberal individualist consensus that had developed over crime, using the language of punishment, and right and wrong' (Gould, 1999: 188). During this period, the future Prime Minister had also visited the newly elected Bill Clinton 'where he had been fired up in part by Clinton's tough line on crime' (Seldon, 2004: 150). Crucially, the Bulger murder involved Blair in a 'spiral of amplification', which reinforced the moral panic which followed the case. He articulated a view, which was to become central to New Labour's position on crime, which was to focus on a very public, though relatively unique crime, and then link this event into the broader nightmare of a morally decadent, disintegrating social order. In practice, children were more likely to die as a result of road traffic accidents or were more likely to be killed by friends and relatives than by strangers. According to the *National Society for the Prevention of Cruelty to Children*, in the mid-1990s, at least one child under five was dying each week from abuse and neglect inflicted by someone known to them. Additionally, 49 children were injured or killed daily by motorists and one in fifteen would be killed or injured before they were sixteen (*The Guardian*, 18 March 1995). These data failed to register with Blair. Rather, the slogan, 'tough on crime and tough on the causes of crime', which was built on a conscious and profound transformation in New Labour's use of language, was to be effortlessly picked up and consolidated further by Jack Straw when he replaced Blair as Shadow Home Secretary. As the next chapter illustrates, it was on this moral and political anvil that Straw forged his iron policies when he became Home Secretary in the pious and authoritarian world of a politically reenergized, but ultimately, ideologically regressive and repressive, New Labour Party.

Strangeways

The debates about crime and, in particular, the emphasis on a resurgent positivism for explaining the deviant behaviour of the irresponsible poor and powerless, took place in the context of a prison system, which once again was experiencing a crisis of legitimacy with respect to its ability to maintain order and control. The events at Strangeways in April 1990 were crucial to this sense of crisis. The 25-day long occupation of the prison by prisoners, the effective destruction of most of the institution's infrastructure and the apparent powerlessness, disorganization and conflict within, and between, state servants, provided a salutary reminder to the governing Conservative party that the tensions, which had been apparent since the 1970s, and identified in earlier chapters, had not been alleviated. If anything, they had become intensified in the years since. In particular, the disturbance indicated that prisoners were unwilling to accept the legitimacy of a penal system that was failing to deliver not only reasonable living and working conditions but also was built on a culture of often-untrammelled prison officer power, underpinned by a militarized hierarchy of masculinity and sustained by violent interventions into their everyday lives. As one noted:

> Within a prison system that had relied so heavily on brutality and an institutionalised denial of basic human rights, the Strangeways uprising represented an eloquent statement that things would never again be quite the same. The old order was indeed changing and never again would regimes that had existed in gaols like Strangeways prior to the 1990 revolt possess the same potency to terrorise and subdue. Prisoners had shown that even one of the most brutal gaols in England, a true bastion of screw power and authority, could be reduced to a burning wreck if and when prisoners

decided that enough was enough. (John Bowden, cited in Jameson and Allison, 1995: 157).

The culture of the prison before the disturbance was dominated by a structured form of authoritarian fratriarchy manifested in a 'strong canteen culture, actively supported and enjoyed by the former governor and ... the celebration of hard drinking and their associated ethic of hard men doing a hard job'. Crucially, even when there were policy changes – what Carrabine labels the 'uneven transition from authoritarianism to professionalism' – an 'aggressive, confrontational approach to prisoners continued to characterise interactions' (Carrabine, 2004: 113 and 190).

Despite endless complaints from the confined concerning prison officer violence, not only in Strangeways but also in other local prisons, the state's response had remained unchanged with respect to how such violence was explained. Officially, it was recognized that there was the odd, atavistic prison officer who was a 'bad apple', whose activities occasionally disturbed what was an essentially benevolent culture whose main preoccupation was the rehabilitation and reform of the prisoner. This, in turn, was underpinned by an often-implicit, and sometimes explicit, construction of the convicted as mendacious, law breaking fantasists who, because they were unwilling and unable to tell right from wrong, could not tell truth from lies. In 2005, Martin Narey, the former Chief Executive of the *National Offender Management Service*, confirmed that in one prison at least it was the accounts by prisoners which *were* indeed true. In describing his time as a prison officer at Lincoln prison, Narey indicated that he saw, 'prisoners in the segregation unit routinely slapped, it was constant low-level abuse. If you wanted to do any good, you had to do it by stealth. The POA ... ran the place. Assistant governors were derided. I can remember getting a real load of abuse for being seen carrying a *Guardian*' (cited in James, 2005: 16).[2]

In the aftermath of the Strangeways disturbance, and the disturbances that took place in over twenty other prisons, the government famously established an inquiry under Lord Justice Woolf and Judge Stephen Tumin (Woolf, 1991). When it was published in February 1991, Woolf's report was regarded by academics, media commentators and policy makers as a progressive model for the future of the prisons. For these groups, the methodology, depth of analysis and the policy prescriptions he propounded were crucial in providing a liberal, considered and humane prescription for the way forward, particularly with respect to balancing the demands of security, control and justice if the legitimacy of the institution was to be reasserted and order reestablished.

However, the prescriptions offered by Woolf, and the version of penal truth he constructed, were flawed and compromized for a number of reasons. In essence, he attempted to introduce what he regarded as a series of apolitical reforms into a highly politicized debate. This meant that while government ministers, in particular, could pay lip service to the impartiality and depth of his recommendations, in practice they were free to choose which policies to implement, which to ignore and which to bend to suit their own law and order purposes. Furthermore, there were a number of internal problems with the report. Woolf employed a methodology which heavily qualified the prisoners' accounts of the disturbances while leaving the accounts by prison officers virtually unscathed; he was reluctant to confront the authoritarian and violent nature of prison officer culture; he adopted a narrow understanding of what constituted a sense of responsibility and contractual relations in the context of an institution deeply undercut with horizontal and vertical intersections of power networks; and finally he based his analysis on a pluralistic understanding of state power (Sim, 1994b).

It was the last failure which proved to be the most problematic. Despite the 'incautious optimism' that had followed Woolf's 'moderately progressive report' (Sparks, 1996: 75), particularly with respect to what appeared to be a falling prison population, the Conservative government quickly reasserted the need for discipline and punishment for those who transgressed. Indeed, the day after Woolf reported, the then Home Secretary, Kenneth Baker, announced that more staff were to be trained in new and improved riot control techniques, that riot control equipment was to be increased, that physical security in prisons was to be reviewed and that 12 new prisons were to be built. Baker went on to say:

> The country will not tolerate the kind of disgraceful behaviour witnessed last April. We must make clear our utter condemnation of it by introducing a new deterrent. We shall therefore, as we have already made clear, bring before the House proposals to create a new offence of prison mutiny, which will carry a maximum penalty of 10 extra years in prison (cited in Sim, 1994b: 42).

He was even more forthright in September 1991 in a speech to the annual conference of the Boards of Visitors:

> Prisoners must understand that they will have to pay the price for rioting – by spending longer in prison and by waiting longer for improvements in prison conditions ... The repairs required will ... have to be made at the expense of other improvements the prisoners themselves would like to see (cited in 1994b: 43).

In his autobiography, Baker revealed that the cost of the Strangeways disturbance was £120 million. For him, 'prisons should not be holiday camps. They should be austere. ... I did not advocate a "softly softly" approach, but I did believe that if society treated convicted criminals as animals then they would behave like animals' (Baker 1993: 454–457). Despite these views, Woolf's report, and his careful analysis (at least from a liberal perspective), was already being sidelined, shunted aside in the Conservative's determined and deliberate push to maintain law and order based around a coercive and militarized state form in which the institutions of the criminal justice system, including prisons, were to play a central role.

Baker was replaced as Home Secretary in April 1992 by Kenneth Clarke. Clarke remained in post for just over a year. In May 1993, Michael Howard became Home Secretary. Howard's stewardship at the Home Office has become infamous, not least because of his first speech to the Conservative party conference in October 1993 where he unambiguously declared that 'prison works'. It is to his contribution to the debate about law, order and prisons to which I now turn.

The moment of Howard

Michael Howard was the seventh Home Secretary since 1979 and the fifth holder of the office since 1987. He saw the Home Office as 'one of the few departments to have escaped the Thatcher Revolution'. It was a place 'packed with defeatist liberals' (Crick, 2005: 271). Howard was antagonistic to the civil service view that nothing could be done about rising levels of crime and the concomitant argument that it was 'very important to keep as many people out of prison as possible, whatever the consequences. I was challenging these long-held views' (Howard, cited in Richards, 1998: 16). Once in office, he surrounded himself with like-minded individuals, including David Cameron as his policy advisor and David Maclean 'a vocal supporter of capital punishment' who regarded 'criminals as "vermin" who should be driven from the streets' and who 'thought the law sided with the criminal'. As Shadow Home Secretary, Tony Blair was reluctant to attack Maclean for these views, pointing out that 'a lot of Daily Mail readers would agree with him' (Crick, 2005: 272).

Howard was critical of the breakdown in the family, lax discipline in schools, the role of television in promoting violence and the lack of individual responsibility for criminal behaviour. All of these themes came together at the 1993 Conservative Party conference. Maclean was instrumental in drafting Howard's speech for the conference, which saw him rhapsodize about his 27-point law and order package and evangelize his slogan that 'prison works'. Two months before the conference, Howard had articulated his views on prisons in a leaked memorandum. Many institutions were ' "too comfortable" and "too lax" '; prison needed to be ' "a more austere experience" '. The leaked document went on:

> "Mr Howard would also like some assessment of the savings that could be made from a change in policy, recognising that this represents quite a departure from some of the commitments set out post-Woolf". Television sets ought to be a privilege, which should be earned Howard thought, and he was in no hurry to end slopping out. "Soft touch jails", he said, "are an insult to victims" (2005: 290).

Howard also pioneered a number of media friendly techniques, which required Home Office officials to construct a grid system for planning all of the key events facing his department for the next two years. It was a strategy, which allowed one senior official to comment that 'those who were working at the Home Office in 1997 said that the best preparation for New Labour was working for Michael Howard' (2005: 284).

Bleak penal times

As noted above, Howard's slogan that 'prison worke[d'] was to become his 'political mantra and provided the ideological justification for locking up people in record numbers'. Additionally:

> This slogan was articulated against a background in which recorded levels of crime had spiralled to over five million in 1994 and where the corrosive impact of deep cuts in the social welfare budget [were] being felt by the poorest and most vulnerable whose behaviour and lifestyle was also under sustained ideological attack by an equally populist Secretary of State for Social Services. "Welfare doesn't work" was the reverse side of the "prison works" coin (Ryan and Sim, 1998: 176).

The effect on the prison population was immediate. The average daily prison moved to 48,000, a rise of 4,200 on the previous year. It was also 'the highest annual rise since 1970' (Home Office, cited in Sim, 2004a: 251). Inside the prisons, the impact was equally bleak:

> Education and preparation for release were scaled down to meet financial targets. Parole and home leave ceased to be normal expectations as an essential aid to rehabilitation and resettlement and became a privilege to be awarded on criteria dominated by possible risk to the public. "Treatment" became a matter not of change but of compulsion and control with its emphasis on drug treatment and incentives (*Prison Service Journal*, cited in 2004a: 251).[3]

Howard also maintained that prisoners should serve their sentences in regimes built around a three-level incentives and earned privileges scheme:

> ... "basic", "standard" and "enhanced" ... each reflecting the individual's pattern of behaviour over a certain period of time. To qualify for privilege levels above the "basic" ... prisoners are required to demonstrate "good" and "responsible" behaviour (Sparks, cited in Ryan and Sim, 1998: 195).

This policy meant that basic regime prisoners in Eastwood Park women's prison could 'spend the period from 5 pm to 7 am lying on their beds, their heads inches from their toilet bowls, gazing into the restricted space between cell walls' (*The Observer*, cited in 1998: 195). As Richard Sparks has noted, what Howard did was to pursue policies that 'convey[ed] a generic feeling of severity ... composed principally of the revival of deterrence and a strong implication of rigour. This ... amounts to the reassertion of the doctrine of less eligibility' (Sparks, 1996: 76).

The impact on prisoners on being socially and politically constructed as less eligible subjects, was immediate and, in some cases, devastating.[4] Campaigning groups such as *INQUEST* linked Howard's policies with the rise in self-mutilations and deaths in custody. In their annual report for 1992 – 1993, the group noted that 77 people killed themselves in British prisons in 1992. The report went on:

> ... Already in 1993, 33 people have killed themselves. There [are] also disturbingly high incidents of self-injury. If Michael Howard's ... suggestions regarding building new prisons, stricter regimes and more custodial sentences, especially for younger people, are implemented, this figure is destined to increase (cited in Goldson and Coles, 2005: 41).

By 1996, the group reported that there were '64 self-inflicted deaths in prison – the highest figure since *INQUEST's* formation' [in 1981] (2005: 42). Overall, between 1993 and 1997, there were 300 self-inflicted deaths in prisons, 23 of whom were minority ethnic prisoners and 10 of whom were women.[5]

In the account of his time at the Home Office, which was published after his sacking in October 1995, Derek Lewis, who was appointed as Director General of the Prison Service by Howard's predecessor Kenneth Clarke, provided an insider's view of the impact of Howard's speech. Crucially, he unconsciously confirmed the point made by Steven Box in Chapter 2, namely that, like their predecessors in the 1970s and early 1980s, judges and magistrates in the early 1990s also played a key role in the intensification in the climate of punishment. Far from being puppets without agency, the judiciary were proactive in this process. As Lewis indicated, 'One judge told me that he had to respond to the prevailing mood: a magistrate noted with pride that he was now sending down more young offenders'. Furthermore, he confirmed that where expenditure sacrifices were needed in order to satisfy Howard's demand for more prisons, then they were made in spending on improving conditions for prisoners, in providing more employment opportunities for them and in failing to 'repair security deficiencies'. For Lewis, 'Howard was concerned almost exclusively with public perceptions. The long-term benefits of educational programmes or maintaining ties with families were, he said, low in his scale of priorities' (Lewis, 1997: 110 and 116).

Howard's bleak doctrine of twentieth century less eligibility was compounded and reinforced by the emphasis on security and control, which was, in turn, intensified after a number of top security prisoners escaped from Whitemoor Special Security Unit and Parkhurst prison. The intensification in security:

> ... had a detrimental impact on the lives of prisoners to the point where pregnant women in labour [were] chained and handcuffed in maternity wards. Other cases included[d] that of a woman who was shackled at the funeral of her 10-day-old baby; an HIV-positive woman who was shackled for 24 hours a day and was compelled to empty her bowels and bladder while chained to a man on the other side of the lavatory

door; and that of a seven stone diabetic prisoner on remand for burglary who was also chained to an outside hospital bed and kept under 24-hour guard by prison officers (Ryan and Sim, 1998: 194).

The escape of the prisoners from Parkhurst instigated an inquiry headed by General Sir John Learmont. As with the majority of state inquiries, the idea that Learmont's inquiry was objective and independent was problematic. According to Lewis, echoing the critique of the May inquiry outlined in Chapter 2:

> ... views, which accorded with those of the inquiry team were incorporated, often verbatim; alternative opinions were rarely debated let alone included in the final report ... unsuspecting MPs may have not realized that the similarity between Learmont's recommendation and the policy that had already been introduced was no coincidence. Members might then have gone on to wonder what was discussed at the meetings between Learmont and Howard, which took place while the inquiry team was preparing its report (Lewis, 1997: 176 and 187).

According to Richard Sparks, Howard's policies 'consolidate[d] under one banner a number of distinct political requirements'. These included: placing the emphasis on the prison as a place of punishment, deterrence and incapacitation; monitoring and centralizing standards, thus intensifying control over staff; and reshaping the internal organization of the prison to emphasis surveillance and situation control. This latter development was 'much more congenial to the world-outlook of neoliberalism than was the lingering welfarism implicit in vocational ideologies'. Sparks concluded that the slogan 'prison works' was a 'populist move', which claimed to:

> ... proffer solutions that seem plausible and intuitively appealing from the stand point of everyday "crime talk" whose presumptions are dominated by the tropes of "system failure" and "social breakdown". ... [It] seeks to turn dissatisfactions that are otherwise directly threatening to the prospects of an incumbent of a party that strongly self-identifies as "the party of law and order" to advantage (Sparks, cited in Ryan and Sim, 1998: 196–197).

The punitive path mapped out by Howard had a desperate converse, namely that the remaining bastions of therapeutic idealism were attacked. In a law and order climate, they were anathema to a political class whose mentality was honed on the retrogressive discourses of punishment and retribution, and the imposition of a sense of responsibility onto and into the bodies and minds of offenders while, as ever, ignoring the callous and irresponsible behaviour of those in their own class.

Dr Bob Johnson resigned from the prison service because of 'the harshness' of Howard's 'current prison policy', which, according to his resignation letter had:

> ... finally grounded my therapeutic endeavours at Parkhurst to a sickening halt. ... Against overwhelming expert evidence you [Howard] maintain a bizarre attachment

> to "austerity", which bears especially hard on mentally ill offenders, which include the most unpredictable and dangerous of all ... (cited in Ryan and Sim, 1998: 196).

Although based in Scotland, the closure of the Barlinnie Special Unit (BSU), in 1995, provides another example of the nefarious impact that a toxic mix of politicians and media was having on radical developments in penal policy in the febrile law and order climate of the mid-1990s. Opened in February 1973, the Unit's empathic philosophy had an immediate impact on those long-termers who were transferred from other prisons where they had been labelled as Scotland's most violent and disruptive prisoners. For Jimmy Boyle:

> It was clear from the start that this prison was different from all others we had been in ... What made the Unit unlike any other place was the way staff and prisoners were allowed and encouraged to sit down and talk together. This was the single most important factor in the Unit. It allowed us to break down all the barriers of hostility between us. ... Ironically, it was a group of prison officers who helped dispel my doubts about the place. It was impressive to see them push forward radical steps for the development of a more humanitarian regime (Boyle, 1984: 8 and 12).

Other prisoners, who served time in the Unit, support Boyle's views that it was a place that induced profound changes in men whose lives had been built on being 'a man in a man's world' (Collins, 1998: 167; see also Steele, 2002). However, the Unit remained an 'experiment' throughout the years of its existence. More profoundly, it was a challenge to the prevailing punitive orthodoxy and therefore generated hostility from the authorities. According to Hugh Collins, it:

> ... had become a political embarrassment over the years. For the main part, the Unit worked but what the prison authorities hated was that they had been proved wrong on the question of treatment. Prisoners like myself had shown that we were not animals: we had shown that if we were treated properly, then we in turn could respond, possibly even change (Collins, 1998: 162).

The Unit's closure was sanctioned by a Working Party established by the Scottish Office whose report was published in November 1994 (Scottish Prison Service, 1994). The construction of the report is a classic case study in the state management of inquiries. This management was pursued in a number of ways (Sim, 2000c).

First, those who wished to submit evidence to the Working Party were only given five weeks to do so. Given that it had taken 21 years to establish an inquiry into the work of the Unit, allowing five weeks to research write and produce evidence provides another example of the state's capacity to control the agenda of inquiries, as well as their outcomes. Second, the request for evidence came during the early summer, which is the busiest time of the year for many academics with respect to student assessment, thereby compromising the ability of those who may have wished to submit evidence.

Third, the Unit's closure was announced on a Friday. For politicians and policy makers, this has become a desired time for disseminating information or making controversial pronouncements given that they are unlikely to be picked up by the media. Those responsible for the closure arguably wanted the minimum of fuss from the Unit's defenders, whom the inquiry disparagingly labelled as 'somewhat idealistic' (Scottish Prison Service, 1994: 15). Fourth, the report's authors claimed to have read widely. In fact, the document contained 26 references, eight of which were written or edited by inquiry members or Scottish Office personnel. The remaining 18 references contained very little acknowledgment to the work of critical academics but did refer to an edited collection, *Prison Violence* (Cohen, Cole and Bailey, 1976), which contained an article highlighting the cybernetic regulation of violence through bolting radios to the heads of violent individuals so that their destructive impulses could be kept under surveillance and control (Moyer, 1976).[6] The inquiry also met with, and drew 'on the experience of a number of experts in the areas of criminality and corrections'. These experts were three North American professors of psychology, two of whom attended meetings held by the inquiry. The document concluded that 'their contributions to the Working Party's work were most helpful' (Scottish Prison Service, 1994: 12). Fifth, a number of media stories carried the clear implication that the Chief Inspector of Prisons for Scotland had recommended that the Unit should be closed. This was untrue. In his annual report for 1993, the Chief Inspector indicated the exact opposite: 'we do *not* recommend closure' (Her Majesty's Inspectorate for Prisons in Scotland, 1993: 33, emphasis in the original). Finally:

> ... the Chief Executive of Scottish prisons was reported to have maintained that inmate costs were running at £80,000 annually. This figure not only remained unchallenged but media commentators failed to note that annual expenditure in 1992–93 on Scottish prisons was over £152 million. The BSU cost 0.05 percent of that figure. This was less than the money spent on postage, travelling and subsistence and stationery and printing (Sim, 1995: 15).

Attacks on those institutions and individuals who did not (and do not), conform to the law and order mentality of politicians, and indeed many state servants, was therefore intrinsic to the state's response to more empathic, welfare-orientated policies towards the confined. I shall return to this point in Chapter 7. For the moment I want to consider two further developments, which began before Howard became Home Secretary but which were consolidated during his time in office.

First, there was the managerial drive towards the contracting out of prison 'services' and the establishment of the prison service itself as a semi-autonomous Whitehall agency on 1 April 1993, the month before Howard became Home Secretary. The appointment of Derek Lewis, a businessman and former television executive, as Director General, at the beginning of 1993, further highlighted the government's determination to outsource a service, which, from the perspective of ministers, represented and symbolized the abject failings of the public sector and, by extension, the postwar settlement between capital and labour. The culture of contracting out was underpinned and reinforced by the emergence of a penal managerialsm with its emphasis on league tables, targets and benchmarks, which, in turn, was legitimated by the discourses of 'economy, efficiency and effectiveness' (McLaughlin and Muncie, 1993). However, this form of managerialism, even on its own terms, was a failure. The autonomy that contracting out was theoretically supposed to engender, thereby undermining political interference in the working of the system, was no more than a chimera. In practice, power remained centralized in the Home Office. As Lewis noted:

> Within eighty-three working days, over 1,000 documents went to ministers, including 137 major submissions. The degree of detailed ministerial involvement was greater than most long-serving civil servants could remember in pre-agency days. It was a far cry from the 'much greater autonomy from ministers and the rest of the Home Office' that Ken Clarke had publicly promised (Lewis, 1997: 156).

More broadly, these managerial developments failed to enhance the democratic accountability of a key institution of the criminal justice system. It was an institution, which (even more than the police) had remained outside the reach of the structures of social democracy – weak, contradictory and inconsistent though these structures might have been. As crucially, they also failed to challenge the power of the prison with regard to what happened in the everyday world of the institution. On the contrary, as Hywel Williams has noted, in this world, prison officers had become:

> ... the custodians of a contracted-out morality, which like all such contractual arrangements, is averse to responsibility and shuns consequences. As a result, the modern prison measures itself by those targets and benchmarks whose hollow sounds mock the modern British state's effectiveness. Modern 'professionalism' excels both at producing targets and at engineering that ticking of the boxes which means that a target can be scored while its real intent is ignored ... (Williams, 2006: 155–6).

Second, these developments, in turn, were underpinned by the ongoing privatization programme, which had begun in 1991 when Group 4 Services signed the first private management contract in Europe, which allowed the company to open The Wolds Prison in April 1992 as a remand prison. In terms of the arguments in this book, the actualities and specifics of contracting out and privatization are less important than the fact that the existence of the prison was not challenged. Furthermore, those who were detained in the new privatized network were the same groups as those who had *always* been detained in the institution since its emergence two hundred years earlier: the economically marginalized, the poor, the powerless: a social detritus whose makeup in the late twentieth century was increasingly racialized and genderized. In that sense, the emergence of a new managerialism and private prison network:

> ... should not be understood as heralding the demise of the prisons. ... There may well be contradictions, contingencies and disjunctures in the government's strategy (as there are in all other areas of social policy) but it is also important to recognise that the emerging public/private prison network is being built on discourses, policies and practices which ultimately unite rather than divide the new penal managers, privatized prison workers and state servants from all levels of the hierarchy in the traditional system (Ryan and Sim, 1998: 199–200).

Happy together: Howard and Straw

Howard's perspective on law and order was sustained and legitimated by the fact that New Labour's Shadow Home Secretaries, Tony Blair and Jack Straw, were in broad agreement with the thrust and direction of his pronouncements. Indeed, according to some commentators, rather than Howard and his predecessor, Kenneth Clarke, setting the agenda, it was *they* who were dancing to New Labour's newly discovered, but desperately corrosive, law and order tune (Downes and Morgan, 2002).

Straw succeeded Blair as Shadow Home Secretary in October 1994. His perspective and position on law and order was underpinned by a number of considerations, including his own ideological inclinations: he admired America's criminal justice policies and Bill Clinton's administration, he was aware of the concerns of the tabloid press and he inevitably responded to Howard's own increasingly authoritarian response to crime and offenders. The implications were profound:

> Both parties locked themselves into an escalating bidding war of ever-tougher proposals. Straw took up the reins with gusto. With Blair's full backing, he came up with a host of policy proposals which indicated that once Labour got into office he would be, as one modernising member of the shadow cabinet predicted, 'the most illiberal Labour home secretary in history' (Anderson and Mann,1997: 255).[7]

Straw and Howard were engaged in a 'policy auction'. It was an auction which was to culminate in an ideological and policy convergence, so that by the end of Howard's time in office 'their bitter duel had turned into a blissful duet' (Crick, 2005: 325). For Larry Elliott, 'Britain now has two parties that support the status quo, two parties that show zero tolerance for the yob who vandalizes the local park but fall strangely silent when it comes to the multinational chopping down large chunks of the tropical rain forest' (*The Guardian,* 13 January 1997). Ironically, it was the ex-Conservative Home Secretary, Douglas Hurd who captured the tone and direction of Straw's time in opposition when he wrote that he 'carried his fervour too far in his determination to match or outdo

Michael Howard. I once predicted in the Commons that we would eventually find him proposing the public hanging of burglars outside a prison gate' (Hurd, 1998: 3).

At the same time, as noted in the previous chapter, the Conservative Party built its law and order policies on a statist/antistatist strategy. Under Michael Howard, the prison took its place on the statist side of this strategy, underpinning the broader, authoritarian policies that the government pursued in its eighteen years in power. In that sense, the Conservative Party constructed a state 'whose capacity for intervention and non-intervention in the febrile arena of law and order (despite being subjected to the new managerialism of ('economy, efficiency and effectiveness') was formidable' (Sim, 2000a: 327). At the same time, the nonpolicing of the powerful, discussed in the last chapter, continued. This was the 'anti-statist' side to the Conservative's law and order strategy. As Larry Elliott and Dan Atkinson noted, in the 1990s, 'unscrupulous financial operators' could be subject to legal proceedings. Crucially, however:

> A major selling point of the new market order was that it would restore the rule of law – battered and bashed about by over-mighty bureaucrats and trade-union militants – as the legal framework within which the market would flourish. But which law and whose courtroom would be reinstated? A feature of the new system is the hiving-off of economic crime into a self-regulatory labyrinth of 'disciplinary tribunals': effectively private courts. Nor do these courts try only 'regulatory offences'. They increasingly hear theft charges. ... Mr Bosworth-Davies, speaking ... in October 1996 warned "[B]ehaviour which would be criminal to any ordinary person if committed outside the City environment, is being allowed to be called something else and increasingly dealt with in a different, quasi-civil, regulatory manner" (Elliott and Atkinson, 1998: 100–101).

The work of the Health and Safety Executive (HSE) also graphically illustrates how, during the first half of the 1990s, the Executive was increasingly restricted, and indeed restricted itself, with respect to the policing of health and safety at work. In the year from April 1996 to April 1997, 302 people were killed at work, an increase of 20 per cent while the number of serious accidents increased to 28,040, a rise of two-thirds: 'The Trades Union Congress blamed "the climate of deregulation" as a key factor in the deteriorating safety record and called for tougher laws to prosecute negligent employers, *as well as an end to cuts to the HSE budget'* (*The Guardian*, cited in Sim, 2000a: 326, emphasis added).[8] Furthermore, between 1990–1 and 1996–7, the number of enforcement notices regarding health and safety fell in each of the three categories used by all of the enforcement authorities, including the HSE: by 55.5 per cent, 27.3 per cent and 12.7 per cent respectively.[9] Thus:

> ... the eighteen years of Conservative rule meant that [the powerful's] activities remained relatively invisible, comparatively unregulated and effectively decriminalized.

> The deregulatory discourses that underpinned the politics of the free market had a precipitous impact on those agencies responsible for ensuring that the powerful, both organizationally and individually, were subject to some degree of regulation, however contingent and fragmentary, under bourgeois legal arrangements (2000a: 324).

However, by the time of the General Election in 1997, the hegemonic appeal of the Conservatives government was fragmenting. Beset by internal contradictions, the government:

> ... had generated its own gravediggers. Internal strife, sleaze and extra-marital relationships led to a crisis point in which the valorisation of a traditional bourgeois morality, juxtaposed against the morals of the ill disciplined and permissive detritus, could only succeed hegemonically if the male members of the government kept their collective mouths shut and their individual zips up (2000a: 327).

Externally, the power of the Party to engage in what Gramsci called the 'elaboration and diffusion of conceptions of the world' (Gramsci, cited in Hall, 1988: 173) with respect to law and order, was contested by New Labour. This contestation was not about the general thrust and direction of the statist/antistatist strategy. As the next chapter argues, New Labour politicians were broadly in support of this strategy. Rather it was about the fact that the Tories had failed to deliver on their authoritarian promises. Thus:

> ... the Party's claim to be the guardians of law and order was crumbling in the face of damning crime statistics, criminal justice inefficiency and an ideological onslaught from Labour which under Tony Blair and then Jack Straw had moved to embrace a new realism on crime and punishment. This led inevitably and inexorably to the claim in their election manifesto that 'Labour is the party of law and order in Britain today' (Sim, 2000a: 327).

Blair and his New Labour colleagues ruthlessly exploited these themes during the 1997 election campaign. One party political broadcast featured 'an obnoxious young couple called Helen and Paul talking about crime' in the following terms:

> Paul: "Number 28's been burgled. I bet it's that gang of yobbos again".
> Helen: "Even if they catch them, they get off scot-free".
> Paul: "If they [the Conservatives] get back in next time there'd be more criminals getting off" (Toynbee, 1999: 16).

By the end of their 18 years in power, successive Conservative governments had bestowed substantial amounts of public money on the criminal justice system. Expenditure had increased by an average of 4.1 per cent each year, making 'criminal justice ... the fastest growing area under the combined Thatcher and Major administrations'. It was a pattern, which, as the next chapter indicates, was to be repeated under New Labour who, after nearly ten years in office, spent 'around £187 billion' on the criminal justice system while the increase on law and order expenditure for the UK was around 3.2 per cent, 'far higher than every other area of government spending apart from health' (Solomon et al., 2007: 18). In that sense, there was serious continuity between the Conservatives and New Labour with regard to their position on supporting what was euphemistically called law and order 'services'. It is to a broader consideration of New Labour's strategy for law and order, which provided the political context and ideological justification for this spending, to which I now turn.

Notes

1 The phrase 'iron times' is taken from Hall (1988: vii).
2 At a conference at the Open University in June 2007, the Director General of the Prison Service, himself an ex-prison officer, also confirmed that violence had taken place in local prisons in particular.
3 In May 1994, Howard also attacked the welfare role and finances of the probation service (Ryan and Sim, 1998).
4 This doctrine had its roots in the 1832 *Royal Commission on the Poor Law*. It 'ensures that the upper margins of prison conditions are guaranteed not to rise above the worst material conditions in society as a whole and that, in times of social hardship, the rigours of penal discipline will become more severe to prevent the weakening of the deterrent effect' (Scott, 2007: 50–51).
5 These figures have been calculated from data, which can be accessed on INQUEST's web site on www.inquest.org.uk followed by Statistics. Thanks to Richard Fontenroy from INQUEST for his help with these figures.
6 Ideas for utilizing technology to control prisoners continued into the twenty-first century. One suggestion for reducing overcrowding in American prisons came from J.C. Oleson in 2002, whose 'modest proposal' for dealing with 'many of the prison's deficiencies' was to place 'prisoners into narcotic (punitive) comas'. Oleson argued that 'if prisoners could be placed into comas, they could be packed tightly into a very limited space with none of the deleterious side effects that are currently associated with prison overcrowding' (Oleson, 2002: 830 and 861). Thanks to Alana Barton for pointing out this reference to me.
7 In September 1995, at the TUC (Trades Union Congress) Conference, delegates voted for the first time to support a prisoner's right to vote. However, Jack Straw rejected the decision of the delegates (*Morning Star*, 15 September 1995).
8 To reiterate a point made in Chapter 3, footnote 4, these figures also undoubtedly underestimate the number of deaths and injuries at work. See Tombs and Whyte (2007: Chapter 2).
9 Thanks to Steve Tombs for providing me with the original data on the work of the Health and Safety Executive.

5

'PIETY AND IRON'[1]: NEW LABOUR AND SOCIAL AUTHORITARIANISM

> I told her [Margaret Thatcher] about my meeting with John Smith. I say, "You've shifted the centre about two hundred miles to the right". She said, "Yes but not far enough yet" (Wyatt, 1998: 107).
>
> I am reminded of a conversation with a senior figure from the CBI. ... On a visit to Downing Street, he and his colleagues had decided on their top and bottom lines in a negotiation with Blair. They never got any further than the top line. To their amazement, Blair was ready to accept all that they wanted. The police, business leaders, intelligence services and Republican presidents of the United States tend to get what they want from Downing Street. Old Labour was perceived as anti-police, anti-business, indifferent to security and anti-American. New Labour must be the opposite at all times (Richards, 2005: 47).

This chapter focuses on the criminal justice policies developed by New Labour in the party's first decade in office. It analyses how Tony Blair's three governments, like their Conservative predecessors, continued with the relentless focus on the conventional criminality of the powerless while simultaneously rolling back interventions for regulating the powerful. For Blair and his ministers, it was the poor and the powerless who were regarded as the primary and intransigent source of criminality in a society that needed modernizing if it was to face the challenges of late twentieth century global capitalism. Before considering specific policy developments under Blair, the chapter outlines the discursive universe, which the party's politicians inhabited. The deliberate use of precise, value-laden language, and binary categories and dualisms, were central to the social construction of a very particular, New Labour reality. This language, and these dualisms, framed who was inside the magic circle of acceptability and respectability, and crucially, who was outside this circle and therefore deserving of intervention by the state and the increasing number of law and order servants employed to reproduce the government's vision of 'compulsory tranquillity' (Elliott and Atkinson, 1998: 80). For some, if this enforced tranquillity could not be generated on the basis of consensual agreement, then it would be enforced by authoritarian coercion.

New Labour's discursive universe

Under New Labour, the use of language was utilized 'to determine political action' (Reeves, 2005: 29). This was achieved through a process of 'framing' or 'ready made moulds for the thinking of thoughts' (Chilton, cited in Reeves, 2005: 30):

> Framing is going on all the time, whether consciously or not. Even apparently banal terms such as "welfare dependent", "yobs" and ... "hard-working families" carry with them a heavy load of assumptions and implications (2005: 30).

The use of dualisms – 'the linking of apparent opposites' (such as tough on crime, tough on the causes of crime) – was central to this process:

> These dualisms are the linguistic heart of the Third Way, which rejects both old left and new right. In this world, there are no difficult choices, no trade-offs; everything is possible. Voters can have their cake and eat it. As a mechanism for persuading people Labour had changed, the language was brilliantly effective. By adding the goals and values of those of the right to those of the Left, Labour successfully offered a smorgasbord of goodies. Why choose between prosperity and social justice when you can have both? ... In many cases, Labour was not really stealing the clothes of the right, just cutting out the labels (2005: 31).

The drive towards constructing definitive discourses around social and political issues in order to control the perception of these issues, derived from a 'new emergent "complex" ... a networking and convergence of interests and perspectives and strategies ...' involving:

> ... central government ... local government, business, the 'third sector' of voluntary organizations, academic research and education and so forth which are being drawn

more tightly together into what is being widely called a form of 'governance' which transcends and makes partly redundant the old divisions between domains. Partnership is a key concept and a key word (Fairclough, 2000: 124).

There were a number of components involved in New Labour's discursive universe, which Blair's administrations strategically mobilized. First, there was the role of primary definers[2] who were classically described by Stuart Hall and his colleagues in 1978 as individuals who establish the initial definition of the topic that 'commands the field' (Hall et al., 1978: 58). In the intervening decades, as Schlesinger and Tumber (1995) noted, a number of new primary definers emerged who were central to the reproduction of dominant ideologies. These groups did not replace the old primary definers but were linked to them ideologically and discursively with respect to their understanding of social problems, and what should be done about them. New Labour's partnership approach to urban governance, for example, meant that at local levels around the country, the relationship between new city centre managers, working with 'older' state servants such as police officers, was crucial in defining who, and what, became defined as deviant in urban areas (Coleman and Sim, 2000).

Second, New Labour politicians shared a 'coincidence of interests' with many in the media in terms of defining what crime was and what should be done about it. This was particularly important with respect to how politicians concentrated on 'bite-sized chunks' of news disseminated to the mass media. According to Stephen Whittle, head of editorial policy at BBC News, 'soundbite thoughts become part of the fabric ... especially in terms of the tabloidisation of formats' (cited in Poole, 2006a: 8). This 'tabloidisation' was underpinned by the self-reinforcing relationship between state servants and the mass media who, while not achieving total synchronicity, nonetheless remained yoked in a cycle of mutually reproducing, narrowly defined discourses around law and order which themselves were not unconnected to New Labour's definition of the same issues. In January 2005, Sir Stephen Lander, the Chair of the Serious and Organized Crime Agency (Soca), and ex-head of MI5, indicated that thirty-three national and regional newspapers had been studied over a five-year period in order to measure 'the number of column inches newspapers give to different types of organized crime'. Not surprisingly, 'organized immigration crime came first, followed by drugs'. He explained the processes involved:

> The brainboxes at the Home Office have been putting together a sort of harm model. The model basically articulates the harm that is caused to the UK under a number of headings ... It also brings into play judgements about the degree of public concern and they have a proxy for this, which is the amount of column inches in the press. ... *It is pretty rough and ready but it is asking the right questions* (*The Independent*, 10 January 2005, emphasis added).[3]

Third, special advisers, and their relationship with the mass media more generally, played an integral part in the attempt to construct a new 'penal common sense' (Wacquant, 1999: 319). These 'messengers of perception' (Young, cited in Fairclough, 2000: 121) were embedded in a process in which 'controlling the presentation and perception of policy is no longer a secondary matter, it is virtually inseparable from policy making' (2000: 122). Their work was further augmented by private sector personnel seconded into the civil service, and by 'a small group of certified market-friendly civil servants, and polling, advertising and media experts'. This development impacted on the issue of evidential support for particular policies. Put bluntly, 'evidence that looks supportive of ideas to which the government is committed tends to be accepted uncritically. Contrary evidence tends to be dismissed' (Leys, 2005: 4 and 15). This process was reinforced by the use of management consultants under the Private Finance Initiative, and public private partnerships, which were 'a goldmine' for private companies. In 1995, consultants 'earned £196 million from the public sector. By 2004, this had increased [by] 850 per cent to £1.87 [billion], excluding the costs of developing information technology systems' (Beckett, 2006: 49). In 2003–04, the Home Office alone spent £46.9 million on consultants (*The Guardian*, 2 September 2006).

As Francis Wheen has noted, New Labour's love affair with consultants, and other secular gurus, began before the party came into government. During the summer of 1996, 100 backbenchers attended a weekend seminar in Oxford. They were addressed by consultants from Andersen on '"total quality service" and "the management of change"'. After they entered government, a number of executives from both Andersen and McKinseys 'were seconded to Whitehall with a brief to practise "blue skies thinking"' (Wheen, 2004: 57–58). More remarkably, in the autumn of 1998, Edward de Bono lectured to officials from the Department of Education on:

> ... his "Six Thinking Hats system" of decision-making. The idea, he explained, was that civil servants should put on a red hat when they wanted to talk about hunches and instincts, a yellow hat if they were listing the advantages of a project, a black hat while playing devil's advocate, and so on. "Without wishing to boast" he added, "this is the first new way of thinking to be developed for 2400 years since the days of Plato, Socrates and Aristotle" (2004: 58).

In a book published in 1985, as Wheen further notes, de Bono pointed to the lessons that readers could learn from the success of a number of entrepreneurial individuals and then ask themselves: "Why not me?" The millionaires he extolled included US hotelier Harry Helmsley, later convicted of massive tax evasion, and Robert Maxwell, subsequently exposed as one of the most outrageous fraudsters in British history' (2004: 59).

Fourth, those who pursued contrary evidence inside Parliament were mercilessly attacked and branded not as 'participants in a reasonable debate about the direction of policy but [as] relics of the party's dark ages, mad lefties jeopardizing the government's future'. Those outside Parliament, including academics – what were to be pejoratively labelled in Blairspeak as the 'forces of conservatism' – had similar experiences: '... consistently pointing to the existence of politically inconvenient evidence leads to professional marginalization or even – if the inconvenience is great enough – persecution' (Leys, 2005: 15).[4] Allied to this development was the presence and influence of American social policy. For Loïc Wacquant England was 'the land of welcome and acclimation chamber' for policies such as zero tolerance policing,[5] 'on their way to the conquest of Europe' (Wacquant, 1999: 327). According to Jamie Peck:

> The cumulative effect of a range of developments – the internationalization of consultancy firms; the broadening policy remits of transnational institutions; the formation of new policy networks around think tanks, governmental agencies and professional associations; and the growth of international conferencing and "policy tourism" – has been to proliferate, widen and lubricate channels of cross-border policy transfer. Many of these channels have become saturated by "ideas from America". (Peck, 2003: 228–229).[6]

Fifth, from its first days in power New Labour constructed itself as *the* party of law and order, thereby symbolically positioning those who disagreed with government policy as being both pro-criminal and anti-victim. Blair's governments built on the historical 'valorisation of victims of crime' (O'Malley, 1996) who, since the 1970s, had become a dominating ideological presence in the 'culture of control' (Garland, 2001), a desecrated figure that was mercilessly mobilized by the political parties over three decades to enforce their vision of order, an order where the victimized would be protected from the ravages of the degenerate, deprived and depraved. As Markus Dubber has noted, extolling victims' rights is both heavily politicized and instrumental in that politicians have understood 'the power of interpersonal identification' and have thus 'surround[ed] themselves with victims of violent crime, or their surviving relatives, when the time has come to re-pledge their commitment to the war on crime'. Crucially:

> The instrumental political significance of the dogged pursuit of their rights becomes clear when one searches for the voices of victims who hesitate to join the communal anticrime chorus. An anticrime politician (and who isn't nowadays?) has no more use for a victim who doesn't call for more draconian punishments of offenders generally speaking than a death penalty prosecutor has for the mother of a murder victim uninterested in venting her hatred for a specific offender in a capital sentencing hearing (Dubber, 2002: 7).[7]

Finally, central to New Labour's discursive universe, and to Blair's world view in particular, was the discourse of modernization, which revolved around the idea that 'anything new must automatically be better than what came before' so that 'any change may be called a "reform": the word symbolizes the central non-idea of all "modernising" rhetoric' (Poole, 2006a: 34). In 53 speeches between 1997 and 1999, Blair, used the word 'new' 609 times, 'modern' 89 times, 'modernize' and 'modernisation' 87 times and 'reform' 143 times (Fairclough, 2000: 18). According to Alan Finlayson:

> New Labour modernisation entails worries about the past (it weighs us down with its slow thinking). It also entails worries about the present (we aren't keeping up with the new), but above all it worries about the future. The future is what we must prepare for, the transformations ahead, the contingencies that must, at all costs, be insured against. *Central to this is the gathering and interpreting of anxiety inducing statistics.* (Finlayson, 2003: 94, emphasis added).

In this doom-laden, political context:

> Blair's 'rhetorical compulsion'[8] as Prime Minister, was pre eminent in articulating a very definite and precise image of criminality. In a Gramscian sense, his compulsive rhetoric was pivotal in tutoring and educating the wider society into, if not embracing, then at least seriously accommodating, commonsense definitions of social harm and criminality. In turn, his reductive evocations were underpinned by an excoriating, evangelical positivism that demanded interventions into the lives of the socially mendicant, those identified as depraved, deprived, desperate and dangerous (Sim, 2008b: 136).

It is to a consideration of Blair's 'rhetorical compulsion' to which the chapter now turns.

Apocalypse now

In July 2004, Blair launched the third of New Labour's five-year strategic plans for reforming public services. Following announcements on health and education, he outlined plans for the further reform of the Home Office and the criminal justice system. Blair's speech was notable for three reasons. First, it came on the back of the ongoing critiques of his actions over the war in Iraq, during which 'British government, in the normal sense of the word, had ground to a halt' (Kampfner, 2004: 291–292). The timing of the speech indicated the government's desperate desire to return the political debate to domestic issues and away from Blair's alleged mendaciousness over the non-appearance of weapons of mass destruction. If Iraq was his perdition, then building schools, hospitals and prisons was to be his absolution. Second, the announcement was built on a plethora of previous initiatives and White Papers, which were intended to reinforce New Labour's 1997 manifesto claim that they, and not the Conservatives, were 'now the party of law and order in Britain today' (The Labour Party, 1997: 2).[9] Finally, he used the speech to launch an evangelical diatribe against the liberal consensus, which he claimed had dominated the debate around law and order since the

1960s. Pointedly entitled, *'A new consensus on law and order'*, he elaborated on one of his favourite themes, the relationship between freedom and responsibility. He argued that in the 1970s and 1980s criminals had increasingly become more violent, while petty criminals had metamorphosed from the 'bungling and wrong-headed villains of old' to 'drug pushers and drug-abusers' who were:

> ... desperate and without any residual moral sense. And a society of different lifestyles spawned a group of young people who were brought up without parental discipline, without proper role models and without a sense of responsibility to or for others (Blair, 2004a: 1).[10]

Underpinning this regressive transformation were various negative developments that had altered and changed 'the established pattern of community life in cities, towns and villages throughout Britain and throughout the developed world'. He concluded that 'people ... want a society of responsibility. They want a community where the decent law-abiding majority are in charge; where those that play by the rules do well; and those that don't, get punished'.[11]

Not for the first time, Blair argued that this was a 'personal crusade' (2004a: 1–2) thus subliminally tying his thoughts in with the broader symbolic and metaphysical conflict between good and evil where the deviant minority would be normalized through penal and professional interventions, thereby restoring individual equanimity and structural equilibrium to local communities. In a speech four months earlier, he described this minority as a:

> ... hard core of prolific offenders – just 5000 offenders – [who] commit around 1 million crimes each year, nearly 10 per cent of all crime. That is only 15 or 20 people for each of the Crime and Disorder Reduction Partnerships. Yet they are wreaking havoc. ... This hard core of offenders may include local gang leaders, drug dealers, vandals, car thieves and others whose prolific anti-social behaviour is causing most harm to local neighbourhoods (Blair, 2004b: 3).[12]

Both speeches contained specific proposals for reforming the criminal justice system further in order to contain the threat posed by the contemporary degenerate. In the July speech, Blair indicated that the government wanted to 'revive community policing'; shift penal interventions from 'tackling the offence to targeting the offender'; and provide local communities and the police with powers 'to enforce respect on the street' (Blair, 2004a: 4). In the earlier speech, he extolled the use of Anti-Social Behaviour Orders (Asbos), local partnerships working in conjunction with central government, the use of fixed penalty notices, Drug Treatment and Testing Orders and the targeting of the hard core of offenders through intelligence-led policing (Blair, 2004b: 4).

The discourse of community, and its imagined benefits, was central to Blair's position. In January 2006, he argued that 'since the self-reinforcing bonds of traditional community life do not exist in the same way, we need a radical new approach if we are to restore the liberty of the law-abiding citizen'.[13] He noted that some things *had* changed so he was 'not ... restarting the search for the golden age. We are not looking to go back to anything'. However, he *did* want to go back in one significant area and that was to 'restore respect' to communities living in a 'modern market economy'. Central to the regeneration of respect was the direct confrontation with the antisocial behaviour of those 'chaotic families' who lacked 'the basic infrastructure of order'. As he noted:

> There are a small number of families who are out of control and in crisis. It is those families whose children are roaming the streets and disrupting the classrooms. We have to help those parents and their children (http://www.labour.org.uk: 2, 4 and 6).

Six months later, Blair returned to these themes in another speech, which contained a litany of his favourite ideas: respect, decency, community, the impact of global social change and the need for summary powers to protect the decent, law-abiding majority from the ravages of the feral, atavistic minority. Once again, the context was modernization, and specifically the need to reform the country's institutions to equip them to respond to the challenges generated by the economic and political demands of a free market, globalized economy that had irrevocably and irreversibly changed the structure and nature of the postwar social order:

> The communities of the Britain before the Second World War are relics to us now. The men worked in settled industrial occupations. Women were usually at home. Social classes were fixed and defining of identity. People grew up, went to school and moved into work in their local environs. Geographical and social mobility has loosened the ties of home. The family structure has changed. The divorce rate increased rapidly. Single person households are now common. The demography changed: the high-crime category of young men between 15 and 24 expanded. The disciplines of informal control – imposed in the family and schools – are less tight than they were (Blair, 2006a: 3).

On returning from a summer break in 2006 in Cliff Richard's Barbados villa, Blair added another dimension to his theme of communities in turmoil. When an interviewer asked about early interventions with problematic children and families by pointing out that, 'a lot of the evidence suggests that you need to be getting in there while the child is still in nappies frankly', Blair took up the point with an enthusiasm redolent of nineteenth-century positivists:

> Or pre-birth, even. You see I think if you look at this realistically and I think in some ways society has been a bit reluctant to face up to these questions fully for very obvious reasons, but let me try, and choose my words carefully, I mean in my view if you have a teenage mum who is not in a stable relationship then you have got a pretty good chance, it doesn't follow absolutely – of course I'm not saying that, but there is a pretty

> good chance that that child will grow up in a difficult set of circumstances and then it maybe only at the age of 7 or 8 that the behavioural problems are so severe that something happens. Now perhaps we should be intervening far earlier, making it clear that in those circumstances from a very early age there is going to be support but also some sense of discipline and framework put in place in order to make sure that that child gets a better start in life because I think if you talk, as I do, to teachers sometimes they will tell you, and I know it sounds almost crazy to say this, but at age 3, 4, 5 they are already noticing the symptoms of a child that when they are 14 or 15 is out on the street causing mayhem (www.number-10.gov.uk/output/Page10023.asp).

As the previous chapter argued, Conservative governments had also mobilized the discourse of community 'as a force for social stability' (Sim, 2000a: 331). Blair was adopting a similar strategy built around what Stuart Hall has termed 'regressive modernisation' (Hall, 1988: 2) in that he ruthlessly mobilized nostalgia as a resonantly powerful individual and collective emotion, in the drive to crystallize and realize his vision of contemporary social arrangements. Thus, while he was looking to the future he was mobilizing the past to justify an authoritarian clampdown in the present. Writing in *The Observer* in February 2006, he justified introducing ID cards, Asbos, new laws to deal with organized crime, as well as changing long-established court procedures through a binary comparison between the traditional old and the modern new:

> In theory, traditional court processes and attitudes to civil liberties could work. But the modern world is different from the world for which these court processes were designed. It is a world of vast migration, most of it beneficial but with dangerous threats. We have unparalleled prosperity, but also the break-up of traditional community and family ties and the emergence of behaviour that was rare 50 years ago (Blair, 2006b: 29).

I shall return to the issue of the discursive power of 'community' in the conclusion to this chapter. For the moment, having established how language contributed to the social construction of New Labour's 'truth' about the social world, and the central role that Tony Blair played in enunciating and disseminating this 'truth', the chapter now turns to the issue of New Labour's law and order policies.

New Labour's interventionist state

In September 1997, at the first Labour Party conference after the party's General Election victory, Jack Straw, the new Home Secretary, provided an indication of his intentions on crime:

> As the wine flowed, I asked him what he plans to do about Myra Hindley, as he has to make a formal decision soon about whether she will ever be released from prison. He smirked. "Well, officially I fully intend to afford her the same rights as any

> other prisoner in Britain ... but unofficially if you think I'm going down as the Home Secretary that released Myra Hindley, then you must be fucking joking!" (cited in Morgan, 2005: 176).

In office, Straw built on the Conservative government's legacy outlined in the previous chapter. It was a strategy centred on a bipartisan approach to law and order issues. As he noted five months before the election, 'we haven't opposed a criminal justice measure since 1988' (cited in Anderson and Mann, 1997: 269). Like the Conservatives, the legislation he introduced strengthened the capacity of the state for intense intervention, overwhelmingly directed downwards towards the powerless. The powerful effectively remained beyond scrutiny,[14] a point I will return to below. This downward gaze was pursued in two ways. First, Straw continued and consolidated Michael Howard's policies in a range of different areas. Thus, the final part of the *Crime (Sentences) Act 1997*, introduced by Howard, was finally implemented in December 1999. The Act allowed mandatory life sentences for offenders convicted for a second time of a serious violent or sexual offence[15]; mandatory minimum seven year sentences for those convicted of trafficking in Class A drugs for a third time; and mandatory minimum sentences of three years for domestic burglars convicted for a third time. Second, he introduced a raft of legislation, built on his own (and Blair's ideological concerns), that was legitimated by the 'selective borrowing from Left Realism ...' (Brownlee, 1998: 333), the self-proclaimed critical paradigm, which had emerged in criminology a decade earlier. For New Labour, and left realists, the concerns of working class communities around crime had to be taken seriously. In his 'flagship' *Crime and Disorder Act*, which Straw described as being 'rooted in the experiences of local people across the country ... a victory for local communities over detached metropolitan elites' (cited in Ryan, 1999:12–13), young people and drug users were elided and particularly targeted. This meant that:

> ... discussion about crime and the undeniable impact that crimes such as burglary will have on the powerless become not just the starting point but also the finishing point for the Labour Party and its political representatives. Consequently, the social harm generated against the young through crime and abuse, the devastating impact of drugs such as alcohol and tobacco on this group and others, and the more general social harm generated by the powerful remain at best marginal and at worst ignored. In the consultation document on crime and justice sent to all local groups in 1998, there are constant references to the young and the drug taker. In contrast, one line is devoted to white collar crime, which in a seven-line paragraph is (wrongly) elided with international crime and terrorism ... (This is one line more than the issue received in the Party's 1997 election manifesto, when it was completely ignored) (Sim, 2000a: 329–330).[16]

Straw was clear about 'which side we are on; the side of the victim, law and order and the people of Britain' (cited in *Prison Review*, 1999: 3). He was also clear about which groups were disruptive and disorderly – 'winos, squeegee merchants [and] aggressive beggars' – whose attitudes, activities and behaviour were to be directly confronted by a policy of zero tolerance. For critics of the government, this policy came 'perilously close to identifying the central problem of society as the need to contain and control the underclass' (Anderson and Mann, 1997: 269).

Furthermore, like the Conservatives, the nuclear family was central to forging New Labour's vision of order. Straw was at one with Blair on this issue. When campaigning for the Labour leadership, Blair had unambiguously declared that 'the break-up of family and community bonds is intimately linked to the breakdown in law and order' (cited in Fairclough, 2000: 42). In November 1998, the Ministerial Group on the Family, with Straw as its chair, produced a consultation document, *Supporting Families*, which argued that, 'family life is the foundation on which our communities, our society and our country are built'. On the specific issue of juvenile crime, the document was no less explicit in its positivist determinism: 'children who grow up in stable, successful families are less likely to become involved in offending' (Ministerial Group on the Family, cited in Sim, 2000b: 174). Other proposals at the time included baby naming ceremonies, stopping 'quickie' marriages, introducing parenthood and marriage classes in schools and housing teenage mothers in specialist hostels. Straw also suggested that more single teenage mothers should be persuaded to give their children up for adoption (2000b: 174). For Ian Brownlee, Blair and Straw's policies meant 'a substantial retreat from traditional socialist thinking on crime [which] has been accompanied by a continuation of the populist punitive discourse of previous Conservative governments, perpetuating the predominance in policy making of a "criminology of the other"'. At the same time, the government had 'persisted with the culture of blaming pathological individuals and families ... a tactic which merely serves to reinforce the punitive expectations of the general public' (Brownlee, 1998: 333–334).

New Labour's punitive drive also extended to welfare claimants. This involved a 're-tooling' of the 'disciplinary state', which underpinned proposed changes to the benefits and welfare system. These changes were based on appealing to the imaginary fantasies and insecurities of the voters of 'Middle England':

> But in appealing to Middle England, the appeal was to be to their sense of insecurity and their fears. These fears were not only about job insecurity, or the problems of negative equity that hit many, including affluent, homeowners who in a declining property market found themselves owing more to mortgage lenders than the value of their property. It was also a fear of social breakdown and disintegration, and in particular the threat of crime that was attached to the so-called 'underclass'. Such fears are a potentially powerful combination for a reactionary politics (Jones and Novak, 1999: 186).

In April 2000, the government intensified this strategy by indicating that the unemployed would be called for interviews. Those who failed to respond to these changes would face benefit cuts. A 'two strikes and you're out' welfare policy had already been announced. Claimants convicted of two counts of benefit fraud would have their welfare payments stopped. According to David Blunkett, the Education and Employment Secretary, 'Tackling fraud sends a clear message that we are transforming the welfare state into the working state'. As the *Daily Mail* acidly noted:

> Imagine the scene. ... The phone rings at 8am. An unsuspecting dole claimant blearily answers. He is ordered to report to the unemployment office within a couple of hours – or lose his benefits. This is but one example of what awaits suspected fiddlers. On top of that, the long-term jobless will be made to sign on every week. You have to rub your eyes in disbelief that a Labour Government could even dream of applying such a big stick. The Tories never dared (*Daily Mail*, 5 April 2000).[17]

Blair's governments also continued to follow the Conservatives in the allocation and direction of expenditure on criminal justice institutions. While these institutions were increasingly subjected to the managerial discourses of 'efficiency, effectiveness and economy' (McLaughlin and Muncie, 1993) described in the previous chapter, concentrating on the impact of these discourses has obscured a more fundamental fact, namely that New Labour's expenditure plans continued to favour the traditional institutions of law and order to the detriment of other, socially useful projects in the criminal justice system. For example, in 1998, MI5 spent £200 million (three times the original estimate) while MI6, spent £80 million (four times the original estimate) on 'fitting' their buildings in central London. The government refused to publish the full report on the overspend (*The Guardian*, 29 January 2000). In contrast, refuges for the 50,000 women and children forced to leave their homes each year due to domestic violence 'remain[ed] under-funded, dependent more and more on uncertain short-term handouts from charities and the national lottery'. Thus, while the government had highlighted this issue, and called for action via various provisions in the *Crime and Disorder Act*, in practice, 'the geographies of domestic violence' meant that abused women and children, in order to feel secure, moved an average of 78 miles away from their homes (Warrington, 2000: 7 and 3). The issue of funding the criminal justice system is discussed more fully in Chapter 7.

From Straw to Blunkett: handing over the authoritarian baton

The end of New Labour's first period in office also meant the end of Straw's tenure at the Home Office. According to Polly Toynbee and David Walker, Blair's first government had failed 'to challenge old fears, prejudices and unreasons on law and order, as on taxation and public spending'. Indeed, 'they were happier following than leading public opinion'. Together, Blair and Straw had 'a chance to allay exaggerated public fear of crime – but too often [they] preferred to exploit it for political effect'. Toynbee and Walker also predicted that as the government had made no attempt to offer any kind of reasoned debate regarding what really worked in social policy terms, then 'those same old inflammatory topics – asylum, drugs, punishment and prison – will burn as fiercely next time for lack of robust and honest political leadership' (Toynbee and Walker, 2001: 179). Writing in *The Guardian*, Hugo Young was equally forthright in condemning the iron authoritarianism of Blair's government, and Straw's time at the Home Office: '... whenever a liberal instinct is required to defend historic freedoms, neither Mr. Blair nor any of his colleagues have a grain of dependability left from the days, when in opposition, they railed against the Tories' systemic authoritarianism. They have become, in the worst of all senses, governmental' (Young, 2000: 20). In a similar vein, Henry Porter provided a damning indictment of Straw's policies:

> ... in a matter of months [he] stifled opposition to a widely and justly criticized freedom of information bill by means of a parliamentary guillotine; introduced a measure to curb the rights of trial by jury after a previous bill had twice been thrown out by the Lords; promoted a bill (now the Regulation of Investigatory Powers Act – RIPA) which allows MI5 and numerous other government agencies to inspect emails without a court order; misled the public in terms of police recruitment – in terms of both quantity and ethnic background; produced a steady rise in the prison population; introduced stringent new immigration controls; and enabled the police to take and retain DNA samples from suspects (Porter, 2001: 19).

Porter concluded that Straw's period at the Home Office was open to:

> Only two interpretations. Either he has been held hostage by his civil servants, or, as I suspect, he has cleverly masked his real nature. Either way, one cannot escape the conclusion to entrust our freedoms to this man, indeed to this government, for a second time would be like committing an elderly relative to the care of Harold Shipman (2001: 19).

In May 2001, Straw was replaced by David Blunkett, 'the most dangerous Home Secretary we have ever had' (Young, 2004: 303). As Home Secretary, Blunkett was 'heavily dependent on his political advisers, more so than most ministers'. He built his reputation on the central planks of citizenship and community. His populist and political emphasis on 'bedevilled communities', and the reductive policy making that flowed from this emphasis, was based on letters from his constituents who became 'his permanent focus group' (Pollard, 2005: 273, 267 and 292). As noted above, hegemonically, the discourse of community was a key galvanizing force in New Labour thinking, as it had been under the Conservatives. The government's modernizing agenda, as exemplified by Blunkett, continued to resonate with nostalgic appeals to an idealized sense of community and for a past in which informal social controls regulated criminality and generated respectable acquiescence in the wider population. Blunkett mobilized this 'communitarian past' and juxtaposed it with a 'vision of an apocalyptic present', which was 'then used to justify an authoritarian future based on a further clampdown on civil liberties and legal rights' (Sim, 2006b: 66).

Following the attacks on New York's twin towers in September 2001, Blunkett reinforced and further extended the state's capacity for intrusive and coercive interventions into the lives of those individuals, organizations and groups whose activities were increasingly regarded as inimical to the preservation of social order. It is not the intention here to explore the various nuances in the different Bills that were brought forward, or Acts that were passed, during Blunkett's time at the Home Office. Nonetheless, given the arguments developed so far in this book there are a number of points that are worth considering. First, legislation such as the *Anti-terrorism, Crime and Security Bill* was 'full of measures that the Home Office had been trying to secure for years, as Blunkett now concedes. "The Tories were right. We did stuff things in that needed to be done anyway to correct anachronisms and sillinesses from the past, so I was guilty of "Christmas-tree-ing" the Bill [hanging all sorts of unrelated measures onto a central spine] ..."' (Pollard, 2005: 276). Second, as ever, particular groups were subjected to the state's scrutiny, and the inevitable processes of criminalization that flowed from this scrutiny. In the three years up to 2004 there were over 100,000 house searches under the Prevention of Terrorism Act, overwhelmingly on Muslim families, which led to 17 convictions 'most of them nothing to do with terrorism' (Cook, 2004: 28).[18] Third, like the *Prevention of Terrorism Act*, passed nearly three decades earlier, the powers contained in the legislation passed in the early twenty-first century, were also increasingly normalized within the wider criminal justice system to the point where the idea that law and order policies and anti-terrorist legislation were separate and discrete areas, was theoretically and politically problematic. In practice, they were increasingly linked across an authoritarian continuum in which one reinforced the other to the point where their deployment as a normal aspect of state power became a matter of commonsense, fact and belief.

This process was not without its contradictions and contingencies, internal divisions and external constraints (Gill, 2008). Nonetheless, as Henry Porter argued, linking the *Terrorism Act (2000)*, 'with issuing Asbos. ... has proved highly effective in controlling demonstrations which offend the government' (Porter, 2006a: 25). The legislation also allowed the state to preemptively intervene into areas of social conflict, a tactic which had been successfully pursued during the year-long coal dispute in the mid 1980s when striking miners were denied the right to picket on the grounds that they *might* engage in behaviour likely to cause a breach of the peace. In 2003, police used their powers to prevent protests against the war in Iraq by claiming that the presence of protesters 'was [also] *likely* to cause a breach of the peace. The state [was] thus engaging in a process of predicting what *might* happen in the future rather than detaining individuals as a result of their past actions and activities' (Sim, 2004c: 45, emphasis in the original).[19]

In November 2004, there was yet another Queen's speech, which contained eight Home Office bills ,which were concerned with 'domestic and global security – from street hooliganism to the threat from al Qaida ...'(*The Guardian*, 24 November 2004). For a number of commentators, the elision of both activities into a general, panoramic nightmare, meant that it was the politics of fear that dominated the political agenda rather than a clear and consistent vision for the future, which recognized the possibility of political violence while simultaneously ensuring that this individual and collective fear did not become the pistons driving social and criminal justice policy. These critics did not simply belong to the traditional liberal press, although they were scathing enough. *The Independent* described the proposed 'illiberal, and mostly unnecessary, measures' as a 'shameless piece of electioneering' (*The Independent*, 24 November 2004) while the *Daily Mail* commented in an editorial pointedly entitled, *'Programme with a hollow heart'*:

> ... this is essentially an exercise in crude electioneering. Nobody, of course, would deny the seriousness of the terrorist threat. But Mr Blunkett has already been robust in tightening the law. So is there really any urgency in his new package – which raises worrying questions about civil liberties – or is Labour just playing the Bush card and trying to terrify the public into voting for it while pulling the rug from under the Tories? (www.dailymail.co.uk)

Blunkett resigned in December 2004 and published his political memoirs in 2006. They were attacked by Martin Narey, the former Director General of the Prison Service, who indicated that after a disturbance at Lincoln prison in October 2002, Blunkett had 'shrieked at me that he didn't care about lives, told me to call in the Army and "machine-gun" the prisoners' (Narey, 2006: 21). Over the next two years, the government rarely strayed from the relentless law and order path laid down by Blair, Straw and Blunkett. Another Queen's speech in November 2006, 'with its almost exclusive emphasis on law and order' (*The Independent*, 24 November 2006), reinforced New Labour's authoritarian tendencies still further, at least for those whose deviant attitudes, dislocated lifestyles and legally defined criminal behaviour put them at the centre of the state's punitive gaze. However, other individuals, groups and institutions were more fortunate in avoiding New Labour's sweeping condemnation of criminal and anti social behaviour. It is to a consideration of their position to which the chapter now turns.

New Labour's anti-statist strategy

If interventions into, and the regulation of the behaviour of the powerless, were an enduring symbol of New Labour's first term in office, so the non-regulation of the powerful, was equally significant with respect to the direction of government policy. As indicated in the previous chapter, this strategy, not unexpectedly, was central to successive Conservative administrations, but the events of January 2000 provided an equally clear and unambiguous indication of New Labour's pursuit of an anti-statist policy with respect to those in power. During that month, the government's timidity and acquiescence towards those individuals and institutions at the pinnacle of the economic and political hierarchy and influence, and who had engaged in activities and actions which were immensely socially harmful to the wider social good, was striking. There were a number of examples of New Labour's acquiescence during this period: failing to pursue war criminals hiding in the UK; indicating that those rail executives who provided evidence to the public inquiry into the deaths of 32 people killed in the Paddington train crash would not be prosecuted; failing to confront police brutality highlighted by the *European Committee for the Prevention of Torture and Degrading Treatment*; resuming selling arms to repressive regimes such as Indonesia after establishing (in theory, at least) an ethical foreign policy; backtracking on a number of key recommendations from the Macpherson report into the racist murder of Stephen Lawrence; and failing to pursue crimes involving insider training.

At the beginning of February 2000, it was revealed that the last successful prosecution for this crime had happened nine years previously when Ivan Goodman, a company director, was sentenced to 18 months imprisonment, nine of which were suspended. As *The Guardian* noted, 'Imagine the public outcry if there had been no successful prosecutions for mugging for nearly a decade. Yet that is the case with insider dealings in the city' (*The Guardian*, 8 February 2000). During 1999, while 33 cases were sent to the *Director of Public Prosecutions* for consideration, no prosecutions were forthcoming (BBC Radio 4 News, 29 February 2000).

Arguably, the most symbolic issue that arose during New Labour's first period in office concerned the detention of the Chilean dictator, and friend of Margaret Thatcher, Augusto Pinochet. Pinochet had been arrested in October 1998. His detention had been engineered not by New Labour ministers but by the Spanish government who wished to see him charged with the murder and torture of its citizens in the aftermath of the coup in Chile in September 1973.[20] On 12 January 2000, using the arcane language of Parliamentary procedure, Jack Straw announced that after taking medical advice from four doctors, he was 'minded' to release Pinochet. Straw had initially refused to release the medical reports on which the decision was based. In contrast to the labyrinth obstacles facing those seeking entry to the UK as political refugees from repressive regimes, Pinochet had visited Britain during the previous decade:

> As an important arms purchaser he had been a welcome guest not just of British Aerospace, Europe's largest arms manufacturer, but also of the Conservative governments. He had also visited Britain after the Labour Party had come to power in Britain

> in May 1997 and, while he may not have been welcomed with open arms, there was no bar to the entry to Britain of a man who a quarter of a century before had been a principal hate figure of the Labour Party (O'Shaughnessy, 2000: 1).

Straw's initial refusal to release Pinochet's medical reports on the grounds of medical confidentiality allowed the dictator and his supporters to:

> Interpret Mr. Straw's ruling as a vindication. Baroness Thatcher, who until this week was ready to fume at the very mention of Mr. Straw's name, has suddenly decided that Mr. Straw is "a very fair man". With friends like that, who needs enemies? ... Despite all the previously highfalutin talk of morality and justice, Mr. Straw has chosen the path of least resistance – using the doctors' reports as political camouflage. Such breathtaking cynicism must at last be overthrown (*The Independent*, 13 January 2000).

Pinochet was flown out of the UK at the beginning of March 2000. Straw caricatured the objections of his opponents as inimical to, and subversive of, the rule of law. The Home Secretary presented himself as a politician who not only transgressed the grubby world of beliefs and ideologies but also had acted to free a sick and ailing man. Bizarrely, Straw's supporters argued that Pinochet's detention was a victory for human rights, because it sent a message to state criminals that they could no longer move across international borders with impunity. For others, however, the image of the plane taking the former dictator to freedom perfectly symbolized New Labour's position on crime and punishment and underlined the government's acquiescent attitude to the powerful. As Francis Wheen argued, New Labour's 'famous slogan should be adjusted: tough on petty crime, feeble on mass murder and torture' (Wheen, 2000: 5).

The antisocial powerful

The forensic focus on the lives of the powerless, and the concomitant lack of attention given to the activities of the powerful, was also clearly evident in how the discourse around, and meaning of, antisocial behaviour was socially and politically constructed in New Labour's first ten years in office, and indeed in their long exile in opposition. For the purposes of this chapter, what is important is not only the political and ideological mechanisms through which antisocial behaviour became associated with the powerless, particularly working class young people, but also how such behaviour became *disassociated* with the activities of the powerful – individuals, groups, organizations, institutions and states. So while Jonathan Simon has made the important point that modern political elites in the USA and the UK, working within neoliberal social arrangements, 'govern through crime' (Simon, 2007), it is also important to recognize that political governance is constructed, developed and imposed through the *nongovernance* of a range of activities – social harms – often generated and indeed legitimated by the activities and ideologies of the powerful. Therefore, in the context of the intense and highly moralistic debates about antisocial behaviour and the powerless, New Labour, consciously and unconsciously, ignored the antisocial behaviour of the powerful and what should be done about it.

The issue of binge drinking provides a potent example of this point. Elizabeth Burney has highlighted the unambiguous, class-based nature of the government's relentless drive against this behaviour and more generally against public begging:

> The cleansing of public space, rather than the protection of neighbourhoods, is the motive for injunctions and ASBOs applied against street drinkers and beggars, now firmly ensconced in the anti-social hit-list. ... It does not seem to have occurred to [Tony Blair] to make the link ... that structural and social deficits underlie much antisocial behaviour, and that therefore, along with crime, concentrations are mainly found in less prosperous communities. Apart that is, from the drunken brawling and offensive antics of better-off youth who can afford to indulge in binge drinking in town centres at weekends. Only lately has the government begun to recognize this as "antisocial" too. But binge drinking is a culture of our times, and a lucrative one at that, which is probably why it has not attracted the same condemnation as daytime homeless street drinkers or "youths hanging about" on impoverished housing estates – in other words, the usual targets for social control (Burney, 2004: 5).

Similarly, Peter Hetherington has noted how 'the seemingly respectable people in the local corner shop, where wall-to-wall cheap drink promotions are invariably the norm, can be accessories to antisocial behaviour. But, they are small fry compared to a cut-price pub chain like the ubiquitous JD Weatherspoon, which slashed prices further last weekend to try to halt flagging sales and compete with the supermarkets' (Hetherington, 2004: 9).[21]

Additionally, Blair and his ministers mobilized a precise and particular definition of responsibility, which the poor and the powerless were expected to internalize. It was *their* behaviour, which needed to be responsibilized, and *their* attitudes, which needed to be normalized, through removing the antisocial negativity that underpinned their thoughts and feelings and which gave meaning to their actions. For Polly Toynbee, 'the language of responsibilities applies to the poor, not the rich – though the poorest fifth of the people (who pay a higher proportion in tax) give 3 per cent of their income to charity while the richest fifth (who pay proportionately less tax) donate only 1 per cent' (Toynbee, 2005: 24). Therefore, enforcing responsible behaviour via Asbos and the Respect agenda was one-way political traffic. As an editorial in the *New Statesman* noted, there were a range of behaviours, which were politically and culturally demonized, and labelled as antisocial, while there were other forms of behaviour, which were also desperately antisocial and irresponsible, but which were regarded as unworthy of intervention or comment by the state, its servants, government ministers and politicians:

> When Mr Blair talks about "enforcement, enforcement, enforcement" he has teenagers from council estates in mind, not corporate giants such as McDonald's. When he talks about beggars, he means scruffy people asking for cash, not market researchers with clipboards asking impertinent details and demanding details of your bank account. When he talks about graffiti, he means laddish scrawlings, not the corporate advertising that increasingly intrudes on public spaces. When he talks about abandoned cars, he means old, often burnt-out bangers, not the illegally parked SUVs that block pavements. When he talks about neighbours from hell, he means tenants in council flats, not Grand Metropolitan pubs playing karaoke (*New Statesman*, 2003: 6).

For Will McMahon, the key issue was how social inequality 'structured' antisocial behaviour, and the response to it, 'rather than a mass outbreak of wickedness by those that have no respect':

> Affluent teenagers "hanging around" at the local pony club, stockbrokers playing heavy metal on their home stereo systems in their large detached houses, or aristocrats tearing around their country estates are all indulging in behaviour that in other contexts would be deemed antisocial. The fact that it is not generally treated as such highlights the fundamental importance of social processes in mediating our understanding of behaviours and their impacts. It is the inequality that matters, not the pathology. ... The power of the concept of "antisocial behaviour" lies not in its analytical clarity, which is conspicuously lacking, but in its flexibility. It mobilises personal fears ... (McMahon, 2006: 3–4).

These critical views made little impact on those inside New Labour's 'big tent' who, like Blair, talked about antisocial behaviour in reductive, class-based and apocalyptic terms. They also offered solutions, which were redolent of nineteenth-century positivist thinking around crime. Thus, Frank Field argued that, 'today's yobbish culture' was striking 'at the very foundations of this peaceable kingdom'. He argued that British politics had to fundamentally change to 'one as obsessed by behaviour as it was once by class' in order to deal with the 'rabble ... [who] hang around in aggressive mood' (Field, 2004: 6, 7 and 8). Central to his vision of a fine-tuned, integrated social order were well-functioning families built on the nurturing skills of women because '*the nurturing of their young is natural to most women*' (2004: 13 and 15, emphasis added).

Maintaining anti-statism

New Labour's institutionalized antagonism in responding seriously to the criminality, deviance and antisocial behaviour of the powerful was to remain central to the conduct of the government's business throughout the first decade of the new millennium. The tortuous parliamentary path followed by the *Corporate Manslaughter Bill* provides a further case study of New Labour's anti-statist strategy in action. The Bill was finally introduced in July 2006. It was the end of a process that had seen 10,000 people killed at work between 1976 and 2006, including 581 in the year before the bill was introduced (*The Guardian*, 20 July 2006; *The Guardian*, 27 July 2006). A promise to introduce laws to deal with deaths at work had been made in New Labour's three General Election manifestos but, unlike their desire to confront conventional criminality with a 'simple, speedy and summary' response, (Home Office, 2006a: 40),[22] the response to corporate criminality was slow, cumbersome and legalistic in the sense that those charged were given every benefit of due process and the rule of law. More fundamentally, the Bill did nothing to focus attention on the individual decision-making of the powerful. For the Centre for Corporate Accountability (CCA), the bill looked:

> ... substantially like the previous draft bill in the essential elements of the offence, and therefore contains the same weaknesses. We welcome that a bill has finally been introduced, but feel the bill may be fatally flawed. Despite the Government's agreement in March to reconsider the 'senior manager test', the language remains unchanged. CCA continues to believe that the senior manager test is so narrow as to undermine the central purpose of the bill. We are also concerned about the limited impact of the bill on deaths arising from the conduct of public bodies such as the police and prisons (www.corporateaccountability.org).[23]

In May 2005, Gordon Brown provided a perfect illustration of New Labour's anti-statist position. He used the model of risk to justify not *more* but *less* state intervention into the operations of big business and proposed a new model of inspection based on 'a one-third cut in inspections – or 1m [million] fewer checks every year – and a 25 per cent reduction in form filling'. This new model was 'quite different' form the 'old regulatory model' that had its origins in Victorian times:

> Under a risk-based approach, there is no unjustifiable inspection, form-filling or requirement for information. Not just a light but a limited touch. ... The risk-based approach will help us move a million miles away from the old belief that business, unregulated, will invariably act irresponsibly. The better view is that business wants to act responsibly. ... So a new trust between business and government is possible, founded on the responsible company, the engaged employee, the educated consumer – and government ... (Brown, 2005: 2–3).[24]

In contrast, at the beginning of 2006, the government launched another offensive against welfare claimants, this time the target was the 2.7 million people receiving incapacity benefits. The Work and Pensions Secretary planned to see this number cut by one million over 10 years. This would be done by enforcing tighter regulations, beginning in 2008, including: a lower initial benefit payment, a more rigorous medical assessment and more frequent interviews, which would lead to 'tougher requirements to seek work or lose benefits'. In typical New Labour style, it was suggested that employment advisors would be allocated to work in doctors' surgeries. Those surgeries, which helped to remove people from the benefits system would be rewarded (*The Guardian*, 25 January 2006). At the same time, those claimants capable of some work would have to draw up an 'action plan, which could mean undergoing training or preparing CVs, or see benefits reduced' (*The Observer*, 22 January 2006).

For critics, this was an example of 'another government economy drive' at a moment when 'DWP [Department of Work and Pensions] staffing levels are being cut and the Citizens' Advice Bureaux report harassment of men in their late 50s in ... deindustrialized areas, who have often experienced life-threatening illness and have only a short life expectancy before them ...' (Letter from Professor John Velt-Wilson, in *The Guardian*, 4 January 2006).[25] The Work and Pensions Secretary developed these plans further at the beginning 2007 when he announced that lone parents, mainly women, were to be forced into work or face sanctions and punishment. Private employment companies were also to be offered bounties if they could keep claimants, lone parents or those on incapacity benefit, working for at least three years.[26] His colleague, the Education Secretary, announced in a Green Paper that teenagers beginning secondary school in 2008 would be fined or face criminal prosecution if they failed to remain in education or training until they were 18 (*The Observer*, 4 March 2007; *The Independent*, 23 March 2007).

These intrusions and interventions by the state into the lives of the powerless again can be contrasted with the state's role in pursuing and prosecuting the powerful. In the aftermath of the cancellation of an investigation by the Serious Fraud Office into allegations of bribery involving BAE systems, it was pointed out that:

> While the existing corruption law is archaic, there are alternative legal routes so the real reason is a lack of will. The same lack of will is exposed not just by the BAE decision but also by the continued non-appearance of the long promised new corruption law – once again postponed, probably for at least two years, despite all the anticorruption conventions, which Britain has signed. There have been objections from certain "stakeholders", home secretary John Reid explained this month – code for big business, those who do the bribing (*Private Eye*, 30 March–12 April 2007).

As Michela Wrong also noted:

> Our anticorruption laws are antiquated. The law-enforcement agencies, which still need the Attorney General's consent to proceed, have brought not a single prosecution for bribery of a foreign public official against any British individual or organisation. Back in 2001, the Home Office said it expected between ten and 20 investigations and one or two prosecutions a year. So much for that (Wrong, 2006: 27).

Furthermore, in 2005–6, the number of offences prosecuted by the Health and Safety Commission 'decreased by 23 per cent to 1012 from 1320 in 2004–5.

The number of offences has been steadily decreasing since 1999–2000'. In addition, the number of convictions decreased by 28 per cent. Prosecutions by local authorities followed a similar trajectory, their number decreased by 19 per cent while the number of convictions decreased by 21 per cent (Health and Safety Commission, 2006: 23–24).[27] In contrast to the ongoing increase in the numbers employed in conventional public and private police forces, staffing levels for the Health and Safety Executive (HSE) fell in the three successive years up to 2004–5. In 1994 there were 4,545 staff employed by the HSE, in 2004–5 this figure had fallen to 3,903. Furthermore, by 2006 the Executive was in 'the vanguard for the government's deregulation message' so that:

> The next health and safety visit to your workplace is increasingly unlikely to be an HSE inspector. It could be a lower grade HSE adviser with no enforcement role. It could be one of the consultants paid to deliver most of HSE's regular safety and health awareness days. Or it could be a Workplace Health Connect adviser who may do everything an HSE inspector does. Except respond to a request from an employee, inspect the workplace or enforce the law (O'Neill, 2006: 7).[28]

Health and Safety at Work was therefore another area where continuity between New Labour and their Conservative predecessors was most evident. Ironically, at the very moment when both Conservative and New Labour politicians articulated the need for more law and order, the number of Enforcement Notices issued by all of the Enforcement Authorities between 1990–1 and 2004–5, fell precipitously in each of the three categories that were utilized by these agencies: Improvement Notices by 39 per cent, Deferred Prohibition Notices by 78 per cent and Immediate Prohibition Notices by 20 per cent.[29] At the same time, in 2006, nearly 4,500 young people were killed or seriously injured at work. This figure represented an increase of 20 per cent compared with five years previously (*The Guardian*, 9 August 2006).

New Labour's 'light touch' with respect to the powerful was complete by the summer of 2006. Seven years after first becoming aware of the scale of fraud surrounding Value Added Tax (so-called carousel fraud), which was reputed to be costing the country £8 billion a year, the number of investigators was increased from 500 to 1,000. Crucially, however, these extra numbers came from removing investigators from other tax dodging activities while '2,000 tax investigation jobs were being cut as part of counterproductive "efficiency savings"' (*Private Eye*, 29 September–12 October 2006). At its annual conference in 2006, although the Party's leadership was defeated when delegates supported a motion demanding that negligent directors should be jailed for 14 years if found guilty of corporate manslaughter, in a fitting climax to almost a decade in power, dominated by acquiescence to the demands of the powerful, Gordon Brown argued that prison sentences for company directors 'would be "crazy"' while an aide to Brown indicated that 'introducing jail sentences would wreck the [Corporate Manslaughter] bill, making it impossible to gain cross-party consensus, *or the support of business*' (*The Guardian*, 29 September 2006, emphasis added).

In 2007, the non-regulation of business was intensified further through the introduction of a Compliance Code which, as Dave Whyte has noted, in practice brought 'the government's renewed neoliberal crusade to the day-to-day work of inspectors by formalising the economic considerations that have always acted to constrain law enforcement'. For Whyte:

> The new model of regulatory compliance that is inscribed in the Compliance Code moves the 'de-regulation' agenda on significantly. The aim of the Code is to replace a logic of minimal economic disruption with a logic of encouraging economic progress. ... Although there is a lack of reliable data to indicate trends in enforcement activity in many spheres of corporate crime, key regulatory bodies charged with controlling social harms indicate major reductions in inspection activity and related enforcement activity in the 10 years that Labour has been in power. Attacks on resources have been experienced particularly in local authority food hygiene, trading standards and environmental protection, and national regulatory bodies responsible for meat protection and health and safety at work. Whilst individual employees are undoubtedly subject to new forms of surveillance, the gaze is invariably downwards and the socially harmful activities of corporations generally escape scrutiny (Whyte, 2007–8: 31–32).

By the end of New Labour's decade in office, while there were just over 1,000 inspectors employed by the Environment Agency, and 1,600 were employed by the Health and Safety Executive, there were 16,000 community support officers employed by the police in the UK, 'more than six times the combined total of HSE and Environment Agency inspectors ...'(2007–8: 32). As ever, conventional crime, committed in the world of the public, remained the overwhelming priority for a government whose attitude towards, and response to, the private criminality of the powerful, was little different from their Conservative predecessors, a point perfectly captured by Christopher Hitchen's view that, 'people who preach law 'n' order for the weak are invariably soft on crime when it comes to the strong' (Hitchens, 2000: 22).

Conclusion

What conclusions can be drawn from the arguments developed above? Fundamentally, as Stuart Hall has argued, New Labour's operational power was built on a '*hybrid* regime', which contained both neoliberal and social democratic components (Hall, 2003: 19, emphasis in the original). For Hall, the neoliberal component dominated New Labour's policy agenda. Additionally, this led Blair's governments to develop a particular form of statecraft, which involved continuing with law and order and social welfare policies developed by the Conservatives while simultaneously articulating their own strategic responses to crime and punishment. New Labour's preferred state form was a 'security state' constructed around an 'amalgamation of conservatism and social democracy' built on 'punitive supply-side reforms' This state form 'had not replaced the welfare state but subsumed it within a society ... of social and spatial polarities ... where social problems are pathologised ...'(Fitzpatrick, 2003: 72). Thus, New Labour's vision of order, and the ideological and material resources mobilized by, and through, state institutions to realize this order, was, both consciously and unconsciously, directed relentlessly towards responding to social problems generated by the powerless and their perceived pathologies. As with the Conservatives before them, the powerful effectively remained beyond New Labour's scrutiny, or indeed their concern.[30] Maintaining order was built on systematically increasing and intensifying the coercive capabilities of the institutions of political society, both with respect to the power of traditional state servants such as the police, and through the mobilization of a dystopian network of private security agents built on CCTV camera surveillance, which made the UK the most surveyed country in the world.[31] At the same time, the institutions of civil society, particularly the mass media, remained deeply embedded both in the social construction of crime, criminality and antisocial behaviour and in the reproduction of a popular consciousness in which the idealization of the contemporary celebrity contributed to the profound depoliticization of the wider culture, to the point where 'gossipy reports about celebrities' ways and means increasingly play the vital role, which was once performed by political gatherings, manifestoes and pamphlets' (Bauman, 2002: 172). The panoptic/synoptic society, with the few surveying the many and the many surveying the few, if not yet fully formed, was beginning to take formidable shape (Mathiesen, 1997).[32]

Furthermore, the language and practice of modernization allowed New Labour to engage in its own form of 'regressive modernisation' (Hall, 1988: 2). In appearing to pull the society forward, in Blairspeak to face the new and more convoluted problems of the twenty-first century, the government simultaneously relied on a vision of an early respectable twentieth-century working class community life that was no less idealistic than Margaret Thatcher's sepia-tinted, Victorian work ethic, discussed in Chapter 3. Both, in their own ways, were built on strangling dissent, curbing diversity, increasing the net of criminalization and normalizing special powers, while simultaneously acquiescing to the rapacious and decadent interests of the powerful. As Will McMahon has noted, New Labour's Respect campaign, and the focus on antisocial behaviour within communities, also operated 'in ideological terms'. This focus was 'important in deflecting criticisms of Labour's failed social policies, crystallized in the one-dimensional thinking of "hard-working families" versus the "lawless minority"' (McMahon, 2006: 3). According to Steven Poole, the Respect Action Plan was built on recasting 'authoritarianism ... as caring' (Poole, 2006b: 24). At the same time, he also noted that 'the term "community" is saturated with nostalgia for forms of life that no longer exist' (Poole, 2006a: 27). Thus, while New Labour in general, and Blair in particular, constructed themselves as ideological visionaries who would provide answers to what appeared to be the most intractable of problems, their vision remained rooted in a past built around a truncated vision of order in which the bonds of social solidarity tied the individual to a Gemeinschaft community as a bulwark against crime. Their arguments, as Adam Crawford has noted, were based on the false premise that 'more community equals less crime' (Crawford, 1998: 243–244). For Crawford:

> ... "community" is not synonymous with social order. "Organised" communities can produce both disorder and foster high levels of crime. Collective values of a community may serve to stimulate and sustain criminality. Communal values themselves can be crimogenic. High crime communities can be both disorganised and "differently organised" (1998: 243–244).

Additionally, both Blair and Blunkett's nostalgia for an idealized community of integrated, socially-networked individuals, was reflected in broader popular culture through phrases such as 'we were poor but we were happy' and 'we never locked our doors'. Clearly, the lived feelings and experiences of the postwar working class were, and remain, very important for understanding how hegemonic visions or order are sustained and maintained in the contemporary world, which is increasingly characterized as untrustworthy, anxious and divided (Buonfino and Mulgan, 2006). However, as I argued in Chapter 1, this vision of the past idealized micro-personal and macro-political relationships and ignored a range of social problems that were deeply embedded in the social relationships of the wider society, not least in relation to the formal and informal, often violent punishment of 'deviant' women (Ballinger, 2000; Spensky, 1992) and the racist ideologies around, and the violence directed towards, minority ethnic men and women (Gilroy, 1987). Therefore:

> ... for many of those living in these idealised communities – women, children, minority ethnic groups, gay men and lesbian women – the fear of crime, and their actual experiences of it, including violence, incest and harassment, was a feature of their daily lives. It is therefore important to recognise this point in order to respond fully and comprehensively to the discourse of modernisation that is so prevalent in the government's thinking, otherwise there is a danger of implicitly or explicitly accepting the premise on which the government's strategy rests, namely that, in many respects, life in the well-integrated communities of the past was both better and less fearful. It is from this nostalgic position that the government makes its zero sum case for radically altering the balance of the criminal justice system away from the 'law breaking minority' towards the victim and 'the law abiding majority' (Sim 2006b: 66).[33]

Moreover, even on its own terms, New Labour's interventions into problematic communities and problem families, was built on a series of contradictions.

Policies such as *Sure Start*, were caught up in the perennial problems of short term funding, insecurity and lack of planning. These problems were compounded by 'arbitrary funding changes, most notably the decision in 2002 that a quarter of the Children's Fund would be set aside for crime reduction projects, which has caused crises in many projects supporting vulnerable families. More measures will simply add to this "initiative overload"' (Fitzgerald, 2006: 27).

Finally, by the midpoint in the new millennium, New Labour's near decade in power had done little to challenge the political and economic direction of the country established under previous Conservative administrations. Importantly, this did not mean the Blair's governments blindly and systematically followed a Thatcherite line, despite his (and Gordon Brown's) publicly expressed admiration for her ideas. In government, New Labour pursued policies which 'previous Conservative administrations had either never espoused or to which they were vehemently opposed' (Sim, 2000a: 327). These policies included: incorporating the *European Convention on Human Rights* into UK law; establishing a public inquiry into the racist murder of Stephen Lawrence; demanding that racist, domestic and homophobic violence be taken more seriously by police forces (though how much the desperately conservative police culture did so is highly debatable); attempting some alleviation of poverty and thereby (in their view) contributing to crime prevention through measures such as *Sure Start*[34]; and supporting the discourse of restorative justice to the point where, according to one commentator, it 'may plausibly be seen as an attempt to revive rehabilitation for a new political era' (Zedner, 2002: 356). In that sense, New Labour's policies were not simply a seamless continuation of the policies pursued by previous Conservative governments. Such a position would be 'sociologically reductionist [and] politically naïve' (Sim, 2000a: 327).

However, it was also clear that the social authoritarianism at the heart of Thatcherism had not disappeared, but in many ways had been intensified under New Labour in defence of a social order described by Tariq Ali as, 'a "model" neoliberal economy' where:

> ... the primacy of consumption, speculation as the hub of economic activity, the entry of private capital into hitherto inviolate domains of collective provision ... reigns supreme. An unrepresentative, unreformed electoral system; a foreign policy whose loyalty to Washington is comparable, in the novelist John Lanchester's memorable phrase 'only to the coital lock which makes it impossible to separate dogs during sex'; the right to a jury trial and the presumption of innocence under heavy attack; an authoritarian social agenda; a conformist media, shamelessly used as a propaganda pillar for the new order. ... Political life in Britain has increasingly come to resemble that of a banana monarchy (Ali, 2005: 6–7).

For Suzanne Moore, after ten years in power, Blair and his governments had built a society where there was 'no trickle-down effect from the City bonuses of millions, no social justice for those without advocates'. It was a 'society in pieces' where insecurity for the majority was underpinned by the social exclusion of the minority from the 'big tent': 'those begging, smoking crack, hearing voices. These chaotic, confused souls wander through our cities and our lives. The hope that things might change for them dwindles' (Moore, 2007: 43).[35]

Hope for such groups might indeed have dwindled in New Labour's neoliberal land of responsibilized, pious citizens. However, if all else failed there was always the prison, and its attendant institutions, where the deviant, depraved, deranged and distressed could be physiologically redeemed and psychologically normalized to take their place in the drone-inducing service economy that they and their Conservative predecessors had constructed over the previous three decades. It is to an exploration of this issue to which the book now turns.

Notes

1 This phrase was coined by Robert Lowell in the 1960s. He argued that while the decade represented a 'golden time of freedom to act and speculate', it would, nonetheless, be ended by 'an authoritarian reign of piety and iron' (cited in Panitch and Leys, 2005: viii).

2 Behind these obvious primary definers stood newspaper owners like Rupert Murdoch. Lance Price, the former media advisor to Blair, noted Murdoch 'seemed like the 24th member of the cabinet. His voice was rarely heard (but then the same could be said of the other 23) but his presence was always about' (Price, 2006: 32).

3 As I note throughout this book , it is important to recognize the contradictions and contingencies in state power. Up to March 2007, Soca's impact had been minimal: drug seizures had fallen rather than risen, drugs were as cheap to buy as before and the number of prosecutions had not met expectations. Soca, it was said, 'was an agency in search of a role' (*The Guardian*, 31 March 2007). However, Soca, despite these contradictions, like many of the other agencies that developed under New Labour and their Conservative predecessors, set the ideological parameters for how crime was understood and what responses were needed to deal with the problem as they saw it.

4 In June 2006, Sir Alistair Graham, the Chair of the Committee on Standards in Public Life, and a critic of New Labour standards in government, indicated that he feared that he was the subject of a smear campaign because of his criticisms of the government in this area (*The Observer*, 25 June 2006).

5 One New Labour favourite was Bill Braton, New York's former police chief, whose views on zero-tolerance policing were uncritically endorsed by the government despite a well-established series of critiques mounted against them. See, for example, Wacquant (2005). Jones and Newburn (2006: 798) take a less critical position and argue that in the area of 'three strikes and you're out' at least, the evidence is 'rather limited ... of direct policy transfer from the United States in this area'.

6 A good example of this process was the conference on the 'third way' held in July 2003, which focussed on modernization discourses such as 'progressive governance', 'disciplined pluralism', 'flexicurity' (combining flexibility with security) and 'entrepreneurial citizenship'. The conference was sponsored by British Airways, Citigroup, PWC, KPMG and the Sultan of Brunei. As Larry Elliott noted, 'the third wayers – baby boomer progressives – are free marketeers who have

learned to play the chords to *Stairway to Heaven*' (Elliott, 2003: 21). Thanks to Roy Coleman for pointing out the articles by Loic Wacquant and Jamie Peck to me.

7 Thanks to Anette Ballinger for the reference. While Dubber is talking about America, the same situation applies to the UK. Politicians, as ever, have implicitly and explicitly construed victims and their relatives as automatically seeking vengeance. However, the evidence is more problematic. In April 2006, a survey by Smart Justice and Victim Support indicated that 'victims support measures which they believe are more effective in stopping further offending, than harsh penalties such as prison' (NACRO, 2006: 10). This is discussed further in Chapter 8. Successive governments' unswerving and unwavering support for some victims can also be contrasted with the prevailing attitude towards the thousands of individuals exposed to asbestos during their working lives and who, as a result, became the victims of asbestos-related diseases. In February 2005, the Appeal Court overturned a ruling allowing compensation for thousands of individuals suffering from an asbestos-related condition. It was estimated that insurance companies would save in excess of £1billion (http://www.tuc.org/h_and_s). Thanks to Steve Tombs for the reference.

8 This was a phrase used by Anthony Beever on *BBC Radio 4 News* on 20 October 2007. It seemed to me to capture perfectly Blair's rhetorical flourishes.

9 Over the next decade, this goal was achieved. By November 2006, there had been 23 criminal justice acts, five immigration acts, seven antiterror laws, 10 education acts and 11 health and social care acts. The government had also created 3,000 new criminal offences 'almost one a day' since they came to power (*The Guardian*, 10 November 2006). According to *The Independent*, New Labour was creating crimes at 'twice the rate of the previous Conservative administration' (*The Independent*, 16 August 2006). Importantly, the government was also using the power of delegated legislation to pursue its objectives. This legislation 'is almost never considered. More than 32,000 such statutory instruments have been passed since 1997' (*The Guardian*, 10 November 2006). Furthermore, not all of this criminalization frenzy was necessarily regressive. For example, the government, in theory, was committed to introducing progressive measures concerning the criminalization of sexual and domestic violence. How these worked out in practice is, of course, an issue, which is discussed later in this chapter. Moreover, the general thrust and direction of criminal justice policy *was* towards greater authoritarianism through a range of net-widening pieces of legislation that increasingly criminalized behaviour which was previously non-criminal.

10 Blair's arguments mirrored those of commentators such as Melanie Philips, who has also talked about 'the creation of a debauched and disorderly culture of instant gratification, with disintegrating families, feral children and violence, squalor and vulgarity on the streets' (cited in Ashley 2006: 8).

11 For New Labour apparatchiks, the focus on law and order was to be intensified in the coming months. In the same month as Blair's speech, one of his advisers indicated that 'we are going to ensure that law and order is debated in the House of Commons every day in the six months before the [general election]' (cited in Garside, 2004: 7).

12 In February 2001, the Home Office published a major report *Criminal Justice: The Way Ahead*. Annex B contains a wonderful overview of the 'active offender population' whose number is put at 100,000. The report notes that this population is 'not static and that as offenders leave the population, a steady

stream of other offenders replace them ... the 100,000 persistent offenders this year are not all the same as the 100,000 next year or indeed last year. The modelling work suggests that approximately 20 per cent drop out and are replaced each year' (Home Office, 2001): 116).

13 This was at the launch of the government's Respect Action Plan which saw no fewer than 16 ministers making speeches (cited in NACRO: 2006: 8).

14 Less than a year after their first General Election victory, doubts were already being raised about the focus of the government's efforts. John Pilger argued that the 'Blair regime' was 'on its way to becoming the sleaziest British government in living memory. In just eleven months it has notched up an aggregate of venality, Tammany and perfidy, which the Tories took years to put on the board' (Pilger, 1998: 23).

15 The issue of America's 'three strikes and you're out' draconian penal policy is important here. By 2006, after more than a decade in operation, Californian prisons held thousands of prisoners imprisoned for crimes such as shoplifting, stealing golf clubs or being in possession of small quantities of drugs. In one case, 'Leonardo Andrade, a drug addict ... was jailed for 50 years for stealing videos worth $153. When his case was taken to the Supreme Court in 2003, on the grounds that the sentence amounted to "cruel and unusual punishment", it was dismissed on a 5–4 majority' (Campbell, 2006: 31). Cavadino and Dignan argue that compared with the justice model of sentencing, 'concepts such as "three strikes and you're out" and "zero tolerance" have made the same Atlantic crossing with considerably greater speed'. However, they also maintain that while these developments might herald 'an acceleration of *penal convergence*, we are still a long way from global *homogenisation of punishment*, which may never occur' (2006: 11, emphasis in the original). It is also important to note that judges did not overwhelmingly endorse the new policy. In 2002, two mandatory sentences were imposed on repeat burglars while no mandatory sentences were given to individuals who dealt regularly in drugs. Altogether between, 2000 and 2003, three drug dealers and eight burglars were imprisoned under the new legislation (*The Independent*, 29 December 2003).

16 According to some commentators, Straw was also not beyond utilizing New Labour's majority to force through legislation even when this legislation had not been discussed in Parliament. Thus, his 2001 Criminal Justice Bill went through when only 90 out of the 132 clauses had been debated. He utilized Labour's majority to ask MPs 'to vote on a motion which stated that 42 clauses of the Criminal Justice Bill had been considered when they hadn't been considered at all. Jack Straw was using Labour's Commons majority to turn fiction into fact'. There was some resistance to this from Conservatives such as Richard Shepherd, who indicated that he was 'concerned about the rewriting of history by deeming things to have happened that have not ... the Order Paper now suggests that what is not true is true' (Oborne, 2005: 73–74).

17 Thanks to Dave Whyte for this article.

18 In 2003, the Immigration Service raided 60 weddings and made 110 arrests (Wall, 2004).

19 New Labour's legislation generated further net widening through extending definitions of, and responses to, deviance. Thus, the Serious Organized Crime and Police Act was used to charge and convict Maya Evans, who was arrested near the Cenotaph in London for simply reading out the names of those soldiers who had died in the war in Iraq. At the beginning of 2006, another part of the Act

came into force, which, 'in effect', allowed 'the police to arrest without warrant anyone for any offence, however trivial, and as a result to be entitled to keep their DNA samples, fingerprints or photographs for evermore, whether or not they are ever charged or convicted' (Berlins, 2006: 12). Furthermore, 'the right to trial by jury was removed in certain cases by the Criminal Justice Act (2003), as was the right of silence and the rule of double jeopardy, which the British have had since Magna Carta .... The right to privacy and freedom to move without surveillance is jeopardized in the Identity Cards Bill. The freedom of association was eroded in the Terrorism Act (2000) as was the presumption of innocence. In just nine years, all the conventions of the rule of law ... have been swept away by a Prime Minister with a winning manner and the instincts of [a] tyrant' (Porter, 2006b: 23).

20 Ironically, given the events of the month, the bombing of the Presidential palace during the coup, which was the final act in the brutal removal of Salvador Allende, was carried out by British-made warplanes (O'Shaughnessy, 2000: 58).

21 Hetherington went on to point out that in a four-week period in the summer of 2004, police and trading standards officers undertook 141 operations by sending underage teenagers into pubs and off licenses and found that half of them were selling alcohol to under-18s (Hetherington: 2004: 9). This kind of research had little impact on government thinking as Cabinet Ministers continued to focus their attention on the use of illegal drugs among teenagers to the point where, in April 2006, the former Education Secretary, Ruth Kelly called for random drug testing for all school pupils (*The Guardian*, 14 April 2006).

22 In the same month, July 2006, the Home Office published *Delivering Simple, Speedy, Summary Justice*, which developed these themes around the delivery of justice in its summary form. The next month, it was revealed that the police were lobbying for new powers to dispense summary justice, including 'the immediate exclusion of "yobs" from town centres at night ... Senior officers say that the powers would be the "modern equivalent of a clip round the ear from the local bobby" and ensure that introducing neighbourhood policing across England and Wales has "bite" and meets public expectations' (*The Guardian*, 15 August 2006).

23 As *Private Eye* noted, 'corporate manslaughter will thus only bring more fines that don't cost directors a penny' and that 'the directors of Thames Trains ... made more from management buyouts of the company than its £2m fine over the 1999 Southall [rail]crash' (*Private Eye*, 27 October/9 November 2006).

24 Thanks to Steve Tombs for pointing this article out to me. In October 2006, *Private Eye* noted that the financial sector paid an extra billion pounds in tax in 2005 compared with that in 1997 'despite profits having multiplied in the meantime (HSBC's alone have quadrupled to £21 bn) ....' Figures obtained by the magazine also showed that the banks 'dreamt up 90 different tax avoidance schemes in less than two years of the operation of laws requiring them to come clean to the authorities' (*Private Eye*, 27October/9 November 2006).

25 By the end of 2006, under provisions in the Welfare Reform Bill, claimants on Incapacity Benefit were to be paid at Jobseekers' Allowance Level 'with similar obligations to find work on notice of further cuts in benefit. As in the US, private firms will be used to police the system, with financial incentives to move people off benefit, or cut the level of benefit paid' (Letter from Charles Hopkins in *The Independent*, 27 November 2006). It is also worth noting that the terms used in this debate can be seen as social constructions. Support for the poor is labelled as a 'handout' while support for big business are labelled as subsidies. As George Monbiot has pointed out, in its submission to the Chancellor's prebudget report,

the *Confederation of British Industry* argued that 'the government should spend less on everything except business. The state should cut its planned spending on health, social security and local authorities, and use some of the savings to protect and enhance its "support and advisory services for trade and business"' (Monbiot, 2005: 27). In 2003 and 2004, Tate and Lyle received £227 million from the EU farm subsidies programme while a new deal that was supposed to cut sugar subsidies to the industry meant that in practice companies would receive £7 billion over a four-year period (*The Guardian*, 8 December 2005).

26 In April 2007, the Work and Pensions Secretary announced that lie detectors – 'voice-risk analysis software' – would be used to attempt to identify 'benefit cheats'. It was claimed that the technology could 'detect minute changes in a caller's voice, which give clues as to when they may be lying'. The lie detectors were to be 'tested on housing and council tax benefit claims first, before being rolled out to job centres later in the year' (http://news.bbc.co.uk).

27 Thanks to Steve Tombs for the reference. It is also worth noting that the banks 'paid £230m less tax in 2004–5 than they did in 1996–7, while their profits roughly trebled to not far off £50bn' (*Private Eye*, 8 December–21 December 2006).

28 Thanks to Steve Tombs for pointing out this article to me.

29 These data were supplied by Steve Tombs. Overall, while there was an 'initial rise' in the number of Health and Safety prosecutions after New Labour was elected in 1997, there was a sharp decline in the following years. Between 1999–2000 and 2003–4, there was a fall of 16 per cent, while between 2003–4 and 2005–06 there was a 38 per cent fall in prosecutions (Tombs and Whyte, 2008: 8).

30 After a decade in power, not only had the powerful consolidated their position in the societal hierarchy but also social inequalities had widened to the point where the richest 1 per cent of the population owned 23 per cent of the nation's wealth, 'compared with 17 per cent at the end of the 1980s. In contrast, the share going to the bottom half of the population has fallen from 10 per cent to 6 per cent. This is more "trickle-up" than "trickle-down"' (Lansley, 2006: 30).

31 In April 2007, it was announced that a network of 'talking' CCTV cameras was to be extended to a further 20 areas in England and Wales after an initial experiment in Middlesbrough. People who were seen to be engaging in antisocial behaviour could be held by staff in a central control room and told to desist from engaging in behaviour such as dropping litter (http://news.bbc.co.uk).

32 Making these points does not mean constructing a reductive, deterministic argument around the impact of mass communications on social consciousness (nor of course does it mean minimizing the impact of state violence in the regulation of the economically marginalized). Clearly, there are contingencies, contradictions and spaces for resistance which cut through the mass communications industry. However, it *is* to say that the ideological parameters within which this industry operates, and the multinational interests involved, are central to the interpellation of the twenty-first century subject. Consequently, knowledge about the ethics and politics of the prison (and the wider criminal justice system) is fractured and mystified, concern about its often-brutalizing role in maintaining social order is minimized, if it is recognized at all while social action to challenge and confront the insidious nature of the system is muted.

33 Paula Wilcox has also made an important point concerning how 'gender-neutral definitions of community' are underpinned by 'idealistic assumptions – that the community will be more democratic and open and less subject to inequitable power relations than the state ... or any other locations of human endeavour. Looking at the community with a gendered lens demonstrates that

the community is as embedded in gendered cultural norms as any other social location, comprising diverse groupings with diverse interests and needs' (Wilcox, 2006: 728).

34 The first evaluation of the *Sure Start* programme found that the behaviour of children of teenage mothers, the unemployed and single parents, the very groups Blair was purporting to reach out to, 'did worse in *Sure Start* areas than those in similarly deprived communities elsewhere' and that 'most of the new resources and services' were 'effectively sucking away support from those in the greatest need ...' (*The Guardian*, 1 December 2005).

35 In September 2006, total consumer debt had reached £1.3 trillion, which indicated the profound levels that individualistic consumerism had reached in the society (*The Independent*, 28 September 2006).

6

'THOSE WITH NO CAPITAL GET THE PUNISHMENT'[1]: NEW LABOUR AND THE WORKING PRISON

> Where the courts sentence or remand an offender in custody, we must provide the necessary prison capacity. Violent and serious offenders are now significantly more likely to get a custodial sentence and to be sent to prison for longer than in 1997. We now have 19,000 more prison places than we did in 1997, and there are around 7,000 more seriously violent offenders in prison, protecting the public from thousands of offences a year, which might otherwise have occurred. Spending on prisons has increased by more than 35 per cent in real terms since 1997 ... (Home Office, 2006a: 32).
>
> For all Blair's early talk of tackling the causes of crime, penal policy has shown much continuity with the Conservative approach (Clark, 2006: 4).

The threat of detention and the unrelenting use of confinement were pivotal to New Labour's vociferous law and order drumbeat in the decade between 1997 and 2007. On one side of the government's penal continuum were proposals to establish 'sin bins' for problem families, which would be patrolled by private security guards. There were also proposals for establishing 'retail jails' in shopping malls and on high streets 'where yobs would be detained for up to four hours' (Hyde, 2007: 32). On the other side loomed the material and symbolic presence of the prison, which was as naturalized in New Labour's collective consciousness as it had been under their Conservative predecessors. Therefore, while the numbers in the average daily prison population varied at specific moments in the thirty years from 1974, the unquestioning myth that the prison was an incapacitating social defence against the depredations of a desperate, parasitic minority remained constant across the political spectrum over the three decades with which this book is concerned.

From the beginning, the New Labour government did little to dispel that myth. In 1997, the average daily prison population for adults was just under 61,500; by 2007 it was over 80,000 (Prison Reform Trust, 2007: 4).[2] Thus, 'while it had taken four decades from 1958 to 1995 for the ... population ... to rise by 25,000' it had taken New Labour 'only eight years to match that 25,000 increase' (McGraw, 2005: 1). For particular groups, the rise in detention rates was spectacular: the number of prisoners aged 60 and over rose by 185 per cent; foreign nationals by 152 per cent; life sentence prisoners by almost 100 per cent; women by more than 100 per cent; 15–17-year-olds by more than 100 per cent and drug offenders by 40 per cent (Inside Time, 2006a). The projected figure for 2013 was a high of 106,550 (cited in Prison Reform Trust, 2007: 39).[3]

As in other Western European and North American jurisdictions, the prison population remained disproportionately racialized and increasingly feminized. At the end of 2005, 25 per cent of prisoners came from a minority ethnic group. Between 1999 and 2002, the population grew by 12 per cent, however, the number of black prisoners increased by 51 per cent.[4] Similarly, the number of women in prison more than doubled in the decade between 1997 and 2007 (Prison Reform Trust, 2007: 22 and 14).

Crucially, however, this figure, based on the average daily prison population, while important, provides only a partial glimpse of the numbers punished by the magnetic power of the penal system as a whole. Roger Matthews has rightly argued that this 'snapshot figure' is not the best method for understanding the movement of offenders between different criminal justice sites. For him:

> The cumulative long-term effect of moving among these different sites is rarely explored, and the combined personal, social and economic costs of this recycling process tend not to appear in the formal calculations of cost-effectiveness. ... What is therefore required is not a snapshot of the distribution of offenders, but rather the tracing of the movement of these offenders through these regulatory agencies. In this way, we are less likely to see custodial and community-based sanctions as two divergent courses. Rather, we are better able to appreciate the collaborative and mutually reinforcing nature of these sanctions (Matthews, 2003: 229).

Following Matthews' suggestion, utilizing other data (which are available in the official criminal statistics but are rarely highlighted by politicians and media commentators) can generate a more profound understanding of the stark reality of penal expansionism. In 2000, the courts sentenced 106,000 people to immediate custody, the highest figure for over 50 years. In the same year, 122,000 people were serving community sentences (Home Office, 2002: 1 and 3). In 2002, the figures had climbed to 111,600 and 186,500 respectively. Both were 'the highest on record' (Home Office, 2004: 2). By 2005, the number of people remanded in custody, compared with 1995, had increased by 28 per cent to 84,850 while the number sentenced was 92,450. Altogether, there were 177,300 receptions into prison in 2005, while at the end of the year there were just over 224,000 offenders being supervized by the probation service (Home Office, 2006b: 1).[5] The prison thus continued on its expansionist trajectory under New Labour.[6] How successive Blair administrations conceptualized the institution's role is the subject of the next part of this chapter.

Judging normality through penal partnerships

For conventionally defined offenders, New Labour's commitment to, and reliance on, the prison, reinforced by other agencies in the criminal justice system, was built on the assertion that penal institutions could be made to work for them:

> ... not by pursuing [Michael] Howard's policy of bleak austerity but through committing staff and resources to developing a range of different programmes specifically designed to change attitudes, challenge behaviour and lower the rate of recidivism. Programme delivery was to be achieved through the construction and consolidation of a web of *partnerships* operating *between* criminal justice and local authority agencies in order to provide a *'joined-up'* response to crime and punishment (Sim, 2004a: 253, emphasis in the original).

Jack Straw's lecture to the Prison Reform Trust in 1998 – *Making Prisons Work* – summed up the government's position. It was a position that was reiterrated in 2001 in *Criminal Justice: The Way Ahead.* This document not only spent 57 out of 107 pages once again discussing one of Blair's favourite themes – the modernization of the criminal justice system – but its authors also declared that:

> ... custodial sentences should not only be there as a punishment and incapacitation but also should help prisoners to lead law-abiding lives after release. To discharge prisoners with the same problems and attitudes as when they went in and with no monitoring of their behaviour afterwards does little to prevent crime or to turn lives around. So we are investing to make prisons work better to prevent re-offending. This requires decent, humane regimes and adequate and appropriate training and employment programmes. Conditions in prisons are very poor and need to be improved (Home Office, 2001: 45–6).

This theme was central to the Halliday report, *Making Punishment Work*, also published in 2001, which recommended:

> ... the virtual abolishment of short-term prison sentences; longer and more intrusive sentences for high-risk recidivists to be followed by community supervision; greater focus on utilizing 'what works' initiatives in prison to reduce reoffending; greater co-operation and integration between the prison and the probation services; the augmenting of proportionality and just deserts with the persistency principle in sentencing rationale; and a transformation in the application of community punishments. ... Halliday's proposals were accepted by the government in the White Paper, *Justice for All* ... and the resulting Criminal Justice Act 2003 (Scott, 2007: 66).

Collaborative partnerships between different professional groups in the criminal justice system were the foundation on which the policy of the working prison was built. In 2000–1, over 1,700 staff were involved in different partnerships at over 100 prison sites (Blud et al., cited in Sim, 2005: 220). Staff from probation, education, psychology as well as prison officers were involved in developing programmes such as *Enhanced Thinking Skills*, *CALM (Controlling Anger and Learning to Manage it)* and *Reasoning and Rehabilitation* (Stewart, cited in Sim, 2005: 220).

Psychological intervention was central to this process. Psychologists were given an enhanced role in developing cognitive skills programmes and applying them to the study of crime and the prevention of recidivism. Between 1999 and 2002, their number doubled to over 600, which made the prison service 'the largest single employer of applied psychologists' (Towl, 2002: 3). In 2004, more than £150 million was spent on cognitive skills programmes (Ford, cited in Carlen and Tombs, 2006: 344). There were also opportunities for psychologists to move into new and novel areas. According to one insider:

> ... the augmentation of the prison/probation partnership offers the, as yet unrealised, promise of the two organisations working "seamlessly" with offenders. For example, there is the potential for a prisoner to begin an intervention while in prison and to continue with it in a community setting. There will be a significant growth in this area of work over the coming years. *Psychologists will need to be adaptable in terms of their roles.* (Towl, 2002: 6, emphasis added).

Unsurprisingly, given New Labour's discourse around offending behaviour discussed in the previous chapter, the new partnership programmes were based on an individualized and reductive presupposition that it was the mangled perspective, and twisted understanding of the world inside the heads of offenders, which needed expert intervention and required programmatic alteration. Women, in particular, were targeted so that adjusting their minds to suit reality became the key to success. The goal was to change 'their *beliefs* about the world; the problem is in their heads, not their social circumstances' (Carlen, 2002: 169, emphasis in the original).

Additionally, as Magnus Hornqvist has noted, the various programmes introduced under the strategy of *What Works?* such as the *Reasoning and Rehabilitation Training* programme mentioned earlier, were closely tied to changes in the labour market and, in particular, the developing relationship between the prison and the demands of the service economy to which the prisoner and ex-prisoner was to be psychologically subservient if he/she was to become a self-governing, socially acceptable subject. Thus, the prison:

> ... has changed along with the nature of work. The factory was at the centre of the prison during the industrial era. But when entry-level jobs are mainly found in the service sector, the cognitive skills classroom has dethroned the factory. *The continuity is also striking.* Now, as then, inmates are trained to become wage-labourers. Now, as then, some inmates will establish a foothold on the labour market, whereas many will not. The impact of the *What works* strategy on recidivism rates is marginal at best, and suggests that the cognitive-behavioural-focus is equally successful – or unsuccessful – as the previous welfare/factory centred approach. Whereas only a minority of inmates will ever establish themselves on the labour market, no inmate escapes its imperatives. The current ideal of the self-controlled, stress managing and submissive service worker saturate the walls, and blurs the boundary between what is inside and outside of the economic exchange (Hornqvist, 2007–8: 20, emphasis added).

New Labour's prison philosophy and practice was therefore built on the idea that the working prison was an institution, which could, and would, play a key role in the lives of the socially excluded via the twin processes of normalization and reintegration. It was a position which inevitably led to a gimlet focus on the individual offender and the characteristics of risk he/she exhibited to the old and new 'judges of normality' (Foucault, 1979: 304) in the treatment and testing rooms behind the walls. Broader, material social divisions, and their impact on the identities, motivation and behaviour of offenders were necessarily, and inevitably, limited to the politically acceptable discourses of social exclusion and integration 'which so easily obscure rather than illuminate patterns of inequality, and which do not question the nature of the society in which people are to be included' (Levitas, 2005: 6). However, the prison was also a place where the old, punitive mentalities, and the often-unaccountable infliction of physical and psychological pain, remained central to the institution's organization and to the everyday interactions that many staff had with the confined. It is to a consideration of this issue to which the chapter now turns.

Life on the inside: retaining the old punitiveness

Pat Carlen has made the point that the developments in penal policy, discussed in the preceding section, should not be seen as necessarily entailing a progressive and enlightened response to offenders. Rather, traditional punitive discourses coexist with modern technologies of penal control, each reinforcing the other:

> ... when this postmodern ideology of multiple programming is cultivated in custodial institutions, its coercive psychological programmes are implemented alongside all the old modernist disciplinarities of placing, normalising and timetabling, and against a backcloth of the even older premodern controls such as lock-ups, body searches and physical restraints, and often in the confused conditions which result from overcrowding. As a result, their possibilities for benign effect are largely neutralised ... the disciplinary transformations in the penal body politic have not supplanted the old disciplinarities designed to keep prisoners docilely and securely in prison. Instead they have added even more layers to the already compacted layers of encrusted disciplinarities (Carlen, 2004: 10 and 17).

With Jackie Tombs, she has also noted how the punitive and the therapeutic overlap and reinforce each other in the contemporary prison setting:

> ... therapeutic programming in prison is always buttressed by all the old punitive and security paraphernalia of previous centuries of creative penal governance; and that such an accretion and layering of disciplinary modes of containment strategies effortlessly produce the mixed economy of the therapunitive prison ... in which any isolated therapeutic attempts to reduce the debilitating pains of imprisonment are inevitably undermined by the punishing carceral context (Carlen and Tombs, 2006: 339).

Therefore, despite (or perhaps because of) ten years of New Labour modernization projects and policies, the old strategies, laid down during the genesis of the modern prison at the end of the eighteenth century, continued to exert a baleful influence on the daily organization of many institutions in the early twenty-first century in a number of interrelated ways.

Table 6.1 Prison overcrowding in England and Wales 1997–2006

Year	Number of places (CNA)	Number of prisoners	Percentage occupation
1997	56,329	61,467	109%
1998	61,253	65,727	107%
1999	62,369	64,529	103%
2000	63,346	65,194	103%
2001	63,530	66,403	105%
2002	64,046	71,112	111%
2003	66,104	73,627	111%
2004	67,505	74,468	110%
2005	69,394	76,079	110%
2006	70,085	77,962	110%

(Adapted from Prison Reform Trust, 2007: 8).

First, the discourse of less eligibility, and the construction of the prisoner as a less eligible subject, which was discussed in Chapter 4, retained a corrosive physical and psychological presence both within and without the prison walls. Many prisoners continued to be kept in conditions, which, in February 2005, were described by Martin Narey, the then Chief Executive of the National Offender Management Service, as 'nothing short of gross' (*The Guardian*, 8 February 2005). In 2006–7, 17,974 prisoners were being held, two to a cell designed for one. This figure had increased from 9,468 a decade earlier while 1,113 were being held three to a cell designed for two (Prison Reform Trust, 2007: 7). Table 6.1 indicates the nature and extent of the problem in New Labour's first decade in power.

Reports by the Chief Inspector of Prisons reinforced Narey's views, highlighting as they did the often appalling conditions in both public and private prisons. In the latter case, one justification for the introduction of these prisons was the role that they would play in alleviating the crisis of conditions and overcrowding. However, at Doncaster prison, privatized in 1994, the evidence gathered by the Chief Inspector a decade later was grim:

> Many prisoners lacked pillows, adequate mattresses, *toilet seats*, working televisions, notice boards and places to store belongings. Some cells, especially on the young prisoners' wing, were dirty and festooned with graffiti. These were examples of an institutional meanness which was also reflected in making prisoners pay to change the PIN numbers they needed to contact relatives, and in the fact that no unemployment pay was provided to those prisoners for whom no work was available (HM Inspectorate of Prisons, 2006a: 5, emphasis added).[7]

In Pentonville:

> … many internal areas remained dirty and vermin-infested, and too many prisoners lacked basic requirements, such as pillows, toothbrushes – and, on one occasion, there was not even enough food to go round at the one cooked meal of the day. Prisoners' requests, through the formal application system, were often ignored. These examples of institutional disrespect again reflected a failure to operate basic systems: a failure that was so endemic that prisoners at induction were told not to expect to have a pillow or to have their applications dealt with (HM Inspectorate of Prisons, 2006b: 5).

In her annual report for 2005–6, the Chief Inspector indicated that her team had inspected 14 prisons in the reporting period and a further three 'shortly afterwards, at a time of maximum population growth. Many reports showed establishments struggling to provide decent and purposeful regimes for prisoners in their care' (cited in Nathan, 2007: 15). Expenditure in the highly emotive and symbolic area of prison food emphasized the ongoing less eligibility of the confined.[8] In 2004–5, the daily cost of food for adult males in public sector prisons was £1.79, for women it was £2.16. Young offenders fared better; the daily cost of their food was £2.26. According to the government, the 47 pence difference in cost 'mainly reflects the general recognition that young people require more vitamins and protein to ensure healthy growth' (*Hansard*, cited in NACRO, 2006:38).

Second, for prisoners, the institution continued to be an alien place of often-bearable pain and desperate tension. In 2004–5, over 21,000 incidents of self-harm were reported, 55 per cent of them in women's prisons. Eastwood Park prison averaged nearly six incidents of self-harms each day, or nearly 2,000 in the year. According to the Chief Inspector, these figures indicated 'the high levels of distress and vulnerability, *which can be exacerbated by inactivity and lack of interaction*' (cited in *Inside Time*, 2006b: 9, emphasis added). Furthermore, between 1997 and 2006, 812 prisoners killed themselves, while the suicide rate for male prisoners was five times greater than for men killing themselves in the community (Prison Reform Trust, 2007: 9).[9] The idea of the seamless transition from prison to community, that was so central to New Labour's image of the modernized, working prison, also failed to materialize with respect to the protection of ex-prisoners. According to Home Office figures, in 2003, 'in the week following release, prisoners ... were about 40 times more likely to die then (sic) the general population' (Shaw, 2007: 1). This situation was compounded by the ongoing and overwhelming emphasis on security, which has been unrelenting since the mid-1960s, and which has justified and legitimated an intense and demeaning level of intrusiveness and surveillance into the lives of prisoners (Fitzgerald and Sim, 1982). Handcuffing a young offender coming out of a coma to a prison officer following brain surgery and using sweatboxes measuring 24 inches by 34 inches for pregnant women prisoners at Styal women's prison, illustrated the extent and impact of the concern with security and control inside and outside of the walls (*The Guardian*, 20 May 2006; *The Guardian*, 1 February 2006).[10]

Finally, violence, and the threat of violence, remained a disturbing presence in the everyday life of New Labour's modernized institutions. In 2006, the Prison Inspectorate noted that in Pentonville 'only 43 per cent of prisoners ... believed that most staff treated them with respect'. Crucially:

> Fewer prisoners than in 2005 felt at risk from other prisoners: but many more felt at risk from staff: 40% (compared with 29% last time) said that they had been insulted or assaulted by staff. ... Some prisoners told us that they were reluctant to complain formally about ill-treatment by staff, in case of reprisals; and the one formal complaint we saw had not been investigated properly. Use of force was high, and recording of how and why it was used was insufficiently precise (HM Inspectorate of Prisons, 2006b: 5).

Prisoners' accounts have consistently reinforced this official line a point I shall return to in Chapter 7.

Additionally, being frightened and feeling unsafe was differentiated by race. In 2005, it was reported that of the 5,500 prisoners interviewed in 18 prisons by the Prison Inspectorate, it was Asian prisoners who faced the greatest bullying and abuse, with 52 per cent indicating that they felt unsafe 'compared with 32 per cent of white prisoners and 18 per cent of black inmates ... while Asian prisoners face[d] most racist abuse from other inmates, black prisoners felt they were least likely to be treated with respect by staff' (*The Guardian*, 20 December 2005). Reports from individual prisons underlined the fear minority ethnic prisoners felt.

In Leeds, 'over a third of prisoners had felt unsafe at some time, and this rose to 43 per cent for black and minority ethnic prisoners' (HM Inspectorate of Prisons, 2005: 5). In Whitemoor, after one prisoner was called a 'fucking nigger' his mother was then called 'a black bitch. I felt frightened that they could kill me at any time but there was nothing I could do' (*The Guardian*, 27 June 2006). At Dovegate, 'safety remained a serious issue' in the prison while 'foreign nationals felt acutely at risk' (HM Inspectorate of Prisons 2007a: 5). In Risley, with a population of 1,100, 'reception staff struggled to cope with the number of prisoner movements in inadequate buildings. ... Over 30 per cent of prisoners (rising to 54 per cent of black and minority ethnic prisoners) reported that they felt unsafe at some point' (HM Inspectorate of Prisons, 2006c: 5). The research conducted by the Commission for Racial Equality into the racist murder of Zahid Mubarek, published at the end of 2003, pointed to the systemic nature of the problems facing minority ethnic prisoners, problems which transcended the cult of the individual prison officer who was a 'bad apple' but instead raised serious questions about the role of prison officer culture itself in the reproduction of racist discourses:

> Prison 'cultures' among prison staff meant race equality procedures could be ignored, staff operated in a discriminatory way, and racist attitudes and behaviour were tolerated. Racist abuse and harassment and the presence of racist graffiti were persistent features of prison life for many staff and prisoners. Action in response to such expressions of racism was generally limited to dealing with the immediate problem rather than rooting out its causes (Commission for Racial Equality, 2003: 45).

I shall return to the question of prison officer culture also in Chapter 7. Before that, I want to consider a number of other issues concerning the prison system under New Labour, beginning with the valorization of the discourse of risk and public protection and its impact on the everyday life of the institution.

Prisons, risk and public protection

> ... new assemblages with risk produce new sites and possibilities for governing (Maurutto and Hannah-Moffat, 2006: 450).

The accelerating use of imprisonment under New Labour was reinforced by the discourse of risk and risk assessment, which was also deeply embedded in the government's law and order mentality. In Tony Blair's first year in office, this discourse was used by a spokesperson for the Prison Service to defend 'chaining a woman prisoner with multiple sclerosis to a hospital bed after she suffered a stroke' (Horlick-Jones, cited in Sim, 2005: 219). More broadly, its impact was seen across a range of penal dimensions, particularly in the number of offenders being recalled to prison. According to the Home Office, the 'year on year rise in the numbers being recalled to custody for breaching licensing conditions [was] a remarkable fifteen per cent' (cited in Solomon, 2006: 18). Or, to put the figures another way, between 2001 and 2006 the number of prisoners recalled for a technical breach of their licence, '... as opposed to recalls for a fresh offence committed on licence ... ha[s] risen by 350 per cent over the last five years' (Higham, 2006: 14). Writing in 2006, the Prison Reform Trust noted that in local prisons, 11 per cent of prisoners had been recalled (Lyon, 2006).

Importantly, this rise took place against an increase of less than 15 per cent in the number of ex-prisoners being released on licence (Dobson, 2007). The Chief Inspector of Prisons noted that 'too often prisoners were not told why they were being sent back to jail; one prisoner hanged himself when he received a piece of paper telling him that he was to serve four additional years. There was no explanation on the paper for this decision (*The Guardian*, 27 January 2006). Furthermore, prisoners were being recalled for behaviour that posed little risk to the public. Data collected by the National Association of Probation Officers (Napo) from both prisoners and probation officers indicated that:

> ... many of the recalls were for technical reasons such as not following rules, or missing appointments. In the majority of the cases of those recalled for technical reasons, there was no evidence of risk to the public. Cases published by Napo include individuals who were recalled for not getting up in the morning, for reporting to the wrong probation office, for losing their permanent address, for being late for appointments, for going absent without leave following a bereavement, because of tags not working, for being arrested but later not charged, for being out after curfew times and for a failure to keep appointments (www.napo2.org.uk).[11]

Additionally, under the Criminal Justice Act 2003, the government introduced Imprisonment for Public Protection (IPP). The Act stipulated that offenders could 'only be released once the parole board judges that they no longer pose a threat to the public. In some cases, this will be never so that life really does mean life' (Home Office, 2006b: 17).[12] Between 2005 and 2006, the number of prisoners serving life sentences, or who had been sentenced under the IPP legislation, rose exponentially to the point where 'nearly one in every ten men in prison is serving these sentences' while the courts were 'using them at a rate of up to 40 a week' (Solomon, 2006: 18). This meant that by 2006 there were over 7,000 individuals serving indeterminate sentences (Higham and Holmes, 2006: 22). According to the Chair of the Parole Board, this figure was expected to rise to 12,500 by 2011

(Nichol, 2006: 7). Other figures indicated that there could be 25,000 individuals serving IPP sentences by 2012 (*The Guardian*, 1 August 2007).[13]

The impact of these sentences on the nature of the prison population was profound. By December 2006 there were more prisoners serving indeterminate sentences – traditional life sentence prisoners and those sentenced under the IPP legislation – compared with those serving less than 12 months. The former group constituted '11 per cent of the prison population' while those 'serving less than 12 months was slightly lower, a situation that has never happened before in the prison system in England and Wales'. The courts were finding the new sentence:

> ... particularly attractive. This is not surprising given that the new sentence casts a much wider net than the automatic life sentence that some see it as replacing. There are 153 specified offences for an IPP compared to 11 offences for an automatic life sentence (which needed two before a life sentence was automatic) and the sentence can be used for a first offence as long as the defendant is deemed dangerous. Recently there have been 50 people a week going into custody on IPP sentences (Solomon, 2007a: 15).

Reid's 'rebalancing' act

In July 2006, in a tone eerily reminiscent of Leon Brittan's speech to the Conservative Party Conference in October 1983, discussed in Chapter 2, John Reid, Blair's fourth Home Secretary in less than a decade, published the pointedly entitled, *Rebalancing the criminal justice system in favour of the law-abiding majority*. Its subtitle – *Cutting crime, reducing reoffending and protecting the public* – reinforced the thrust and direction of Reid's thinking (Home Office, 2006a). The document attempted to respond to various crises that had gripped the Home Office and which had led to the sacking of Charles Clarke the previous May. Crucially, its anonymous authors maintained that it was important to 'rebalance the criminal justice system' away from what the government saw as the system's misplaced concern for the rights and welfare of the atavistic, parasitic minority and towards the rights of victims and the law-abiding majority through pursuing yet more policies to redress this alleged imbalance. These policies included: building an additional 8,000 prison places; increasing the maximum penalties for certain offences and changing the parole system so that 'any decision to release an offender into the community must be made unanimously' (2006a: 6). The document was replete with references to the victim to the point where:

> ... every new member recruited to a parole board will have direct or indirect experience as a victim of crime, or will be able to demonstrate a sound awareness of victims' issues. We will also enhance training for all parole board members in victims' issues. We intend

> to introduce a Victim's Voice, which will enable the concerns of victims in the most serious sexual and violent cases to be put powerfully to the panel hearing the case, as well as dealing with public safety issues (2006a: 15).

Rebalancing the criminal justice system thus reinforced New Labour's commitment, discussed in the previous chapter, to 'privileging and institutionalizing the voices of victims, or rather those victims who [were] regarded ... as legitimate victims of crime' (Sim, 2006b: 66). It was also 'underpinned by implicit and explicit categorical juxtapositions: the law-breaking minority and the law abiding majority; the victim and the offender; balance and imbalance; the communitarian past and the anomic present; and the formal and the informal' (Sim, 2008b: 138). In terms of the prison, it was clear, indeed boastful, about the place of the institution in New Labour thinking:

> Prison capacity should be determined by the need for places. If people need to be in prison, the places will be made available. There are policy changes in this document which will increase the need for places – for example, toughening our response to bail breaches; better enforcement of community sentences; and new proposals on serious and prolific offenders. To accommodate the impact of these changes, we will look for more effective ways of focusing the existing prison estate on those who should be in our prison system (for example by doing more to return foreign prisoners to their country of origin) (Home Office, 2006a: 33).

The proposals came after yet another round of political one-upmanship between the main political parties as they continued with the authoritarian 'policy auction' (Crick, 2005: 325) discussed in Chapter 4. At the Conservative Party Conference in October 2004, David Davis, the Shadow Home Secretary had returned to the theme of 'prison works'. He maintained:

> ... prison does work. It is a deterrent. Criminals fear it. And it takes criminals out of circulation – while they are locked up, they cannot commit crimes. Half of all crimes in Britain are committed by the same 100,000 persistent criminals. But at any one time, just 15,000 of these are actually in jail ... our criminal justice system is in crisis. We will solve this crisis by scrapping Labour's early release scheme, by increasing the proportion of the prison budget that is spent on education and rehabilitation; and by starting a prison building programme that will allow judges to send prisoners down for the sentence they deserve (Davis, 2004: 5).

In February 2005, Michael Howard returned to the theme that had made him famous twelve years earlier. He indicated that under a future Conservative government, burglars caught for the third time would serve at least three years and hard-drug dealers would serve at least seven years. Not only would this strategy increase sentences by a fifth but it would also add another 14,000 offenders to the prison population. An extra £760 million would be spent on building new prison places. For Howard, 'the decline of individual responsibility, the proliferation of so-called "human rights" and government's failure to draw a clear distinction between right and wrong [had] left Britain in a moral quagmire'. In the grim political world of penological auctioneering, the then Home Office minister, Hazel Blears, boasted that the government had added 17,000 places to prisons since 1997 while also promising that a further 3,000 would be added to the system (*The Guardian*, 8 February 2005).

In June 2006, the Conservative Party indicated that they were considering spending £15 billion to create additional prison places. David Davis was ' "quite sure" that more prisons [were] needed' while Jack Straw commented that 'we have built more prisons and prison places and the chances are that more have to be provided. I have never had a problem about building more prisons' (http://news.bbc.co.uk/1/hi/uk_politics/5091720.stm). At the end of July, and in the light of Reid's expansionist plans, the Home Office announced that by 2012 the prison population could be somewhere between 88,980 and 102,280 (*The Independent*, 28 July 2006).[14]

This grim political one-upmanship was also evident in the continuing focus on the criminal 'underclass'. Thus, while Blair and Reid discussed the criminal minority who lacked a moral and familial compass in communities buffeted by the forces of an untrammelled globalization beyond political and state control, Norman Tebbit, one of Margaret Thatcher's closest political associates, was equally clear when asked about the 'greatest challenges' facing the UK:

> Leaving aside climate change and terrorism, which we share with other nations, the most serious is the social instability consequent upon unlimited, unmonitored, uncontrolled immigration unwilling to integrate or abide by British customs, cultures and laws. This is made worse by the progressive collapse of educational standards leaving a skills shortage and a surplus of near unemployable semi-illiterate and innumerate school leavers, undisciplined, without moral standards, living in urban areas with inadequate policing, and a judiciary infected by political correctness and imported legal concepts which fail to distinguish between rights and entitlements (Tebbit, 2006: 25).

By the beginning of 2007, Reid's plans were being contested within the state itself and by external commentators. As the overcrowding crisis deepened, prisoners were sleeping in basement court cells, while Reid's much-touted plan to build 8,000 new places risked being undermined. While the government had agreed to underwrite the cost of building the prisons by the private sector to the tune of £1.7 billion, the Treasury was not prepared to provide funds to actually run the prisons (*The Guardian*, 18 January 2007; *The Guardian*, 17 February 2007). In February 2007, in the annual Prison Reform Trust Lecture, the Archbishop of Canterbury talked of a 'custodial fundamentalism' and 'custodial obsession' being imposed on an already 'overloaded and ineffectual prison system'

(Williams 2007: 5) while in evidence to the Home Affairs Select Committee two months later, Lord Justice Woolf raised serious concerns about the prison building programme and what should be done about it:

> What I have learned over the period in which I have been involved is that if more prisons are built they will be filled and the policies that result in the overcrowding now will continue that overcrowding. What we have to do is make a proper assessment as to the fair proportion of the economy of this country, which it is right to devote to imprisoning individuals. If you say that that fair proportion is unlimited, you can make it work; you build more prisons and ensure that they have very effective regimes, but in practice we find that that does not happen. One may have another 800 places available over a relatively short period of time but they will not be sufficient to deal with the problem. But even if it was sufficient to deal with the problem it would be only a very short-term solution. I just do not think that it would work. That is why I would like a brave government to say that it will not have an open door policy as far as concerns prisons, that *this* is a sensible number for the community and sentences must be produced which will use them in the most effective way (Woolf, 2007: 7, emphasis in the original).

Thus, despite ten years of unambiguous New Labour support, the prison was racked by its own internal contradictions and crises and remained, as it had been since its genesis at the end of the eighteenth century, a site of contestation and conflict. The question of contestation, and the nature of the hegemonic challenges that could be mounted to challenge the institution's dominant ideological and material position within a law and order society, will be addressed in the next chapter. Before doing so, I want to consider four broader conceptual themes and issues regarding the institution's place within New Labour's punitive world.

Conceptualizing the modern(ized) prison under New Labour

First, and most obviously, like the Conservatives before them, the prison was a central component in New Labour's commitment to both constructing and defending their particular vision of social order. In doing so, the institution continued to work at an ideological level through the ongoing reproduction of a deeply embedded popular and political discourse, in which crime was socially constructed as the prerogative of a 'scientifically identifiable', atavistic minority of feral individuals, families and communities who could be normalized by exposing them to the rigours of professional intervention. Again, like their Conservative predecessors, New Labour's criminal justice and penal policies were relentlessly focussed on the powerless. As ever, the powerful remained beyond scrutiny, a process reinforced by the distracting role that the prison played in diverting attention away from their behaviour and criminality (Mathiesen, 1974). Furthermore, the 'action' function of the institution described by Thomas

Mathiesen in 1990, seven years before New Labour came to power, remained as resonant in 2007 as when Mathiesen first conceptualized it, and indeed provides the political umbilical cord that linked New Labour politicians with their Conservative predecessors. 'Taking action' invariably and inevitably involved expanding the number of prisons:

> By relying on the prison, by building prisons, by building more prisons, by passing legislation containing longer prison sentences, the actors on the political level of our own times ... obtain a method of showing they act on crime as a category of behaviour, that they do something about it, that something is presumably being done about law and order. ... No other sanction fulfils this function as well (Mathiesen, 1990: 139).

Additionally, the institution was increasingly working at a material level with respect to its connection to the service industry labour market, which was discussed above. As Alessandro De Giorgi has noted, what has emerged is a 'paradigm of global less eligibility', built around a 'punitive assemblage' which:

> ... includes both penal and extra-penal strategies, ordinary prisons as well as immigration detention centres, tough anti-crime policies as well as restrictive 'anti-poor' welfare reforms – through a punitive *continuum* targeting those inside prisons as much as those entrapped in the surrounding wastelands, in a constant reminder of what awaits them if they refuse to surrender to the imperatives of an over-exploitative economic order ... (De Giorgi, 2007–8: 18, emphasis in the original).

Within this 'punitive assemblage', the institution was also being utilized to warehouse foreign national prisoners, once more with desperate consequences for the mental health of a number of those detained. Here, and again in contradiction to the fantasies expressed by New Labour ministers concerning the smooth-running, normalizing working prison, the human consequences were grim. In February 2007, the Chief Inspector of Prisons in a report which followed an earlier study described:

> ... the anxieties, uncertainty, frustration and at times despair that many foreign national prisoners were experiencing. Those prisoners included people who had lived here since childhood, or were responsible for small children; as well as people who were clearly not deportable or who were held on inaccurate information. One stark indicator of their predicament was the increased prevalence of self-harm – which we had not found to be an issue in the research for the thematic review, a year earlier. Foreign nationals described feeling suicidal, due to the uncertainty of their position; and IMBs [Independent Monitoring Boards] and establishments reported increased self-harm and suicide attempts (HM Inspectorate of Prisons, 2007b: 5).

Additionally, between 2000 and 2007, there were eight suicides in immigration detention centres (medicaljustice.org.uk), while between 2006 and 2007 alone, there were 199 attempts at self-harm that needed medical treatment. In Yarl's Wood, women detainees alleged that:

> ... staff regularly refer to them as 'black monkey', 'nigger' and 'bitch'. They claim vital faxes from solicitors are going amiss and information on basic legal rights is being withheld. Detainees also complain they are given days-old reheated food in which they have found hair, dirt and maggots (*The Observer*, 24 May 2007).

Second, given the nature of its incapacitated population – the unemployed, the homeless, the mentally distressed, the institutionally brutalized, the sexually traumatized and the substance dependent – the institution continued to materially engage in the 'penal management of poverty and inequality' (Hallett, cited in McElligott, 2007: 31), however contradictory and fragmentary that process might be. For David Wilson:

> Prison is already performing a huge disappearing trick, sweeping under the carpet huge swathes of the population, hiding them from public view – and thus removing them from the scope of public policy and the home secretary's inbox. At a time when we are reducing welfare provision, prison plugs the gaps that must emerge when there are fewer community mental health nurses, hostels and drug treatment programmes. Prison removes from our streets all the young men who have been excluded from school and then can't find jobs because it is cheaper to outsource the work to the developing world. And it mops up those who don't quite fit in, those whom we would all therefore prefer to ignore (Wilson, 2006: 26).

The research conducted by David Downes and Kirstine Hansen has reinforced Wilson's point concerning the relationship between the rolling back of social welfare programmes and the rolling out of punitive, penal policies. While urging caution in the treatment of cross cultural data, they nonetheless noted that in the 18 countries they studied, '... the seven countries with the highest imprisonment rates, all spend below average proportions of their GDP on welfare, while the eight countries with the lowest imprisonment rates all spend above average proportions of their GDP on welfare, with the exception of Japan' (Downes and Hansen, 2006: 4). The UK came fourth in the list of 18.

Thus, after a decade of New Labour, what was in place in England and Wales was a 'perpetual prisoner machine' (Dyer, 2000), which cycled and recycled known offenders around the system. This recycling was reinforced by the lack of provision in the resettlement of offenders, both before and after release, to the point where the annual prisoner survey carried out in 2006 by the prisoners' newspaper, *Inside Time*, found that 'on average, 80 per cent of males and females who were within 12 months of release had not been offered any resettlement help' while 'of those who had, approximately two-thirds of respondents said it had not helped' (*Inside Time*, 2006d: 1).

Third, the prison was embedded in a structure of power in which old and new strategies and policies of social control were supporting and reinforcing each other. As Christian Parenti has observed:

> The discourse of the liberal policy wonk operates on the assumption that rational plans will displace irrational ones. But in reality any soft form of control can easily be grafted on to the most repressive form of police state. One could conceive of a regime that routinely uses capital punishment, genetic fingerprinting, militarized police *and*, for the barely deviant, ladles out endless hours of anger management, therapeutic probation, public shaming, and elaborate forms of restitution. Therapy and the gas chamber are by no means mutually exclusive. Newer, softer, more rational forms of control do not automatically displace repression, surveillance and terror (Parenti, 1999: 242–243, emphasis in the original).

This elastic connection between the punitive and the therapeutic, discussed earlier via the concept of the 'therapunitive' (Carlen and Tombs, 2006: 339) was reflected in, and reinforced by, developments outside of the prison gates.[15] The impact of the 'therapunitive' was apparent in government plans to employ 10,000 new clinical psychologists and therapists and open 250 new treatment centres to combat 'depression and anxiety' through utilizing cognitive behavioural therapy (*Open Mind*, 2005: 5). This development was taking place at a time when prescriptions for drugs such as Prozac had reached 3.5 million, an increase of 120 per cent in the decade between 1996 and 2006 (*The Independent on Sunday*, 16 April 2006).[16] It was also apparent in at least one of the provisions in the 2003 Criminal Justice Act, which stipulated that:

> ... in addition to the normal fixed term, judges must impose a new "indefinite public-protection sentence" on anyone convicted of a serious violent or sexual crime whenever they think there is a "significant risk to members of the public" that the prisoner might re-offend. ... The more dangerous you are thought to be, the longer you will serve, in effect being punished for crimes you're deemed likely to commit in the future, as well as those in the past. *This represents a historic transfer of power: away from the judges and evidence tested in open court towards the state and its forensic psychiatrists* (Rose, 2005: 28, emphasis added).[17]

Public protection, narrowly and circumspectly defined, therefore justified and legitimated the intensification in the intrusive capacities and capabilities of risk-based experts and their claim that they now possessed the clinical and methodological expertise to predict the future with respect to the deviant and dangerous behaviour of the powerless. However, as Nicola Gray and her colleagues have noted, there are a series of issues concerning this development which (inevitably) have been (and continue to be) ignored by New Labour including: the ability, or (indeed the inability) of those working in psychiatry and psychology '... to reliably and validly diagnose "severe personality disorder"';

their 'ability to accurately identify, assess and manage "risk"; and ... the ethics (professional and personal) of indefinitely and compulsorily detaining individuals purely on the basis of the risk that they pose ...'(Gray et al., 2002: 4).

For Zygmunt Bauman, the old – what he termed the 'Big Brother' strategy – was 'alive and better equipped than ever – but now he is mostly to be found in the off-limits, marginalized parts of social space such as urban ghettoes, refugee camps or prisons'. The new 'Big Brother' was concerned with exclusion and with 'spotting the people who "do not fit" into the place they are in, banishing them from that place and deporting them [to] "where they belong", or better still never allowing them to come anywhere near in the first place' (Bauman, 2004: 132). In other words, 'hard forms of control are not receding, but soft forms are expanding' (Marx, 2005: 36).

Fourth, the discourse of privatization continued to play an important role in New Labour's modernized penal vision of the prison. As I noted in Chapter 4, the private sector managerial discourses of 'economy, efficiency and effectiveness' (McLaughlin and Muncie, 1993) were mobilized and applied by the Conservatives to the criminal justice system. Jack Straw, and his successors, continued to pursue these policies, which included the ongoing privatization of the penal system, a policy to which he and New Labour were hostile while in opposition. By the end of 1999, four private companies were operating seven prisons. Another four were due to open over the next three financial years, adding 2,500 extra places to those already in use, while three other institutions were at various stages in the planning process (Prison Reform Trust, 1999: 15). This trend was further reinforced by the government-appointed Carter Review, which was published in January 2004 and which led to the establishment of the National Offender Management Service (NOMS) six months later. Carter argued that increased private sector involvement should be encouraged in the prison service through greater 'contestability', which, according to David Scott was:

> ... intended to encourage the privatization of rehabilitative services in both the community and the prison. In future, if a prison should fail to 'work' in reducing reoffending or protecting the public, the problem will not be identified as the broader structural contexts shaping the prisoner's agency and choices, but the combination of a problematic prisoner with failings on the part of the delivery of rehabilitative programmes (Scott, 2007: 66).[18]

However, the principle of contestability identified by Carter, and the strategy of bifurcation advocated by Halliday, were unlikely to offer either greater protection to the public or deliver a greater sense of justice. On the contrary:

> A bifurcated strategy rooted in the persistency principle will undoubtedly cause greater discriminatory outcomes, lead to net widening, probably to just catching petty and minor offenders and to expanding the penal gaze further on to those from impoverished or minority ethnic communities (Scott, 2007: 66).[19]

By 2007, there were 11 privately run prisons in England and Wales, the majority of institutions therefore continued to be managed by the state. Nonetheless, despite this apparently low number, New Labour was presiding over the most privatized prison system in Western Europe with 10 per cent of prisoners incarcerated in private institutions (Prison Reform Trust, 2007: 37–38).

As in the USA, in at least one case in England and Wales, commercial interests were beginning to impact on the prison population. In Dovegate, a therapeutic unit within the main prison, the Chief Inspector of Prisons found that prisoners were not being reallocated quickly enough from the unit. This was 'blamed by the prison on crowding elsewhere in the system, *but we were also concerned that there was a commercial imperative to keep numbers up on the unit*' (HM Inspectorate of Prisons, 2007c: 5, emphasis added).[20] Additionally, half of the 8,000 prison places due to be completed by 2012 were to be built within three, privately run, institutions, each holding 1,300 prisoners, which was double the capacity of existing, individual prisons (*The Guardian*, 1 December 2006). Furthermore, private companies were not only amalgamating, as in the government approved takeover of Wackenhut by Group 4 in early 2003, but they were also moving out from the prison and into other areas of social control such as 'electronic tagging and tracking systems for convicted offenders'. This development had:

> ... the blessing of the Home Office. Companies such as Memex have also moved into the market for CCTV cameras in England and Wales while simultaneously supplying technology to the Joint Chiefs of Staff at the Pentagon, the CIA and the Defence Intelligence Agency (Norris and Armstrong, cited in Sim, 2004c: 43).

In December 2006, in a further twist to, and intensification in, the privatization drive, it was reported that due to the Treasury's refusal to fund the 8,000 new prison places announced by John Reid, Home Office financial directors were considering offering members of the public the opportunity to purchase shares in new prisons under a 'buy to let' scheme. Investors would be involved in:

> ... a new-style property company that would build jails and then rent them out to private prison operators. This would provide a steady guaranteed dividend from the "rental income". One incentive for small investors is that the government's punitive penal policy has seen prison numbers rise relentlessly over the past 10 years and would appear to guarantee a steady stream of rental income with no apparent shortage of prison "tenants". ... The model uses "real estate investment trusts" (Reits) which are to be launched by the Treasury in January [2007] and will enjoy tax exemptions. They are designed to encourage a wider range of investors in property. This model has already been used in the United States by the Corrections Corporation of America to finance several new privately run jails. ... Under the proposed system, the prison operator would rent the facility from the Reit and the income would be channelled back to the investors. Private prison contracts tend to be long-term in Britain, with 25-year leases common (*The Guardian*, 1 December 2006).

Conclusion

There was a grim irony to New Labour's defence of their version of the modern prison. Not only did Tony Blair's three governments preside over the highest prison population in Western Europe, which, in the aftermath of the changes announced by John Reid, was likely to accelerate further to the point where the country would move 'from the leading incarcerator in Western Europe into a new league, that of the former Warsaw Pact states in the east' (Prison Reform Trust, 2006c: 3), but across a range of other social, cultural and political areas, the country was also a European leader. As noted in the previous chapter, it was a country ruptured and riven by social divisions and deep rooted, social inequalities, sustained by a £1.3 trillion record level of debt, to the point where individual Britons had twice the level of debt compared with other Europeans (*The Independent*, 28 September 2006). Additionally, as a contributor to *The Guardian* noted, the country had: 'the highest rate of child and pensioner poverty; the lowest-paid workers working the longest hours; the most under-funded healthcare and education provision; the highest-paid corporate and management executives. ... Life expectancy for males in the poorest parts of the country are comparable to developing countries and we hold the onerous title of the most violent society in the western world, according to UN figures' (John Wright, Letter to *The Guardian*, 29 June 2006).

It was therefore a society, which differed significantly from Blair's messianic fantasy that 'Britain under his stewardship [was] well on its way to becoming "this other Eden"' (Elliott and Atkinson, 2007a: 26). For Elliott and Atkinson, the reality was very different. Speculators dominated a society that was more easily regarded as 'one big offshore hedge fund ... while asset-strippers' planned to turn 'the few remaining factories ... into industrial theme parks'. Furthermore, far from being at the forefront of a new, highly paid, twenty-first century workforce leading the world, the fastest growing occupation between 1992 and 1999 was hairdressing while there were three times as many people working in domestic service as there were in the 'creative' industries such as advertising, video games and film (2007a: 74 and 88). Finally, 'the proportion of the population employed by the well-off to do their cooking, cleaning, childcare and gardening [was] as high as it was in the 1860s' (Elliott and Atkinson, 2007b: 5).

The brooding presence of the multilayered, hybrid prison, and those it incapacitated, perfectly symbolized the nature and direction of the country and its desperate search for political and cultural modernization. It was an institution, which, two hundred years on from its birth in another era of frantic, ruthless, bourgeois modernization, continued to 'command(ed) the reflexive assent of the propertied and the powerful' (Ignatieff, 1978: 210). Culturally and politically, it was deeply embedded in the collective consciousness of the society despite the debates about developing and adopting alternatives to the institution in response to offending behaviour. Thus, in the first decade of the twenty-first century the question for New Labour politicians, and their Conservative counterparts, was how could the institution be sustained at minimum cost while ensuring the maximum benefit for their potent law and order agenda? For critical thinkers, there was an alternative question: what radical strategies could be developed in order to contest and transcend the place of the prison in political rhetoric as the immediate and 'natural' response to crime and deviance? The next chapter explores this question by outlining the case for abolishing the institution in its present form.

Notes

1 This was a phrase used in an interview with C.S. Smith on *Channel 4 News*, 11 June 2001. One example of those with no capital getting the punishment occurred in Scotland, in June 2006, when Alexander English was jailed for four months for stealing a single shoe for his friend whose leg was in plaster. He had 45 previous convictions and also admitted stealing two soft toys. Sheriff Watson asked 'Did he have a market for one shoe?' His defence lawyer replied 'He didn't have a market for one, my lord, but his friend who has a leg in plaster did' (http:news.bbc.co.uk/1/hi/Scotland/Glasgow_and_west/5060956.stm).

2 The government also boasted that there were a record number of police officers, 141,270, as well as over 6,300 Community Support Officers (CSOs). In the latter case, in the 2006 Budget, it was announced that an extra £100 million was to be spent on recruitment to take their numbers up to 16,000 by 2007. The goal was to employ 24,000 additional CSOs (*The Guardian*, 23 March 2006; Home Office, 2006a: 23).

3 The inexorable rise in the average daily population meant that the Home Office's projected figures for the prison population needed to be constantly revised. In January 2005, officials claimed that a 'low scenario' projection would see the population rise to 76,170 by 2011. That figure had already been passed by October 2005. A 'high scenario' projection indicated that the figure would be 87,550 by 2011 (Home Office, 2005: 29).

4 According to the Home Office, in 2001 the incarceration rate for white people was 170 per 100,000 of the population. This compared with 1,140 per 100,000 for black people, 536 per 100,000 for Chinese and other groups and 166 per 100,000 for South Asians (Home Office, 2003: 106 and 113).

5 The Home Office always cautions against using these data, particularly with respect to simply adding figures together. Some individuals will be in one category of having been sent to prison while also being counted in another category, for example, being on probation in the same year. However, the Home Office argument misses the point. The data can be used to provide an indication of the level of actual interventions made by the agents and agencies of the criminal justice system, which inevitably may involve a smaller number of individuals but which nonetheless do involve a direct hit or contact with an individual in each case whether or not that individual has been through the system before. In other words, it is immaterial whether the same individual is dealt with by both the

probation service and the prison system in the same year; it is the actual number of interventions that are made which serve to reproduce, in a Foucauldian sense, a criminal class targeted by the criminal justice system, which legitimates its further expansion.

6 The prison was also increasingly being used to detain those suspected of having some involvement in political violence. Between December 2001 and December 2003, 14 people were detained under the *Anti-Terrorism Crime and Security Act* (2001) in Belmarsh. One of the detainees had polio; another had no arms while a third had been transferred to the state mental hospital at Broadmoor. Half of the detainees showed signs of mental illness while the mental health of the detainee who had polio had deteriorated to the point where he could not recognize his fellow inmates, nor was he able to communicate with them: 'his condition worsened after he was confined to his cell by his illness. The prison authorities refused him a wheelchair, and inmates' offers to carry him to classes and prayers were refused' (*The Observer*, 14 December 2003). However, in line with the arguments developed in Chapter 1, how new and unique this development is remains a matter of debate given the role of the prison as a place of detention in Britain's colonial wars and the normalization of special powers that arose from thirty years of political violence in Northern Ireland (Hillyard, 1987), a point reinforced by McEvoy et al. (2007: 314) who have argued against adopting 'an ahistoric perspective' regarding political prisoners while noting that 'there are direct links between past and contemporary experiences of political imprisonment'.

7 In April 2007, Richard Davison argued in the High Court that being charged £70.08 over a two-month period to make phone calls was a human rights issue. His case was based on the fact that the same calls on a payphone would have cost £15.20. His case also highlighted the fact that the Prison Service received a commission of 10 per cent from British Telecom on prisoners' phone credits (*The Guardian*, 2 April 2007).

8 The perennial issue of the food prisoners receive at Christmas is still invariably contrasted with the view that pensioners cannot afford food cooked to the same culinary standards. In 2003, the Soil Association also used prisoners in their critique of school meals, in this case arguing that 'more money was spent on prison food than school lunches' (*The Guardian*, 6 October 2003).

9 Thanks to Richard Fontenroy of *INQUEST* for his help with these statistics. The figures from the Prison Reform Trust publication are different from those here, as they had been wrongly calculated in the initial publication.

10 Eric Allison, the journalist who revealed this scandal was subsequently banned from visiting Styal.

11 Time on licence was also likely to increase significantly as a result of provisions under the Criminal Justice Act 2003. Thus, 'those serving sentences of under a year will be under supervision for the first time; those serving long sentences will be under supervision for the whole sentence instead of until the three-quarters point, and the new public protection sentences will include long periods of licence' (Prison Reform Trust, 2006a: 14).

12 According to the Prison Reform Trust, such prisoners were regarded as short term life sentence prisoners who had tariffs of five years or less and who should have been prioritized for places on 'offender behaviour courses if they are to have a chance of release at tariff expiry'. Inevitably, given the state of the prison system, there were problems with prisoners 'getting on to courses' (Prison Reform Trust, 2006b: 4).

13 These sentences were declared unlawful in August 2007 by two Appeal Court judges, who ruled that it was 'arbitrary, unreasonable and unlawful' to keep prisoners beyond their tariff date without access to rehabilitation programmes in order to reduce their risk of reoffending (*The Guardian*, 1 August 2007).

14 The government continued to defend the prison despite the fact that 58.5 per cent of offenders released from jail or beginning a community sentence in 2002 had reoffended within two years of their sentence. In 1997 the figure was 53.1 per cent while in 2000 it was 57.6 per cent (*Inside Time*, 2006c: 1).

15 As with any social process, there are contradictions and contingencies in these developments. It is important to recognize that therapeutic techniques might benefit some individuals at particular moments of difficulty and distress as opposed, for example, to isolating them in segregation units. What I am concerned with identifying here, however, is the individualizing tendencies of these processes, and their role in enforcing social discipline and structures of domination, rather than inducing and generating social change. There is also the question of the disproportionate use of officially prescribed drugs and psychiatric labels with respect to women (Sim, 2005) and minority ethnic groups. In the latter case, a report by the Health Inspectorate, published in December 2005, noted that black people were 'three times more likely than the rest of the population to be admitted to mental hospitals' were 'twice as likely to be sent there by the police or the courts' and were '50 per cent more likely to be placed in seclusion' (*The Independent*, 7 December 2005).

16 In 2006, the global market in antidepressants was valued at £25 billion (Schoch, 2006: 34).

17 Others have pointed to the shift towards a justice system 'based on probabilities'. In 2006, the then Lord Chancellor, Lord Falconer 'talked of Violent Offender Orders ... to control those suspected of possibly committing acts in the future – no previous conviction or police record required. Falconer cited Asbos as the precedent set, issued on a balance of probabilities' (Letter from Robin Tudge in *New Statesman*, 26 March 2007: 8).

18 The Offender Management Bill, which was passing through both Houses of Parliament in 2007, allowed the probation service to be opened up to further competition and also included allowing private prison directors to carry out prison disciplinary adjudications (Nathan, 2007).

19 However, as noted in Chapter 1, it is important to recognize that policies are never implemented in fully formed ways from the moment they are articulated either by ministers or by their policy advisors. Contestability was challenged by the Prison Officers' Association, which led to a government 'rethink [which] meant that substantial changes in competition would not be as quick or as extensive as originally conceived' (Bennett, 2007: 10).

20 Again, as in the USA, private companies were also targeting areas of high unemployment. Doncaster prison was built in the local area by Wackenhut because 'there was a reserve army of unemployed steelworkers and miners in Yorkshire with little option to take jobs on pitiful terms' (Cohen, cited in Sim, 2004c: 43).

7

FOR ABOLITIONIST PRAXIS: TRANSCENDING THE PRISON MENTALITY[1]

Institutions as they exist at the moment are a danger to the community (Boyle, 1984: 34).

It should be possible – using, for example, the current struggle for justice – to develop middle-range policy alternatives, which do not compromise any overall design for fundamental social change. This does not mean simply employing this overall design to develop a theoretical critique of the justice programme, but actually being brave enough to speculate on some policy alternatives, however unfinished and unworkable they might appear. When the world goes out of frame – as it has tended to in the past – we lose the chance of influencing it. Conservative interests have always kept the world in focus, for they are part of the frame. A critical criminology has to combat not just knowledge, but the power of knowledge (Cohen, 1979: 49–50).

In many ways, this book is a story of reification and naturalization in that within the political consciousness of both Conservative and New Labour administrations, and the common-sense consciousness of the wider population, the prison has become an indestructible presence in the fight to maintain law and order.[2] In England and Wales (and indeed internationally as indicated by accelerating rates of imprisonment in even the most liberal social democracies) the institution exists in the collective mind as an existential comfort blanket for the protection of the globalized citizen against the material and psychological insecurities generated by the predations of the criminal and the deviant. In other words, it has become hegemonic in the sense that its presence has come 'to be taken-for-granted as the natural and received shape of the world and everything that inhabits it'. In short, it has become 'habit forming' (Comaroff and Comaroff, cited in Hirsch and Lazarus-Black, 1994: 8).

The unrelenting support for the prison from politicians, and the mass media, has only added to the seeming impregnability of the institution to any ideological or material challenge. Therefore, while New Labour might have rejected the more overt and blatant retributive elements in Michael Howard's bleak doctrine of neoliberal less eligibility, the government's strategy, as Chapter 6 indicated, was, and is, no less dependent on the prison as a key institution in the reformulation of social control practices that 'fit' with the ideological and material concerns of capitalist modernity espoused by Blair and his coterie of Home Secretaries: Straw, Blunkett, Clarke and Reid. In fact, the construction of the prison as a seemingly benevolent place of progress for 'at risk' groups has entrenched the institution even further in the political landscape and popular consciousness of the country, an embedded presence in the war against crime that delivers only good news to the wider population with respect to the punishment of the offender.

Challenging this prevailing orthodoxy, and the institution's valorization, particularly if such challenges espouse the principles and precepts of abolitionism, remains a difficult, sometimes lonely task, especially in a society and culture dominated by a 'climate of retribution and revenge' (van Swaaningen, 1997: 174). Such a society produces 'an increasingly fearful public whose idealization of the past, and trepidation about the future, legitimates the populist clampdown in the present' (Sim, 2004b: 129).

Thus, while suggestions for reform from pressure groups still carry some social democratic weight and influence, and while limitations are placed on what state servants can and cannot do to the confined (at least in theory), the idea that the prison could be partially or even fully abolished has come to be regarded simply as an idealistic anachronism stemming from the subversive, but doomed libertarianism, of the 1960s and 1970s, a naïve and sacrilegious demand that has no place in the 'real' world of the twenty-first century and the everyday concerns around crime that beset and lay waste to the lives of 'ordinary' people. Liberal pressure group politics espousing policies (*not* demands) that are acceptable and realistic, it is argued, is the respectable way forward as it was in the 1970s (Ryan, 1978). Prison reform as industry is simply the continuation of these politics in the early twenty-first century. Therefore, the *idea* of the prison appears to have won in the hegemonic struggle to define and actualize contemporary responses to the problem of crime. It has become a taken-for-granted presence in the society's culture in that 'it is difficult to imagine life without [it]'. At the same time, prisons are absent from this culture in that the society 'is often afraid to face the realities they produce' (Davis, 2003: 15).

However, as Gramsci recognized, while a bloc or an idea can strive for hegemonic domination that domination is never completely achieved. In short, hegemony is 'fought for, won, lost, resisted ...' (Bennett, 1986: xv). Following this logic, the question to ask is how can Wacquant's 'penal common sense' referred to in Chapter 5, be transformed in a Gramscian sense into nonpenal 'good sense'? This remains an extraordinarily difficult question to answer, and indeed task to undertake, given the symbolic and material power of the prison within contemporary culture and politics. At the same time, the contradictions in the system – its huge financial cost (notwithstanding the input of the private sector), the rates of recidivism, suicides, disturbances and the lack of democratic accountability mean that there are contradictory spaces where radical interventions can be made which can transform liberal possibilities into abolitionist probabilities with respect to definitive penal, and indeed, wider social change. Allied to these contradictions, is the intensification in the harm that the institution generates in the lives of those whose sense of psychological and material well-being will have already been fractured by their pre- and postprison experiences. In the case of short term offenders, when released 'a third lose their accommodation, two-thirds lose their employment, over a fifth come out facing increased financial problems, over two-fifths lose contact with their families' (Morgan, 2004: 4).

In the light of these contradictions, and in response to the annihilation of the spirit that the prison engenders, this chapter focuses on two areas. First, it discusses the challenges that confront abolitionists in their attempt to provide a radical alternative to the prevailing discourses around prisons and punishment. Second, it outlines a number of radical proposals, which would form the basis for an abolitionist strategy for challenging, contesting and ultimately fundamentally transforming penal institutions as they are presently constituted.

The state and abolitionism

Thomas Mathiesen has argued that the capitalist state is 'highly absorbent', in that it encourages a reformist gradualism towards penal policy and correspondingly generates a spirit of cooperation within the liberal prison reform lobby. For Mathiesen, absorption operates at two interrelated levels. First, a strategy of 'defining in' allows the state to co-opt those organizations concerned with the development of social policy in general and penal policy, in particular. These organizations are allowed to comment on 'official reports, legislative bills, etc', so that "'everyone is heard" – and thus everyone is involved' (Mathiesen, 1980: 286). There are different strands to this 'defining-in' process:

> In the first place, you are invited to try and *persuade* the representatives of the state, rather than to struggle for demands. Secondly, you are invited *to show by example* how things should be done, rather than struggle against the way things are being done. In the third place, you are invited to *participate* in the decision-making process of the state representatives. The defining in which takes place through the latter form, participation in decision-making, generally takes one of three forms. Firstly ... through *encapsulation* ... anything new is permitted only in so diminished a form that it does not break with the premises of the system. Secondly, it occurs through *initiation*: the rebel is initiated into the secrets of the system, and thereby silenced as regards external criticism, through his pledge of secrecy. Thirdly, it occurs through the *creation of responsibility*: as a participant in the system, you take part in decisions and actions for which you in turn are held responsible. The latter process, the creation of responsibility, in particular governs your further actions: your co-responsibility makes it impossible for you to renounce, let alone denounce, actions, which lead away from your long-term abolishing goal. The processes mentioned here, encapsulation, initiation and creation of responsibility, are psychologically extremely pressing, as they force the individual to yield with regard to contradiction and they transform contradiction into accord (Mathiesen, 1980: 287–288, emphasis in the original).

Second, an equally powerful strategy 'define[s] out' those policies and practices that challenge the punitive fundamentals of the system. Critics are ideologically constructed as individuals and organizations who are irresponsible, nonconformists, divorced from the realities of life, whose support network includes extremist organizations and who are 'oppose[d] to short-term improvements'. Taken together, these processes operate hegemonically to construct an 'objective truth' around prisons. Thus, 'the more absorbent and defining-in the state becomes, the more *reasonable* it will appear *to define out those who nevertheless are unwilling to conform*' (Mathiesen, 1980: 288–291, emphasis in the original).

Nearly three decades on, Mathiesen's insights remain powerfully (and painfully) relevant for thinking about the construction of dominant discourses around penal 'truth' and the marginalization of alternative discourses around punishment. Indeed, it could be argued that the state's hegemonic capacity to direct and control the debates concerning the need for the prison, and an increasingly expansive and intrusive system of social control, has become *more* not *less* powerful in the intervening years. Why? There are a number of reasons for this.

Mystifying punishment

First, there is modern prison's extraordinary capacity for mystifying its punitive capabilities for inflicting pain and inculcating fear, and if need be terror, into the lives of the confined. In a process described by Pat Carlen as 'absurd obfuscation(s)' (Carlen, 2002: 116), the systemic harm generated by the prison's culture is masked and mystified by a rhetoric of benevolence and paternalism. The culture's legitimating rationale (the odd 'bad apple' of a prison officer notwithstanding), is premised on enhancing the care of the confined and thus encouraging their redemption to normal citizenship. However, the ongoing issues of deaths in custody and self-harm raise serious questions about the benevolent underpinnings of the prison's culture.

In 2003, a record number of women – 14 – committed suicide, a rise of 64 per cent on the previous year. In October 2004, Katherine Jones became the second woman in just over two days to die in prison. These deaths brought the total number to 13, including 11 who had died since the previous April (*INQUEST*, 2004). Overall, between 1990 and 2007, 115 women died in English prisons; 88 of these deaths were self-inflicted (Sandler and Coles, 2008). In addition, in the year up to February 2004, there were over 1,500 incidents of self-harm in New Hall women's prison, a rise of 200 per cent (*The Observer*, 8 February 2004). Between May 1997, when New Labour took office and January 2004, the prison population rose by 14,000 while there was a five-fold increase in incidents of self-harm. This amounted to nearly 15,000 prisoners damaging themselves (*Private Eye*, 20 February–4 March 2004).

In 2004, the *Joint Committee on Human Rights*, whose membership was drawn from both Houses of Parliament, indicated that it was 'shocked' by some of the discoveries its members made during their inquiry into deaths in custody. In particular, the Committee pointed out that the human rights of the confined, and the attempts by those staff who were attempting to deal with them, were 'thwarted by an *under-resourced and ramshackle physical and administrative environment*' (House of Lords, House of Commons, 2004: 8, emphasis added). Family members of the deceased also presented the Committee with:

> ... compelling evidence of failings throughout our systems of detention, and of the grievous personal consequences of those failings. The family members with whom we met, primarily parents whose sons and daughters had died, told us of their belief that the state had failed them in its duty of care (2004: 8).

In Woodhill, there were 10 deaths between 2002 and 2005. These included:

> ... nine within the first month of custody and five within the first week. Yet none of our recommendations in the last report on improving early days in custody had been implemented. ... Prisoners who were at risk of self-harm or suicide were poorly supported and managed; some were unnecessarily sent to the healthcare centre. Anti-bullying procedures were not implemented properly; indeed many staff were unaware of them. For example, no action was taken to discipline or work with a prisoner who had threatened to kill his cellmate, and crucial

information was not exchanged about identified bullies (HM Inspectorate of Prisons, 2006d: 5).

The position of asylum seekers also provides a further, powerful indication and indictment of the dire state of the prison system, in this case in the increasingly privatized immigration detention centres where detainees 'suffered from hopelessness, despair and suicidal urges' (McFadyean, 2006: 36). Between 2001 and 2006, there were 17 suicides in detention centres and prisons while 185 people attempted suicide and 1,467 were placed on self-harm watch between March 2005 and January 2006. According to Melanie McFadyean:

> It's our money that is spent on this barbarism most of us are happy to ignore while private companies fill their coffers. In its mania for privatization the government is planning to sell us shares in the new prisons it is planning to build, while Britain now has the highest rate of imprisonment in western Europe. It gets away with it, because asylum seekers are the lowest of the low – and so-called failed asylum seekers are our version of the *Untermensch*, the expendable (McFadyean, 2006, emphasis in the original).

Furthermore, the debate about the prison, both in the media and in the narrowly defined world of what still passes for social democratic politics, is based on focussing on the institution's overt goals: rehabilitation, individual deterrence, general prevention, and incapacitation. These goals, allied with a narrow conceptualization of prison officer culture, are both the starting *and* the finishing point for liberal analyses and debates around the prison. Thus, the social harm that the institution engenders, and which many of its workers perpetrate, as well as the *systemic* discourses of punitive degradation, which underpin the prison's culture and which often legitimate that harm, are rarely if ever discussed by liberal prison reformers or those responsible for managing the system. Indeed, in discussions about the impact of the prison's culture, it is *state servants* – prison (and police) officers – who are conceptualized as victims of that culture, usually with respect to the violence that they face in their everyday lives. This process is:

> ... sustained by *exaggeration* in relation to the numbers who are assaulted and murdered and *overdramatisation* in relation to the seriousness of the violence against them. At the same time, violence committed *by* state servants is also mystified ideologically through a process of *individualisation* and *circumspection* ... this means focussing on the few 'bad apples' allegedly responsible for institutional violence while narrowly defining the nature and extent of the violations against those who are in the care of the state. ... In a Gramscian sense, this accreditation, consecrated and blessed by the vast majority of the mass media and government and opposition spokespersons, has been integral to the construction of a common-sense, populist discourse concerning what state servants do and *what is done to them* on a daily basis (Sim, 2004b: 126–127, emphasis in the original).[3]

Incorporating reform and extending normalizing judgements

Second, Pat Carlen has pointed to the power of the prison to engage in what she has called 'carceral clawback'. In the years since Mathiesen's initial intervention, the prison has continued to incorporate even the most radical critiques, such as those mounted by feminist scholars in Canada, subverting their programmes for dynamic, structural penal change and facilitating their metamorphosis into passive prescriptions for individual governance (Carlen, 2002). This process has been legitimated by the interventions of the new phalanx of professional groups, the 'judges of normality' (Foucault, 1979: 304) discussed in the previous chapter:

> At the beginning of the 21st century "the prison" is as much a laboratory for all kinds of social engineering/reform as it has ever been. Moreover, it is becoming a lucrative and staple source of funding for many newcomers to the prison industry who appear not at all unwilling to legitimate the use of imprisonment by reference to the "effectiveness" of their "programmes" in reducing crime (Carlen, 2002: 120).

Despite a range of significant methodological problems (Hope, 2002), 'what works' has legitimated the programmes of intervention mobilized inside prisons, which are underpinned by the search for the holy grail of criminological endeavour, the causes of, and perfect response to, crime. This has led criminology (and indeed liberal reform groups) away from directly confronting structural and institutional issues and the corrosive dehumanization of the individual that they generate. Underpinning the consolidation of this discourse has been the drive towards marketization that has spread through higher education built on the commodification of knowledge and the search to finance research *from whatever source* in order to cope with the crisis in funding faced by universities. It has led to the reinforcement of criminology's ties with the state as academics, in the scramble for funds, have proactively and increasingly worked within the agenda set by successive governments and state servants, with their inevitable focus on the lives and activities of the powerless and a concomitant, indeed cavalier, disregard for the crimes committed by the powerful (Tombs and Whyte, 2003; Walters, 2003).

This development has further reinforced the marginalization of the reverse, but equally important question, namely 'what does not work' with offenders inside and those deemed to be 'at risk' when released. In terms of penal policy, warehousing prisoners in appalling conditions, allowing prison officers to use unfettered and often brutalizing discretion, denying basic human rights such as the right to fresh air and utilizing drugs to control 'difficult' behaviour, are only four of many examples of state-sanctioned behaviour that operates in prisons to repress, control, humiliate and induce pain. For those on the outside, the lack of employment opportunities, exclusion from the housing market and the more general processes of stigmatization endured by ex-prisoners, also contribute to the systemic failure to respond to them in a way that transgresses the social and symbolic divide between the respectable majority and the atavistic minority. Therefore, asking what does not work with offenders is as important as asking what works with them, but it is a question which has been relegated to the political and policy margins as it raises some difficult and awkward questions concerning the gap between official rhetoric and the brutal reality of everyday existence inside and outside of the prison walls.

Undermining and ignoring successful policies

Third, the official and dominant definition of 'what works' mystifies another set of key issues, which relate to those policy developments that *have* worked with offenders over the last four decades but which have not been extended and embedded into the rest of the penal system. Grendon Underwood provides a good example of this process.

Opened in 1962, the prison offers 'something of an antidote to the simply coercive and repressive', which Christopher Cordess sees as the dominant political and policy response to offenders, particularly to the conventionally defined dangerous individual. Cordess also makes the important point (still very much neglected in mainstream criminology and other disciplines) that it is not just dangerous individuals who abuse power but 'in settings of detention [there are] the ever present tendencies towards quite subtle, as well as gross, abuses of power. Our "criminal institutions" are every bit in need of assessment as the dangerous people held within them, but they are frequently even more resistant' (Cordess, 2004: v–vi).

In 2004, over forty years after it was first opened, the Chief Inspector of Prisons praised the work of the prison and its staff, describing the institution as:

> ... exceptionally safe ... a remarkable achievement given the nature of the population. ... Self harm was minimal and systems to prevent it were first rate; in fact the Prison Service *may have much to learn from the success of the therapeutic model.* ... Grendon deserves recognition and support (Her Majesty's Chief Inspector of Prisons for England and Wales, 2004: 3 and 6, emphasis added).

Pointedly, the Chief Inspector also commented that the history of the prison had been a 'struggle for recognition and acceptance ...' (2004: 3).

This last remark leads to a profoundly important question, which goes to the heart of penal policy developments in England and Wales. Why have successive governments been so circumspect in recognizing Grendon's achievements? As Eric Allison pointed out at the time of the Chief Inspector's report, the prison:

> ... has always been under siege from reactionary elements of the penal system. ... Grendon's inspection report begs some serious questions: why doesn't the prison

service embrace a system that, while not perfect, clearly works better than conventional imprisonment? Why has it taken 40 years to put another Grendon on line? Why is it that after a 1993 study showed that at least 2,500 prisoners would benefit from therapy there are fewer than 500 therapeutic community places in the whole system? (Allison, 2004: 5).

David Jones maintains that therapeutic communities such as Grendon provide:

> ... a treatment structure which integrates social and interpersonal approaches with psychoanalytic psychotherapy. A defining feature has involved attempts to flatten the division between the doctor and the patient, recognising the impact of the social structure and context on psychological disorder. This notion emphasises that organisational structures and internal relationships are crucial to an understanding of how a disorder is maintained and addressed (Jones, 2004: 193).

In January 2007, the Chief Inspector published another report on the prison and again pointed to its strengths, particularly with regard to the relationship between staff and prisoners, which 'remained amongst the best we have come across'. Ominously, however, the Inspectorate also noted that 'the need for financial savings had put added pressures on staff and prevented them from being deployed as regularly as they had been on our last visit, which hindered consistent support and supervision of groups' (HM Inspectorate of Prisons, 2007d: 5).

Despite the emphasis on therapy (or rather, perhaps because of it), 'most therapeutic units within the Prison Service experience isolation and precariousness in terms of continuity ... and some are not permitted to survive' (Medlicott, 2001: 221). Medlicott's last point is important, because she highlights another dimension to the politics of penal antagonism, namely the closure of ideologically troublesome units (such as the Barlinnie Special Unit discussed in Chapter 4) often after sustained and vitriolic attacks against them by a combination of media and politicians with academics often assuming the role of 'bystanders' in terms of defending them (Cohen, 2001). In the case of the therapeutic community at Glen Parva, 'twenty years in the making were 20 minutes in the breaking' (MacKenzie, 1997: 26). The antagonism to the philosophy and practice of Units of this kind was also identified by the *Prison Reform Trust* as far back as June 1986. As the Trust noted at the time:

> Those few innovations of which we can be proud – Grendon Underwood, the Wormwood Scrubs Annexe, the Barlinnie Special Unit – have not been repeated elsewhere in the system and, indeed, have been regularly threatened with closure. The one other special facility usually mentioned in this connection – Holloway's Therapeutic Unit – is now, to all intents and purposes, abandoned (Prison Reform Trust, 1986: 5).

The controversial raid on Blantyre House resettlement prison in May 2000 – an institution described by the former Chief Inspector of Prisons Sir Stephen Tumin as 'an example of all that is best about the Prison Service' (cited in *House of*

Commons Home Affairs Committee, 2000: paragraph 1) – provides another example of continuities in the state's hostility towards those individuals and institutions interested in pursuing progressive and empathic policies with offenders.

The Home Office argued that 'emerging intelligence' (cited in 2000: paragraph 21) indicated that the prison was awash with contraband material and therefore this legitimated an unprecedented intervention by 84 prison officers from other prisons who carried out a search of the prison after the governor had been removed. *The Select Committee on Home Affairs* conducted an investigation into the events and was scathing not only in its criticism of what had transpired, but also the attempt by the Home Office to justify the search on the basis of flawed intelligence as well as the subsequent attempt at a political cover-up. The Committee's report indicated the nature and extent of its concerns:

> We were completely unconvinced that the search was a proportionate response to the intelligence, which has been used to justify it. We do not believe that the reasons given to us in public justify the exceptional search or the way in which it was carried out. Nor do we find the evidence given in private persuasive. ... On the basis of all the evidence we have heard, we conclude that the search was a failure aggravated by the unnecessary damage caused. It was an exceptional operation in Prison Service terms and it was neither planned nor carried out with an appropriate degree of care. ... This was not a normal search and it should be judged by a different standard. We believe the items found fell well below the level of contraband, which would justify an exceptional search of this nature. It appears to us that none of the illicit items were found in the areas to which entry was achieved by forcing locks and breaking doors. If this was all that the "emerging intelligence" anticipated would be found, that intelligence did not justify the search. If the "intelligence" led officers to believe that more would be found either that intelligence was flawed or the search was. ... We are dissatisfied at the attempts made to mislead the Committee and public over the significance of what was found. We were told on 16 May that a "quite frightening amount of contraband material" was found. ... A parliamentary answer on 25 May referred to "98 finds of unauthorised articles ..." ... In fact the Prison Service's own internal inquiry concluded "there were no significant finds" (House of Commons Home Affairs Committee, 2000: paragraphs 37–44).[4]

Why have empathic policies been ignored and marginalized while supportive staff have pejoratively been named and shamed? Simply put, they have generated a powerful challenge to the often-unforgiving political and cultural claim that the prison is primarily and unequivocally about punishment. This claim, and the hostility towards the institutions discussed in the preceding section and in the previous chapter, is not the result of an instrumental conspiracy involving various levels of the state and its servants coming together to crush challenges to the prevailing penal order. As indicated in Chapter 1, the mobilization of state power is both complex and contingent. Indeed, interventions by state servants can often result in consequences, which are unforeseen and unplanned, as the initial decision to establish the Barlinnie Special Unit indicates (MacDonald and

Sim, 1978). However, the cultural dynamics of the prison, from the landing culture to the rarefied bureaucracy of the senior civil service, and the hegemonic power networks involved, are orientated towards a vision of confinement, which emphasizes collective and individual punishment over collective support and individual empathy. The stark reality is that modern penality is based on a punitive discourse out of which the prison derives its legitimation. Policies and practices, which articulate a different reality, and which transgress and threaten the hegemonic discourses of pain and punishment, remain in a subaltern relationship to these discourses, to be brutally dispatched to the political and policy margins when they become too difficult to manage.

Criminality, criminology and 'crime science'

> Crime and punishment are too important to be left to the criminologists (Sutton, 2004: 185).

Fourth, many of the policies and practices pursued under the discourse of 'what works' have been further legitimated by the explanatory paradigm within which crime has increasingly been explained in the early twenty-first century. The state's activities remain focussed on the small group of individuals – Blair's 'hard core of prolific offenders' (Blair, 2004b: 3) discussed in Chapter 5. The criminality of this dangerous and disruptive few has been increasingly explained through a classicist/positivist dyad, which is also differentially *genderised* (Sim, 2005). Therefore, while the discourse of rationality is mobilized to explain the offender's behaviour, the roots of criminality still lie within the individual and therefore it is *they*, or their family structure, or their community dynamics, and not the wider social and economic arrangements and circumstances that need radical transformation, a point I will return to below. This, of course, is not a new phenomenon. The discourse of criminology as a science, based on the doctrines of longitudinal prediction, individualization and the search for the holy grail of criminological endeavour, the causes of crime, has a long history and in its positivist form, has dominated both criminological theorizing and policy interventions since Lombroso's time. This quest continued right into the twentieth century with places such as the Institute of Criminology at Cambridge, at the forefront of research and theorizing in the area. For example, Donald West's study of delinquency, which began in 1972, was able to proclaim that the best predictor of criminality was 'family income inadequate'. How did the Cambridge academics arrive at this conclusion? The children in the study were subjected to various tests: 'a Spiral Maze test, a Body Sway test ... and ... the Pencil Tapping Test ... [where] the subject taps a pencil on a blank piece of paper for ten seconds, this reveals the extra punitive personality type, and it was confidently expected that "boys with delinquent personalities would tend to scatter their dots more widely". Elsewhere psychiatric social workers rated the attitudes of the boys' unfortunate mothers. Forty-two boys were said to have "cruel, passive or neglecting mothers", and were more than twice as likely to become early delinquents as the remainder of the boys' (Cohen, 1968, 50).[5]

Thirty years on, similar ideas underpinned the announcement by the Youth Justice Board and the Ministry of Defence that school children as young as six, deemed to be 'at risk' through showing 'early signs of aggressive or disruptive behaviour' were to be targeted and subjected to a programme of discipline. Those who completed the programme would 'not only win a certificate but automatic referral to a cadet force. The children will learn to obey orders and meet strict standards of discipline, cleanliness and fitness. The scheme is similar to America's "boot camps" for disruptive children' (*The Independent*, 26 October 2004).[6]

This positivist emphasis is embedded in the DNA of conventional, contemporary criminology, as manifested in the emergence of 'crime science', which continues to build on the predictive capacities of experts – an 'intellectual priesthood' (Cohen, 1982: 108) – who, in utilizing the seemingly neutral and utilitarian language of science, particularly psychological science, construct themselves as criminological diviners whose soothsaying is able to predict the trajectory of individual criminal behaviour through employing various strategies: offender profiling, psychological profiling, geographical profiling, crime mapping, forensic podiatry and optimal foraging behaviour, described by its proponents in the following terms:

> ... when hunting for resources (e.g. food), animals aim to maximise the resources acquired while simultaneously minimising the consequent chance of getting injured (or eaten!) and the search time (or effort) involved. To what extent do offenders behave in this way? (Johnson et al., 2005: 149).

Other contemporary researchers have not been immune from attempting to identify patterns of individual criminal behaviour. On receiving the prestigious Sutherland award in 2002, David Farrington pointed to his theory of 'Integrated Cognitive Antisocial Potential' (ICAP), which focuses on 'the translation from antisocial potential to antisocial behaviour [which] depends on cognitive (thinking and decision-making) processes that take account of opportunities and victims' (cited in Soothill, 2005: 15). While there might be theoretical and methodological differences between Farrington and the new crime scientists, the end result is the same. Like crime scientists, his (and their) research is 'explicitly designed to explain offending by *lower class males*' (2005: 16, emphasis in the original).

Thus, in terms of historical continuity, the discourses of psychological individualization and prediction, as ever, remain central to contemporary criminology's theoretical and methodological orientation, just as they did at the moment of criminology's birth in the nineteenth century. However, as Foucault wryly observed, clinical psychology is built on 'an eclecticism without concepts', which is reinforced by the 'lingering belief' that 'the involuntary fasting of rats' provides 'an infinitely fertile epistemological model' (Foucault, cited in Macey, 1993: 121–122). Furthermore, Philip Tetlock has pointed out that the idea that experts can predict human behaviour by virtue of their ability to reason and think through problems is also problematic:

> ... when we pit experts against minimalist performance benchmarks – dilettantes, dart-throwing chimps, and assorted extrapolation algorithms – we find few signs that expertise translates into greater ability to make either "well-calibrated" or "discriminating" forecasts. ... Even the most astute observers will fail to outperform random prediction generators – the functional equivalent of dart-throwing chimps – in affixing realistic likelihoods to possible futures (Tetlock, 2005: 20 and 41).

As he also notes, Yale undergraduates will engage in 'specious reasoning' to the point where they did 'a worse job than Norwegian rats in guessing, which side of [a] T-maze would contain ... yummy pellets' (2005: 287).

The theoretical and methodological myopia that has dominated academic criminology's history, and the narrow, reductive presuppositions and conservative 'domain assumptions' (Young, 1981) about human behaviour that have underpinned the definition of crime, remain firmly embedded in twenty-first century political and policy circles. Discussion and debate is restricted to a narrow ideological and discursive terrain, which means, as argued in Chapter 1, the massive, and incapacitating social harms generated by the powerful, increasingly well-documented in the work of critical criminologists, still remain on the academic and political margins (Hillyard and Tombs, 2004). 'Establishment criminology' (Sumner, 1982: 3) has returned with a vengeance. This, in turn, has generated an insensate and sometimes hypocritical torpor within the discipline to the point where it appears to have suffered an 'historical and political lobotomy'[7] with regard to recognizing the social and cultural complexities surrounding crime and punishment and the more general, but vital questions, around state power, social divisions and crimes of the powerful (Coleman et al., 2009).

The reassertion of 'establishment criminology' has a further insidious dimension to it. In constructing its theoretical and methodological arguments on such a narrow discursive terrain, it, intentionally or otherwise, contributes to the wider political discourse in which diversity, tolerance and pluralism (the mainsprings of new deviancy theory in the late 1960s (Cohen, 1979) have been undermined by the doctrinaire and authoritarian vision of social order propounded by politicians over the last three decades. It is a vision which, as earlier chapters have indicated, is ideologically sustained by a regressive, naïve and idealized view of the past, which does very little to reassure those living in the present that their psychological and social security will be maintained. Neither does it offer them a compelling and inclusive vision of the future that transcends these contemporary insecurities. Rather, it is a criminology which has been protected from the neo-liberal buffeting sustained by higher education institutions, fuelled as it is by the heady prospect of research grants to further investigate the psychologies, habits and miseries of the powerless, their families and their communities.

Demythologizing the prison[8]: towards abolitionism

The final part of this chapter outlines a number of 'negating reform[s]' (Mathiesen, 1974: 208) that could be mobilized and utilized to challenge and contest the lamentable political and criminological failure to confront the often-deleterious effects of the prison on prisoners and their families, its collateral impact on the wider society and its insidious influence on the debate around law, order, crime and punishment. It is concerned with outlining radical alternatives that transcend the current reformist and restricted rhetoric around the prison, while at the same time recognizing that in the current political climate 'the incorporation of radical critiques into the neutralizing administrative machinery of the penal apparatus' (Carlen, 2002: 117) remains a constant source of philosophical and strategic tension for abolitionist thinkers. There are three specific areas I want to highlight – introducing a moratorium on prison building, redirecting criminal justice and prison expenditure and dismantling the culture of prison officers – before turning to a number of broader suggestions for radical change in this area.

Stopping prison building and closing existing prisons

The exponential expansion of the prison system, driven relentlessly forward by a seemingly endless building and refurbishment programme, is the first key area for radical intervention. Demanding a moratorium on prison building, and the closure of particular institutions, would underpin an abolitionist strategy for confronting the social problem that the prison has become. In the current retributive climate, this remains an easy case to articulate but a much more difficult one to see implemented, in the sense that proponents of this position are unlikely to be taken seriously by the mass media, politicians and policy makers whose ideological commitment to, and reliance on, the prison guarantees the institution unequivocal support. For Thomas Mathiesen, however, relying on an endless building programme, dominated by the prison/industrial/state complex, means that the spiral of prison expansionism will be sustained:

> if radical criminology and sociology of law could now gather around and focus upon the short-term goal of *a halt in prison expansion,* rather than focussing on a variety of goals and issues, as we usually do, headway might be made in this area. ... The prison system as a social institution is never satisfied – it is like an

> animal whose appetite increases with eating ... new prisons, even new prisons expressly intended as substitutes for rather than as additions to old prisons, in practice and fact tend to become additions (Mathiesen, 1986: 88 and 91, emphasis in the original).[9]

More specifically, Pat Carlen has argued that the majority of women's prisons could be abolished immediately without any great danger to the wider society:

> To reduce the prison population we must first reduce the number of prisons; to reduce the number of prisons we must first abolish certain categories of imprisonment. Women's imprisonment is, for several reasons, a prime candidate for abolition. Those reasons can, first, be derived pragmatically from the characteristics of the female prison population and, then, be related more fundamentally to *possible* shifts in the social control of women and *desirable* shifts in the relationships between women and men. ... *I am suggesting that, for an experimental period of 5 years, imprisonment should be abolished as a 'normal' punishment for women and that a maximum of only 100 custodial places should be retained for female offenders convicted or accused of abnormally serious crimes.* ... The choice is between continuing to squander millions of pounds on prisons or taking bold steps to stop legislators and sentencers seeing the prisons as being the ultimate panacea for all social, political and penal ills (Carlen, 1990: 121 and 125, emphasis in the original).

In 2006, Carlen returned to this argument. She noted abolitionists had a number of enemies including 'populist politicians':

> ... who are less interested in adopting rational and effective measures to ensure that responses to women's crimes address the situations leading to the lawbreaking in the first place, and much more interested in courting public favour (and votes) by arguing that despite all the evidence to the contrary, only a *punitive* response will stop women going to prison again ... most politicians have been ready to buy into two other myths (or lies) inherent in contemporary populist and punitive rhetoric: the myth that in-prison programmes can 'reintegrate' people who have never been 'integrated' in the first place; and the myth also that non-custodial penalties must be tough and backed-up by the threat of imprisonment if magistrates and judges are to be persuaded to use them (Carlen, 2006: 1–2, emphasis in the original).

Carlen again argued that women's imprisonment '*should be abolished as Part of a Staged Experiment in Prison Abolition which will eventually be extended to Men. BUT, that because of women's non-threatening criminal profiles, all women coming before the courts should comprise the first Prison Abolition Experimental Group*' before concluding that, '... societies must stop seeing prison as a panacea for all social ills, and, instead, see it as an unusual and abnormal punishment which must be used sparingly rather than promiscuously' (2006: 5–6, emphasis in the original).

As I noted in Chapter 1, abolitionist ideas should not be dismissed as idealistic and utopian but rather should be understood in a Gramscian sense as hegemonic, impacting on more traditional views on crime and punishment while leading, again utilizing Gramsci's insights, those individuals and groups who articulate these more traditional ideas onto a new, critical terrain. This process was evident in March 2007, when Baroness Jean Corston published her review, officially commissioned, of women in the criminal justice system and concluded that 'the existing system of women's prisons should be dismantled and replaced by smaller secure units for the minority of women from whom the public requires protection' (Home Office, 2007: 5).

Stopping the prison-building programme would therefore be a first, but important step, towards radically redefining the terms and direction of the debate about prisons. Making demands for alternatives to custody *without* a critique of the prison building and refurbishment programme will do little either to alleviate the current prison crisis or challenge the central role of the prison within contemporary political and popular consciousness.

Redirecting the prison and criminal justice budget

> If I were still chief justice, I would be concerned with the prisons' amazing capacity to absorb money as the population increases more than expected (Woolf, 2007: 2).

Jon Vagg has argued that during periods when law and order campaigns dominate political debate, substantial amounts of money are spent on prisons. This expenditure usually involves providing more prison spaces as governments demand that this money is spent efficiently while issues such as improved prison conditions receive scant attention until they are 'condemned as scandalous' (Vagg, 1994: 326). In the period covered in this book, Vagg's point is entirely pertinent, particularly when coupled with the antistatist strategy to which earlier chapters have alluded. Thus, in 1984–5, expenditure on social housing was 1.4 per cent of GDP. In 2001–2, this fell to 0.5 per cent. Expenditure on social security fell from 11.9 per cent of GDP in 1984–5 to 11.2 per cent in 2001–2. In contrast, expenditure on law and order rose from 1.9 per cent in 1984–5 to 2.3 per cent in 2001–2 (Glenneristeг, cited in Pemberton, 2005: 26).[10] More specifically, when extra resources have been allocated for offenders, the ideological and material bias has remained firmly with the prison. In November 2002, the government allocated an extra £70 million to the National Probation Service while allocating an extra £275 million to the prison service (Edgar, 2003: 24). This represented an 11 per cent increase in the prison budget, raising it to £2.8 billion in 2003–4 and was designed to deliver 2,320 extra places inside (Prison Reform Trust, 2003: 4). By 2006, the government's often-unthinking commitment to the prison meant that it failed 'to shift funds from custody to prevention: billions are spent on the criminal justice system, but just £370 million on youth justice programmes. Prison is swallowing up the cash that might stop crime – and it doesn't work' (Toynbee, 2006a: 27). Rod Morgan made a similar point in June 2006 when he noted that 70 per cent of the Youth Justice budget was spent on custody (BBC Radio 4 News, 23 June 2006). Furthermore, while the government had allocated £115 million to over 150 local authorities to 'provide "innovative" facilities for teenagers', for Yvonne Roberts this figure did not 'add up to much, particularly since sports grounds have been flogged, youth clubs closed and street projects axed because of a lack of funding. We spend only 17p a day for each teenager on youth clubs, sport and leisure' (Roberts, 2006: 32). At the same time, the legal aid budget was slashed from £378 million in 1995–6 to £210 million in 2004–5. In comments by the judiciary to a government review of legal aid services, judges complained that civil legal aid had been 'scraped to the bone over the last 10 years' (*The Guardian*, 24 April 2006).[11]

Mary Riddell has made a similar point regarding funding for outdoor activities for young people at risk of offending. Biker schemes, involving 200 children which cost £220,000 annually or just over the £172,300 spent on keeping to keep one child in a secure training centre, 'were foundering. Two collapsed recently [June 2007] and most are chasing the same scraps of short-term funding never certain that the wage bill can be paid. Welcome to the charity world. The only oddity is that such awesome amounts of state cash and head scratching are invested in what fails' (Riddell, 2007: 31). It is also worth noting that when yet another prison and probation crisis erupted in late 2006, treatment programmes for sex offenders and for those accused of domestic violence were cut back (*The Guardian*, 19 September 2006).

By March 2007, the UK was spending more on law and order as a proportion of its national income than any other industrialized country, including the USA. This meant that nearly £23 billion was spent in 2007–8. Moreover, as Envar Solomon has noted, even in their own terms, such expenditure patterns are problematic in that, rather than spending money on supportive services for offenders, the 'largest proportion of expenditure goes on staffing costs, including salaries, pensions and other employee costs, accounting for around three quarters of overall spending'. Furthermore, the impact of the prison-building programme has been such that between 1997 and 2007 'at least £2 billion has been spent on accommodation'. At the same time, 'resources are becoming more thinly spread as the Prison Service faces more substantial reductions in its budget over the next three years. The advances that have been made could easily and quickly be lost' (Solomon, 2007b: 22). By the end of a decade in power, New Labour was spending £32 billion on public order and safety, the highest expenditure in the Organisation of Economic Development and Cooperation, the group representing the world's richest nations (*The Independent*, 31 January 2007; *The Guardian*, 24 November 2006). At the same time, as Chapter 4 noted, in those ten years, £187 billion was spent on law and order 'services' (Solomon et al., 2007). Additionally, the average cost of each prison place built between 2000 and 2006 was £99,839 (*Hansard*, cited in Prison Reform Trust, 2006a: 5).

Therefore, the direction of expenditure towards law and order solutions to social problems has led abolitionists to argue for a radical reallocation and redirection of criminal justice resources in two particular areas. First, as Mathiesen notes, there would be financial support for victims including economic compensation and 'symbolic support in situations of grief and sorrow, shielded places where victims who need protection can get it, support centres for battered women ... the victims get nothing out of the present system, and get nothing out of enlarging and accelerating the present system ...'. Second, Mathiesen argues that 'the war on crime should become a war on poverty' (Mathiesen, 2000: 343–344). This would include changes to living accommodation, work, education strategies and drugs policies:

> You may ask, "Who should pay for this?" The answer is that the prison should pay for it: The dismantling of the prisons would give us extremely large sums of money, billions and billions of US dollars, which we could spend generously on the victims and the offenders (2000: 344).

Mathiesen's argument regarding support for women who have been beaten and murdered as a result of domestic violence is graphically illustrated by the situation in England and Wales. In 2007, domestic violence remained the biggest killer of women under the age of forty-four (*Dispatches*, 19 March 2007). Despite this figure, and the widespread nature and extent of violence against women more generally, successive governments remained trapped in an ideology which prioritized public criminality. In Thames Valley, the apparent downgrading of this violence was caused by the pressure generated by central government to improve detection rates for crime and 'drives emanating from Downing Street to focus on particular areas, such as street crime'. In the words of one police officer, 'You don't improve performance indicators by preventing a domestic murder. ... And police have an old saying – "what gets measured, gets done"' (Rose, 2007: 11). Additionally:

> ... the women's refuge movement has prioritized shelter and services to safeguard women and children's safety. Resourcing of the women's refuge movement has always been, and remains, insecure and pitifully small, placing severe restrictions on what can be achieved (Wilcox, 2006: 725).

In 1985, 1,842 rapes were reported to the police; by 2005, this figure had increased to 14,449. In 1984, there were 68 rape crisis centres for women, by 2006, there were 'only 32 women only sexual violence support services, because of a lack of funding, and our information from the Survivors Trust suggests they're closing at a rate of two per month' (Women's Resource Centre, 2006: 1). By the beginning of 2007, the services provided by Rape Crisis Centres were 'facing an unprecedented funding crisis exacerbated by government policy. Half of rape crisis groups have closed over the past decade and a further ten face imminent demise' (Letter from

Professor Liz Kelly in *The Guardian*, 15 February 2007). By July 2007, it was reported that half of the 32 remaining rape crisis centres could close, or have their activities severely curtailed, because of government funding cuts (*The Independent*, 5 July 2007).

The direction of expenditure on law and order and who benefits from this expenditure, therefore, remain key issues and important points of contestation with respect to thinking about constructing a viable and radical alternative to the current dominant narrative surrounding the criminal justice system and the voracious appetite of the system and those who work within it, for more resources which, for women in particular, has meant less protection.

Dismantling prison officer culture

In many ways, prison officer culture is the elephant in the corner with respect to political and criminological debates around prisons. The analysis of this culture has been premised on the belief that its essential benevolence is occasionally disrupted by the presence of an idiosyncratic or deranged 'bad apple' whose removal will restore the paternalistic equilibrium of the institution. Thus, for the Prison Reform Trust, most prison staff carry out their duties with 'skill and integrity' (cited in Sim, 2004b: 115). Within criminology, the positivist perspective of liberal reform groups has been reinforced by a resurgence in the literature on prison officers (Liebling, 2004; Coyle, 2005: Chapter 5). This work, while offering a number of insights into the dynamics of staff culture, nonetheless conceptualizes this culture in either morally progressive or morally neutral terms (Sim, 2008a). In one study, the focus was on 'the best aspects of prison officer work and very little on the "dark side"'.[12] For these authors, the everyday work of officers was built on the 'under-use of power' and the 'diligent and skilled use of discretion' (Liebling and Price, 2001: 108 and 124).

In contrast, abolitionists would argue for a critical analysis of prison officer culture that challenges, (to borrow a phrase from Zygmunt Bauman) criminology's 'unperturbed equanimity' (Bauman, 1989: 212) towards it. The everyday dynamics of this culture are central to the reproduction of the prison as a place of punishment and pain. This culture is built on: its untrammelled, corrosive masculinity; its discretionary use of often, nonaccountable power; its capacity for seriously inhibiting the desire of prisoners to change and its role in reinforcing an everyday politics of indifference built on the 'neutralisation of moral responsibility' for prisoners, 'the social production of distance' between the confined, and prison officers as a group and the opprobrium directed at prisoners where 'being for the other' is replaced by 'the sober, rational calculation of costs and effects' (Bauman, cited in Pemberton, 2004: 77–81). Finally, there is the question of prison officer violence, which, within criminology has been overwhelmingly conceptualized 'in rigorously positivist terms, the result of an individual, unmanageable state servant deviating from cultural and institutional norms that are otherwise benevolent and supportive'. In effect, this 'means that the often-insidious role of prison staff in maintaining the vulpine order of the prison is ignored' (Sim, 2004b: 115). However, as Richard Edney has noted, not only has the question of prison officer violence been neglected in criminology but criminology also needs to attempt to theorize:

> ... and make problematic the nature of violence against prisoners. In that sense it requires that the 'stories' of prisoners are accepted as legitimate offering as they do the experience of those subject to great power and the possible basis for a theory of such power. ... In comparison with earlier prisons with their filth and overcrowded nature, 'modern' prisons are viewed in progressive and positive terms. Unfair and brutal practices are posited as antithetical to the prison project and contrary to penological objectives. Moreover, the implicit assumption is that the community has moved *beyond* such prisons. However, the prison remains an institution with totalitarian features. A necessary by product of such a regime is that prisoners remain vulnerable to abuse (Edney, 1997: 38–39, emphasis in the original).

Accounts by prisoners themselves reinforce Edney's argument and highlight the banality of the violence they experience on a daily basis.[13] These accounts – 'penology from below' – (Sim, 2008a), remain as valid as a truth about penal life as the dominant, official accounts from above. In a letter to *Inside Time*, the national monthly newspaper for prisoners, one prisoner noted that:

> In our closed environment, mistreatment and punishment have become acceptable; it is part of the routine of prison life. Officers are ill-equipped; with insufficient training to deal with the multitude of problems they encounter. ... The attitude of being 'hard' towards inmates has become part of the Officer's subculture. It is no longer seen as being only necessary in certain situations, but as being essential in dealing with everyone. ... While other professions have evolved into the twenty-first century, the prison system remains firmly entrenched in the past. The reality of the role of [the] Prison Officer has become distorted; the central principle seems to be that inmates are objects to be 'kept' rather than people to be 'cared for'. Perhaps if this inhibitive attitude changed, if Officers interacted with inmates, respected boundaries, involved prisoners in their own long-term plans, listen[ed] to problems and responded to needs, then the role could be redefined, making the job rewarding and fulfilling. In short, if Officers became 'carers' instead of 'keepers' then both sides would benefit greatly (Tolmaer, 2006: 3).

It has become commonplace to dismiss accounts by the confined who, because they have been convicted, are constructed as mendacious fantasists. Three points are worth considering here. First, why would the prisoner quoted above lie about life inside and therefore put himself at risk of official retaliation? Second, taking a longer historical perspective, radical prisoners' rights groups and prisoners themselves, consistently complained about violence in prisons in the 1970s and 1980s. This was usually and inevitably denied by those responsible for the system.

However, twenty years later, Martin Narey, the then Chief Executive of the *National Offender Management Service* (NOMS), confirmed these complaints in describing his time as a prison officer at Lincoln prison: 'I saw prisoners in the segregation unit routinely slapped, it was constant low-level abuse. If you wanted to do any good, you had to do it by stealth. The ... Prison Officers' Association ... ran the place. Assistant governors were derided. I can remember getting a real load of abuse for being seen carrying a *Guardian*' (cited in James, 2005: 16). Finally, and more broadly, given the level of what Leo Panitch and Colin Leys have called the 'generalised pathology of chronic mendacity', which has become institutionalized within the circuits of power within advanced capitalist societies, and the 'unprecedented levels of secrecy, obfuscation, dissembling and downright lying that now characterise public life' (Panitch and Leys, 2005: vii), then in the current political climate, accounts from above should also be subjected to the same level of scrutiny and scepticism.

The culture of indifference, and the moral opprobrium directed at prisoners, which, following Bauman, I referred to above, begins, as Elaine Crawley has indicated, in the training school where a highly masculinized, punitive discourse prevails:

> ... a female officer commented that "at training college you're taught never to trust the bastards!" ... Numerous new officers were shocked at the degree of verbal and psychological abuse meted out by their trainers. ... They claimed that corporate promotions of "excellence", "caring", "quality" and "respect" – terms that they had heard a great deal during their initial interviews – were barely evident in the organisational realities that they had experienced during this element of their basic training. ... Many of my interviewees, male and female, remarked upon the militaristic, paternalistic and abusive nature of their basic training (Crawley, 2004: 69–70).

Training included 'games' such as 'shag-tag', which involved trainee officers bending over and touching their knees so that they could 'only be "released" by three thrusts (indicating sexual intercourse from the rear) from another officer (again male or female)' (2004: 73).[14]

This culture also systematically corrodes the psychological well-being and career prospects of those staff who are concerned with promoting change among prisoners through offering them empathy and support. The attitudes of such staff:

> ... indicate that it *is* possible to break down the deeply embedded, apparently unyielding cultural edifice of penal negativity ... and develop radical alternatives built on a proactive respect for prisoners. However, if such officers continue to leave the service, or fail to be promoted, or are psychologically lacerated on a daily basis, then the punitive and demeaning discourses which dominate the prison will continue to be reproduced. On the other hand, if they were unequivocally supported ... then it is possible to imagine a different model of confinement developing for those who need to be detained. Anything less, and the system will remain locked into the discourse of a sanctified 'us' and a despised 'them', offering nothing but daily frustration and

> denigration to good staff and ongoing humiliation to prisoners while providing little by way of sustained protection to the wider society (Sim, 2008a: 204, emphasis in the original).[15]

Therefore, introducing the kind of 'negative reforms' advocated by Thomas Mathiesen would involve dismantling this culture and redesigning and refocusing staff training so that the discourses of human rights, social justice and democratic accountability, as well as interpersonal empathy, respect and support for the confined, as exemplified in the philosophy and practices of the Barlinnie Special Unit, discussed in Chapter 4, become normalized in the everyday practices of prison officers. These policies and practices would also be institutionalized so that they become central to the promotion prospects of all staff within the prison service. Such a fundamental change would fulfil Mathiesen's criteria for reforms that both contradict, and compete with, the prevailing orthodoxy around prison officers and would be integral to an 'abolitionist policy' that 'is offensive and tries to do away with the repressive established systems' (de Folter, 1987: 38).

Abolitionism, criminal justice and social inequalities[16]

The specific 'negative reforms' outlined above, have a more general context with respect to a number of broader changes and interventions, which would form the basis of a programme for radically transforming prisons. For abolitionists, these changes would include: reforming sentencing policies; democratizing the judiciary and radically transforming legal training more generally so that lawyers, judges and crucially, magistrates, become socially conscious as well as legally aware; removing private companies from their involvement in planning, managing and running penal institutions; decentralizing prisons by making them democratically accountable to locally elected monitoring groups; developing social policy and welfare responses to crime beyond the prison gates, especially with respect to the question of illegal *and* legal drug taking; rejecting both Conservative and New Labour's obsession with American neoconservative politicians and their law and order and social welfare policies; challenging, and indeed categorically rejecting, simplistic banalities such as 'tough on crime, tough on the causes of crime'; and shifting the terms of the penal debate regarding alternatives to custody so that decision-makers in the criminal justice system would have to 'justify prison not the alternative' (Tombs, 2003: 8).[17]

Angela Davis has also argued that broader changes in criminal justice policy are crucial to the process of radical transformation in that abolitionists should not look for:

> ... prisonlike substitutes for the prison, such as house arrest, safeguarded by electronic surveillance bracelets. Rather, positing decarceration as our overarching strategy,

> we would try to envision a continuum of alternatives to imprisonment – demilitarization of schools, revitalisation of education at all levels, a health system that provides free physical and mental care to all, and a justice system based on reparation and reconciliation rather than retribution and vengeance (Davis, 2003: 107).

For Davis, these changes are inevitably and inextricably tied in with the need for a 'radical transformation' in the wider structures of power that generate the profound social inequalities and dislocations that dominate the national and international social order in the twenty-first century. Thus, 'alternatives that fail to address racism, male dominance, homophobia, class bias and other forms of domination will not, in the final analysis, lead to decarceration and will not advance the goal of abolition' (2003: 108).[18]

Articulating a profound desire for radical social change, as Angela Davis does, sits uneasily alongside the cynical, decadent, political and popular culture that prevails in a technologically advanced, but increasingly crisis-prone capitalist society. Here, critical ideas and radical programmes for social action are treated by the political class as both ill-conceived and irrelevant to their strategies for governing and maintaining social order.

Politicians have taken refuge in their unrelenting articulation and desire to be *seen* to be doing something – anything – about crime (which, in turn, is tied in with their desperate compunction to hold onto parliamentary power *whatever* it costs). In turn, they position those who step beyond the 'acceptable' limits of criticism as unacceptable and uninvited intruders into the 'real' business of government. The prison – 'understood as one of the epicentral institutions of these neoliberal times' alongside 'a parallel set of institution-building processes [which are] at work, many of them geared to the reorganized imperatives of labor regulation, social control and the governance of systemic socio-economic insecurity' (Peck, 2003: 226) – as different chapters have shown, remains deeply embedded in their strategies and policies for delivering that political vision. However, these strategies and policies, like the wider neoliberal, social arrangements, which underpin and legitimate them, are also beset by internal and external contradictions and contingencies. It is to a consideration of these contradictions with which the last chapter is concerned and to which I now turn.

Notes

1 The idea of 'transcendence' is taken from Herbert Marcuse who used it to describe 'tendencies in theory and practice which, in a given society, "overshoot" the established universe of discourse and action toward its historical alternatives (real possibilities)' (Marcuse, 1972: 11).

2 This is what Pierre Bourdieu called '*doxa* to connote that which is unquestionable and taken for granted within a culture. *Doxa* is something you do not discuss

or debate, because it is inherently good and therefore undebatable' (cited in Mathiesen, 2000: 346, emphasis in the original).

3 Twenty-nine prison officers died between 1988 and 2000. One was murdered, while twenty-eight died from heart attacks, suicides, accidents, illnesses and road traffic accidents. See Sim (2004b) for a discussion of these figures.

4 In a final twist to the story, the prison's ex-governor was charged with failing to properly receipt some items that the institution's prisoners had collected for the charity Mencap. No disciplinary action was taken (*Private Eye*, 1–14 June 2001). An alternative account of the search has been provided by Tom Murtagh who was area manager where the prison was located. The subtitle of his book – 'Lessons from a Modern-Day Witch Hunt' – expressed his views on what had transpired (Murtagh, 2007), a view reinforced by Martin Narey, the former Director General of the Prison Service who wrote the book's Foreword. Murtagh himself argued that the events 'serve[d] to highlight the ease with which a few powerful individuals, maybe under subtle pressure from criminal elements, can subvert the system to the highest level' (2007: xvii)

5 It is also worth remarking that Professor West could have saved himself journeying to South London for his study and could simply have stayed in Cambridge and studied the delinquent antics and activities of Cambridge undergraduates out on the weekend. These activities, of course, are usually described as 'high jinks' not delinquency or antisocial behaviour.

6 Joint projects had already been established between youth offending teams and the Devonshire and Dorset Regiment, RAF Halton and the Royal Navy's Sea Cadet Corps (*The Independent*, 26 October 2004). In January 2006, it was announced that children *under three* as well as pregnant teenagers were to be targeted in Scotland 'as part of the national drive to cut violent crime' (www.theherald.co.uk/news). Needless to say those who were to be targeted lived in deprived areas. In July 2006, it was reported that a similar scheme was being mooted in England and Wales with babies and toddlers under two being targeted as part of the drive against antisocial behaviour in problem families (*The Observer*, 16 July 2006).

7 This phrase is taken from the review by David Stubbs of the film *Uncovered: The War* on Iraq, published in *Uncut*, 91, December 2004: 179.

8 'Demythologizing the prison' was a phrase used by Andrew Jefferson and Peter Scharff Smith at a lecture to the Danish Institute for Human Rights in October 2005. I am grateful for their contribution to my thinking in this area.

9 Jerome Miller's strategy in closing Massachusetts's juvenile institution in the early 1970s provides a paradigmatic example of what could be done if the political will existed and if politicians could transcend and transgress their reluctance to see beyond the prison as the place for punishing the offender (Rutherford, 1992).

10 Taking a longer time frame, the number of houses built in 1977 by local authorities was 146,444; in 2000–1 915 were built. Private companies built 155,296 houses in 1977 and 153,633 in 2000–1 (Glennerster, 2003: 167).

11 It is also worth noting that while the legal aid budget rose from £1.5 billion to over £2 billion between 1997 and 2006, this rise was to cover all legal aid services from crime through to asylum, divorce, housing, mental health and children in care. In contrast, the budget for other criminal justice agencies had increased significantly during this time: the police grant for 2005–6 increased by 15 per cent to over £4.5 billion; expenditure on the Crown Prosecution Service (CPS) increased by 75 per cent between 2001 and 2006 to £604 million, while the numbers employed by the CPS increased by 40 per cent (Independent Defence Lawyers, 2006: 2). Thanks to Avtar Bhatoa for providing me with the information on this point.

12 One wonders how a critical study, which simply focussed on the worst aspects of prison officer work, would be received by funding bodies and those who grant access to penal institutions.

13 I have paraphrased Hannah Arendt's famous phrase, 'the banality of evil' coined at the time of the trial of Adolph Eichmann and am using it to challenge the positivist assumption that violence against prisoners can be explained through the individualized lens of positivist determinism. Instead, it is 'quite ordinary, commonplace, and neither demonic nor monstrous' (Arendt, cited in Jacoby, 2005: 79).

14 It has also been asserted that 'the quality of the training offered is of such a low standard that recruits are routinely given the answers to exams before they sit them, thereby making a mockery of the whole process' (Paxton, 2006: 19).

15 The power of the culture to punish deviants also extends to those who speak out against it. Carol Lingard, who served for 15 years as a prison officer, and who complained about the bullying and intimidation of prisoners by officers in Wakefield, was treated as a 'grass' by her fellow officers while managers 'failed to take her complaints seriously'. She eventually lost her job, had to take medicine for anxiety and found herself in a situation where 'work became a very hostile, unsafe environment...I was made to feel that I had done something dreadful and that I was going to pay for it'. She eventually won a claim for unfair dismissal and received an apology from the Director General of the Prison Service (*The Observer*, 26 June 2005). In April 2008, another officer, Emma Howie, who, because she had reported assaults against prisoners in two high security prisons was also labelled a 'grass' and was sent grass clippings and a wreath in the post. Before deciding on the amount of compensation she should receive, an employment tribunal was stopped because a senior governor was told by the tribunal to Email the head of the prison service to ask for an apology over her treatment (Allison, 2008: 4; *Society Guardian*, 9 April 2008).

16 In August 2006, the top 1 per cent of the population in the UK owned 23 per cent 'of everything' while the bottom 50 per cent owned 'just 6 per cent. If you take homes out of the equation, then the top 1 per cent owns 63 per cent of all other assets. The bottom half owns just 1 per cent' (Toynbee, 2006b: 27). In the same month, bonuses for those working in financial 'services' in the City of London increased by 16 per cent to reach £19 billion (*The Guardian*, 17 August 2006). Between 2006 and 2007, the combined wealth of the richest thousand people in the UK rose by 20 per cent or by £59 billion. In May 2007, despite ten years of New Labour government, inequality in the country was as high as the inequality experienced during Margaret Thatcher's time in power (*The Guardian*, 30 April 2007; *The Guardian*, 18 May: 2007).

17 In many respects, liberal prison reform groups would not disagree with a number of these proposals. In a letter to *The Guardian* on October 10 2006, the Deputy Director of the *Prison Reform Trust* outlined a number of suggestions for alleviating yet another prison crisis, including: a national network of court diversion schemes together with a range of mental health facilities; residential drug treatment places; local authority secure care; specialist fostering; intensive supervision and mentoring for children; properly funded locally run community sentences and politicians desisting from inflaming the fear of crime. Abolitionists would not disagree with many of these suggestions but would contest their ability to induce serious penal change without immediately halting the prison-building programme, recognizing the vulpine nature of the prison officer culture and dealing with the profound levels of social inequality that scar the national and

international landscape. I will return to the issue of reform in the final chapter of this book.

18 On a global scale, these inequalities were profound, indeed grotesque: the richest 500 people on the planet had a combined total of over 1,500 billion dollars; the richest 50 million people in Europe and North America had the same income as the poorest 2.7 billion people; 11 million children under five were dying each year through preventable diseases, often generated by a lack of clean water. Conversely, state-subsidized support for the average cow in the European Union in 2005 was $2.62 a day while half of the world's population lived on less than $2 a day. One third of deaths, around 18 million people a year, were caused by poverty.

8

ABOLITIONISM IN AN ANTI-UTOPIAN AGE

> ... we can place a high-tech vehicle on Mars that moves on cue; but we cannot muster the will or resources to fix a defective social order (Jacoby, 2005: 149).
>
> Forget about reform; it's time to talk about abolishing jails and prisons. ... Still-abolition? Where do you put the prisoners? The 'criminals'? What's the alternative? First, having no alternative at all would create less crime than the present criminal training centres. Second, the only full alternative is building the kind of society that does not need prisons: A decent redistribution of power and income so as to put out the hidden fire of burning envy that now flames up in crimes of property – both burglary by the poor and embezzlement by the affluent. And a decent sense of community that can support, reintegrate and truly rehabilitate those who suddenly become filled with fury or despair, and that can face them not as objects – 'criminals' – but as people who have committed illegal acts, as have almost all of us (Waskow, cited in Davis, 2003: 105).

In presenting an abolitionist case against the contemporary prison, this book has implicitly and explicitly also been concerned with providing a critique of the politics of liberal reform. Importantly, taking this critical position does *not* mean that reform organizations, and the often-benevolent motivations behind the work of those individuals involved with them, have not had some success in highlighting, and sometimes changing, the iniquities and injustices of prison life, as well as in a range of other social arenas. As Foucault has noted:

> There are hundreds and hundreds of people who have worked for the emergence of a number of problems that are now on the agenda. To say that this work produced nothing is quite wrong. Do you think that twenty years ago[1] people were considering the problem of the relationship between mental illness and psychological normality, the problem of prison, the problem of medical power, the problem of the relationship between the sexes, and so on, as they are today? (Foucault, interviewed in Kritzman, 1988: 154).

Liberal reform groups have therefore played a central role, since the birth of the modern prison, in making visible what was invisible with respect to the individual and collective mistreatment of prisoners. However, despite their involvement in progressive, if limited penal change, abolitionists remain justifiably sceptical of their lobbying activities, with their emphasis on pragmatic expediency, together with their myopic and misguided faith in the sanctity of piecemeal change. For abolitionists, reform organizations have not only failed to challenge the fundamental presuppositions underpinning the commonsensical world views of Conservative and New Labour governments regarding crime and punishment, but also the very language they use often reinforces their incorporation into the dominant discourses and structures of power mobilized to justify the nature, relevance and, above all, the *need* for the prison. So while these organizations argue for alternatives to custody, for limitations in the use of prison, for reducing overcrowding and for the curtailment of sentencing discretion, the continuing *existence* of the prison remains unquestioned, its fundamentally destructive capacities unarticulated. As Thomas Mathiesen has noted:

> The more we use the language of the powerful, the more attuned we become to defining the problems at hand *as the powerful usually do*; in other words, the more integrated we become into the old system. We define the problems in this way in order to persuade the powerful that our contradiction is sensible. But competition is then maintained at the cost of the contradiction itself; the contradiction is abolished and turned into fundamental agreement; the forms which compete are both integrated into the old system, tested out, and finished (Mathiesen, 1974: 19, emphasis in the original).

Reform organizations continue to exert an important but ultimately baleful influence on the political and policy debates around prisons and on popular consciousness more generally, precisely because of the lobby's often-slavish, expedient emphasis on reform as an end in itself. They remain tied into what Foucault called 'the monotonous critique' that has endured since the genesis of the prison during another moment of frantic, bourgeois modernization at the end of the eighteenth century which was noted above in Chapter 6. As he pointedly made clear, since then the institution has been subjected to a range of scathing critiques: it does not diminish the crime rate, it causes recidivism, it produces delinquents, it encourages loyalty between prisoners, it stigmatizes offenders and it differentially impacts on the families of prisoners through condemning them to living in poverty (Foucault, 1979: 264–268). This long history of abject failure has effectively been ignored by the reform lobby and by those who voraciously demand more prisons and more prison places. At the same time, whenever a crisis has erupted, the prison has 'always been offered as its own remedy' to its problems. It is a remedy built on 'the repetition of a reform that is isomorphic, despite its idealism, with the disciplinary function of the prison ...' (Foucault, 1979: 268–271).

Contemporary policy reforms, as Pat Carlen and Jackie Tombs have pointed out, have also fallen into the same punitive trap as their historical predecessors. The partnership approach to offender management, for example, one of the central pillars in New Labour's penal policy, has been legitimated by the 'advocates of penal reform' who in:

> ... becoming disillusioned by repeated failures of governments to reduce prison populations, have repeatedly accepted the invitation of prison administrations to help shape new prison regimes ostensibly designed to reduce both the pain and the damaging effects of imprisonment but which in effect often merely help to hide them ... (Carlen and Tombs, 2006: 341).

They also note that liberal notions of reintegration and community sentences have not resulted in a decrease in the prison population. Rather, the increase in the women's population, in particular, provides a further example of 'penal creativity and plasticity' in that the prison:

> ... is always and already changing its discourses of legitimation and its strategies of governance for keeping the already-excluded in their place. The distinctly new twist to all these many previous reconfigurations of penal discourses is the finding of the Scottish sentencing study ... that the move to make community sentences more rigorous so as to increase their popularity with sentencers perceived by governments to be imprisoning women because they think community sentences are *too soft* has backfired: the evidence suggests that some Scottish judges are now sentencing women to prison because they think the new style community sentences are *too harsh!* Until, therefore, carceralism is decentred from governmental and popular thinking about how to respond to crime, until, in effect, the punishment/reintegration couplet is abolished and prison populations reduced, it is likely that all attempts both to civilise the punitive response and reduce racialized, class-based and gendered patterns of social exclusion will be thwarted ... (2006: 356–7, emphasis in the original).

The doctrine of gradual reform has moved the organizations that support this doctrine into the dangerous position, however unconsciously, of 'philosophizing the disgrace'[2] that penal institutions have become, thereby reinforcing 'the stultifying idea that nothing lies beyond the prison' (Davis, 2003: 20). However, despite its apparently indestructible ideological and material presence, as we reach the mid point of the new century's first decade, there are a number of overlapping contradictions, contingencies and points of contestation, which, taken together, continue to deny the prison an all-embracing hegemony within the contemporary apparatus of punishment. There are five, in particular, I want to consider in the next part of this conclusion.

Contradictions, contingencies and contestations

First, there is the process of carceralisation and what appears to have been the unyielding consolidation of the modern prison within this process. In *Discipline and Punish*, Foucault outlined a number of key characteristics, which constituted the 'carceral'. These included the principle of 'relative continuity' whereby different institutions were linked not only by 'mechanisms of surveillance and punishment' but also by a 'continuity of punitive criteria and mechanisms, which on the basis of a mere deviation gradually strengthened the rules and increased the punishment'. The 'carceral' was also organized around "'disciplinary careers" ... and the establishment of a specified criminality'. Ultimately, it succeeded 'in making the power to punish natural and legitimate, in lowering at least the threshold of tolerance to penality'. Foucault concluded: 'by operating at every level of the social body and by mingling ceaselessly the art of rectifying and the right to punish, the universality of the carceral lowers the level from which it becomes natural and acceptable to be punished' (Foucault, 1979: 299–303).[3] Intensifying punishment for conventional criminal behaviour, punishing increasing numbers who have deviated from officially defined norms and values, reinforcing specific and particular views of criminality, and lowering the level of acceptability with regard to who gets punished and why, have, as this book has argued, been central to criminal justice and penal policy in the last three decades.

However, this process, like any governing activity, state or otherwise, has been, and remains, imbued with contingencies and contradictions. The construction of the carceral, penal state is not an unrelenting, historical inevitability where the will to power, which has been ideologically and materially ratchetted-up over the last three decades, will continue to be imposed on an unsuspecting population. Furthermore, the state *cannot* guarantee that punitive policies will inevitably 'work', even taking into account the limited definition of success within which its servants and politicians themselves discursively operate. At its simplest, there is the problem of unintended policy consequences. For Bob Jessop, '... as in all cases of social action, there will always be unacknowledged conditions influencing the success or failure of their [state officials'] actions as well as the unanticipated consequences which follow from them' (Jessop, 1990: 367).

Second, and more specifically, both historically and contemporaneously, the prison has been denied hegemony through being confronted by major and minor individual and collective acts of subversion, refusals and confrontations. As Amy Myrick has pointed out, the 'ultimate carceral institution', which was the American prison 'at the turn of the 20th century' never truly captured the hearts and minds of the confined. According to Myrick, 'prisoners' self-representations fit uneasily into the parameters of Foucault's carceral state: prisoners "escaped" through religion, generic writing that defied progressive individuality, and the mirroring of their audiences['] values, fear, and identity' (Myrick, 2004: 93).[4] In short, the power of the 'carceral's objectifying gaze' has always been confronted by the 'living, breathing criminal' (Myrick, 2004: 107). Thus, at particular moments, state servants may achieve a grudging, fractured and superficial legitimacy in the eyes of the confined but the presence of 'living, breathing criminal[s]', and the activities they engage in inside – from writing to rebelling – makes it difficult, if not impossible, for the prison, and more importantly, those who represent its power in the form of prison staff, to achieve complete, hegemonic domination over them.

Third, these internal refusals and confrontations have, as various chapters have shown, been supported externally by radical prisoners' rights organizations and, more recently, by law firms offering legal representation to the confined. These firms, in alliance with nongovernment organizations such as *INQUEST*, have breached the often-paranoid secrecy of the prison (and the state more generally), and, while not overthrowing its ideological and material power to punish, have succeeded in at least imposing limits on the discretion that state servants enjoy at various levels of the penal bureaucracy, making them aware that they are under surveillance and could be called to account for the policies they implement, or conversely, do not implement on a daily basis.[5] In short, these developments have placed limitations on the power to punish. To put this point another way: if such groups had not been established what kind of untrammelled power would the confined have faced in the nonaccountable world of prisons, in general, and in the sepulchral isolation of segregation units in particular? The publication of newspapers such as *Inside Time* has also provided a platform to challenge dominant ideologies and 'truths' around life inside. Like the workers' newspapers of the nineteenth century, described by Foucault (Myrick, 2004: 107), the articles in these publications, and the letters from prisoners they contain, can be seen as part of 'a whole effort' that is being made 'to reverse [the] monotonous discourse on crime, which sought both to isolate it as a monstrosity and to depict it as the work of the poorest class' (Foucault, 1979: 288–289).[6]

Fourth, as Chapter 4 noted, the prison has been defended on the grounds that victims of crime are propelled by an atavistic desire for vengeance and more retributive punishment. Yet, even here, despite the sustained media and political focus on victims and their rights, particularly over the last three law and order decades, this intense campaign again has not achieved hegemony.[7] For example, victim surveys have revealed that victims are sceptical towards the prison as a means of solving crime. In 2006, research by *Smart Justice* and *Victim Support* found that:

> ... almost two-thirds of victims of crime do not believe that prison works to reduce non-violent crime and offences such as shoplifting, stealing cars and vandalism. There is overwhelming support for programmes that focus on prevention i.e. more support for parents, more constructive activities for young people and more drug treatment and mental health provision in the community (*Smart Justice*, 2006: 1).

Additionally, the authoritarian demands for intensive punishment, which Conservative and New Labour politicians have led and exploited over the last three decades, have been centred on those individuals and families whose lives have been devastated through the violent loss of a relative or friend. They have particularly focussed on those family members who, in their grief, have called for a retributive response to the perpetrators. Again, however, these demands have not achieved total domination. Crucially, there have been other voices whose hurt, pain and raw sense of loss has been no less acute but who have *not* resorted to the clamour for vengeance. In July 2005, after her son's brutal, racist murder, Anthony Walker's mother did not call for revenge and retribution. While politicians, and many media commentators, rightly condemned Anthony's murder as an act of racist barbarism, they were much less forthcoming regarding her plea for understanding and forgiveness regarding Anthony's killers. Why was this? The answer lies in the obvious fact that her sentiments did not chime with the dominant, retributive law and order philosophy which government ministers and many in the media have constantly articulated. In that sense, those who espouse punitive retribution have not managed to completely dominate the social and political agenda by leading the society down a punitive road, where every signpost points only towards punishment and pain for offenders, even where those offenders have committed the most outrageous and dehumanizing acts of violence.

The final contradiction concerns the issue of violent crime, dangerous individuals and what should be done about them. The stalking figures of the irredeemable psychopath and the monstrous, sexually licentious paedophile, and the dangers they pose to an already beleaguered and fearful population, have been mobilized to justify and legitimate the need for the prison as a crucial bulwark in protecting the wider society from their murderous and perfidious actions. Again even here, the question of serious crime, and what it means, is less clear-cut and open to contestation and debate. As Barbara Hudson has noted, 'serious crimes and crimes which are taken seriously are not necessarily the same ... seriousness of law enforcement ... does not relate to seriousness of crime if the latter is to be judged by any rational calculus of harm as suggested by the more liberal justice model theorists' (cited in Sim, 1994a: 280).

Hudson's point is very important, suggesting as it does that even those actions and activities, which often involve horrendous levels of violence may not be treated in an appropriately serious manner, or even defined as such. For example, the twentieth century was '... the century of "megadeath" ... and "politically motivated carnage"'. This carnage resulted in the deaths of up to 175 million people as a result of 'state sponsored massacres or other forms of deliberate death ... excluding military personnel and civilian casualties of war ...' (Morrison, 2006: 54). What do these data tell us about the definition of violence, the practices of dangerousness and the relationship of both to the 'normal' individuals who have killed and maimed on such a vast scale? In asking these questions, it is not the intention to labour the point about how dangerousness is socially constructed. It is simply to indicate that the link between social protection, dangerous individuals and punishment is more complex and nuanced than is recognized in the dominant discourses concerning risk and serious crime when considered against the background of violence noted above.

Furthermore, even on its own terms, the role of the prison in protecting particular groups from the ravages of violent and dangerous individuals is also more complicated, complex and contestable than defenders of the prison have been prepared to recognize. Male violence against women provides a pertinent and powerful example of this point. As I argued in Chapter 1, despite the often-stated commitment from state servants that they are there to offer protection to women, in practice the personnel and institutions of the criminal justice system, often desperately fail to do so. Given the culture of the modern prison, it is questionable whether incarcerating the dangerous men who are caught and processed through the criminal justice system, actually changes their behaviour when they are detained. The discourse of masculinity, which is deeply embedded in this culture, and which cuts across what appears to be an intransigent divide between prisoners and prison officers, offers little by way of changing the misogynistic attitudes that underpin the violence of many men and which reside at the very centre of their being. At the present moment, the prison simply reproduces normal men, with all of the subsequent problems, and concomitant risks, for many women (and children) that normal prison regimes generate (Sim, 1994c). The rocketing prison population has done little to alleviate the desperate levels of violence, and the 'intimate intrusions' endured by women of all ages in their everyday lives (Stanko, 1985). Taking this position does *not* mean dismantling the walls of the prison and releasing into the community those men who have been caught and sentenced for serious crimes of violence against women. However, it *is* to say that the level of violence against women (and also against minority ethnic groups)[8] raises significant questions about the need to think more critically about the definition of serious crime and dangerousness, about the nature of the response to dangerous individuals and, more particularly, about the role of the prison *as it is presently constructed and constituted* in the policing and regulation of dangerous individuals, again however they are defined.

Facing the future: a (re)emerging radicalism?

Loïc Wacquant has made the point that relying on the prison is 'not a destiny in advanced societies but a matter of political choices ...' (Wacquant, 2001: 85). Consequently, opposition to the prison should be developed along three dimensions. First, the *'words and discourses'*, which are used to stifle and restrict debate, and the use of 'vague and incoherent notions such as "urban violence"' should be challenged. Second, critics should 'thwart the multiplication of measures tending to "broaden" the penal dragnet and [should] propose a social, health or educational alternative whenever feasible. We must stress that, far from being a solution, police surveillance and imprisonment typically aggravate and amplify the problems they are supposed to resolve'. Third, he argues for links to be forged 'between activists and researchers who work on the penal front and those who battle on the social front, and this *on the European level* so as to optimize the intellectual and practical resources to be invested in this struggle'. For him, '... the true alternative to the drift towards the penalization of poverty, soft or hard, is the construction of a European social state worthy of the name. The best means of making the prison recede is, again and always, to strengthen and expand social and economic rights' (2001: 86, emphasis in the original).

Abolitionists would concur with these arguments. Internationally, the forging of social and political links between different anti-prison groups, and other new social movements, has become a significant dimension in contemporary abolitionist praxis. In America, the commitment of anti-prison groups such as *Critical Resistance* and *No More Prison* is not to the tribal sloganeering of conventional party politics, or to the tired expediency of the traditional penal reform lobby, but to the new social movements that have emerged around the anti-globalization protests and the war in Iraq (Sudbury, 2004).[9] Specific issues affecting prisoners have also generated new grassroots organizations, including *Families Against Minimum Sentences*, the *Women's Advocacy Ministry* and *Stop Prisoner Rape* (Bosworth, no date). For grassroots organizations, 'the overall message is clear: reducing the prison population and prison spending is the only way to create genuine public safety' (www.criticalresistance.org).

Other developments in America have indicated that the prison's dominance is far from complete. In 2005, the number of states who had rejected mandatory minimum sentences had reached twenty-five as legislators shifted their position towards supporting early release and community programmes (Dean, 2005). Other states had closed prisons altogether (www.criticalresistance.org). These developments have less to do with the conversion of Republicans and Democrats to an abolitionist position on prisons, and have more to do with the fiscal crisis gripping and destabilizing a capitalist economy in which the budget deficit is counted in trillions, rather than millions, or even billions of dollars. Nonetheless, anti-prison groups have been instrumental in creating a space for more critical debates and policy interventions to emerge.

In England and Wales, visible strategies of contestation have included demonstrations outside prisons in order to draw attention to the often-ignominious deaths of prisoners through focussing on the deleterious impact of vulpine regimes, which have underpinned the decision to take their own lives. These demonstrations have challenged the traditional invisibility of the prison and its 'circumscribed and specific' role as a 'place of memory' within capitalist modernity (Auge, 1995: 78). Instead, public protest has made the prison visible. It has become, however fragmentary, a part of contemporary, collective thought as opposed to existing on the forgotten margins of a culture, which, in the words of Zygmunt Bauman, is built on '*disengagement, discontinuity and forgetting*' (Bauman, 2004: 117, emphasis in the original). One such demonstration took place at Holloway in November 2005 to highlight the death of Karen Fletcher, the fourth death in the prison since April 2004. This was followed by another demonstration at the prison in July 2007 to highlight the death of Marie Cox who was awaiting sentence for trespassing with intent. She was the sixth woman to die in prison since the beginning of the year. This was the twenty-fifth demonstration outside women's prisons since the protests began in April 2004. There were also a number of arrests over the same period.[10]

The demonstrations have been supported by the re-emergence of *Radical Alternatives to Prison* as a campaigning group, with a new name, *No More Prison*. One of the group's first actions was to organize a demonstration outside Styal prison in April 2006 in order to highlight the failure of that particular prison to provide a duty of care to the vulnerable women held there.[11] The group's unambiguous, abolitionist position was espoused in its manifesto:

> Prisons are failed institutions that do not work. They are places of pain and social control and are brutal, abusive and damaging to everyone who is incarcerated in them. Prisons are fundamentally flawed and all attempts to reform them have failed. We are committed to their abolition by:
>
> - Exposing the reality of imprisonment today;
> - Stopping the building of new prisons and the expansion of existing prisons;
> - Highlighting the fact that prisons not only fail prisoners but also have a negative impact on families and friends, victims and survivors and the whole community;
> - Campaigning to close existing prisons;
> - Opposing the criminalization of young people, working class and minority ethnic communities;
> - Promoting radical alternatives to prison that focus on social and community welfare rather than punishment (*No More Prison*, 2006).

The majority of politicians, policy makers, media commentators and, indeed, many of those in the liberal reform lobby itself, will regard the arguments outlined in the preceding section as hopelessly idealistic while constructing abolitionists as no more than '... dinosaurs, unreconstituted hangovers from the profound but doomed schisms of the late 1960s, who are marginal to the "real" intellectual [and political] questions of the 1990s and beyond' (Sim, 1994a: 264). In living in what Russell Jacoby has called 'an anti-utopian age', democratic politics have been reduced to often-infantile political manoeuvring and grim, focus group populism. In this political context, radical suggestions for penal *and* societal change, which stray beyond this narrow political and populist terrain, leave their protagonists open to the charge that they are motivated by a starry-eyed utopianism. However, 'in an age of permanent emergencies' the problem lies *not* with utopianism but with focussing on the present to the point where 'more than ever we have become narrow utilitarians dedicated to fixing, not reinventing the here and now' (Jacoby, 2005: ix). Thus, dichotomizing the discourse of reform with the discourse of utopianism (or, in this case, abolitionism) misses a fundamental point:

> ... the choice we have is not between reasonable proposals and an unreasonable utopianism. Utopian thinking does not undermine or discount real reforms. Indeed, it is almost the opposite; *practical reforms depend on utopian dreaming – or at least utopian thinking drives incremental improvements* (2005: 1, emphasis added).

This is a point that those who are responsible for delivering penal policy, and those who engage in reformist politics, might consider as they contemplate introducing and supporting yet more reforms in their search for the holy grail of penology, the ideally reformed prison. However, like Samuel Beckett's characters in *Waiting for Godot*, the anticipation of those awaiting its appearance is futile. Indeed, the final irony is that it *is* prison reformers who are the idealists, because, unlike abolitionists, their desire for the oxymoron that is the ideally reformed prison is one that will never arrive or will ever be realized.

> I want to end this book with the words of a 58-year-old male prisoner.
>
> As we get older we all get more ailments because that's the way of life, as we get older our bodies start to wear out, things go wrong so we need that extra little bit of medical care ... and irrespective of what people may think, we are still a person, we may be behind the wall, we may be behind bars but we are still people, it will never be altered from that; we will always be people, we may be older people, we may not be, shouldn't be in here, it's probably our own fault we are in here but we are still people and that's the way it will always be and they can't change that.[12]

This account is used here *not* because of a naïve, idealistic belief in the higher, angelic consciousness of the confined, or as an uncaring snub to the victims of conventional crime. Rather, such accounts not only contribute to challenge 'the politics of excommunication' (Foucault, cited in de Folter, 1987: 41) that confronts prisoners but also they subvert their ideological construction as inarticulate, irrational and unfeeling 'outlaws of humanity' (Schmitt, cited in Critchley, 2007: 142), who are qualitatively different from the 'respectable' majority and are therefore beyond redemption. As this book has shown, this orthodoxy has done little either to generate genuine public protection, and a sense of individual safety, despite the unrelenting presence of the prison, or to arrive at a less hypocritical view about the nature and extent of crime and offending behaviour. Indeed, his words suggest that those of us outside the prison's gates should reappraise our attitude towards prisoners (and towards crime more generally) before demanding that *they* – the other – reappraise *themselves* and their attitudes towards their offending behaviour. This reappraisal concerning crime, and indeed the place of the prison itself, would be a small but important step in the process of recognizing the corrosive futility, which has been intrinsic to the system of punishment as it has developed over the last two centuries and may help to contribute to its eventual demise before another two centuries have passed.

Notes

1 Foucault made this point in 1981.
2 The phrase 'philosophizing disgrace' is a variation on the term 'philosophize disgrace' and is taken from Bob Dylan's song, *The Lonesome Death of Hattie Carroll*. Prison reform groups have also been keen to stay on the inside track politically in terms of the support they enlist from 'the great and the good'. Thus, the former Conservative Home Secretary Douglas Hurd became Chair of the *Prison Reform Trust* in November 1997 and was succeeded in September 2001 by Sir Robert Fellowes, the former Private Secretary to the Queen. It is also worth noting that the liberal reform lobby is big business. In 2004–5, the Howard League for Penal Reform showed a surplus of £499,151 for the year while its accumulated surplus was £1,186,359. The *Prison Reform Trust* had a surplus of £191,942 for the year and an accumulated surplus of £562,366. Thanks to John Moore for providing me with these figures, which are taken from The Charity Commission overview of the organizations' annual accounts.
3 In an interview with *Ideology and Consciousness* in 1981, he also discussed 'the processes of "carceralisation" of practices of penal justice (that is, the movement by which imprisonment as a form of punishment and technique of correction becomes a central component of the penal order) ...' (Foucault, 1981: 6).
4 Thanks to Roy Coleman for pointing this article out to me.
5 This point was made in a discussion I had with a prison worker in 2007 with respect to the work of INQUEST.
6 I have taken this idea from Amy Myrick who discusses it in Myrick (2004).
7 The fact that those who had been victims of serious miscarriages of justice, were being asked to pay 25 per cent of their compensation back to the state, because they did not have any living expenses when in prison, only serves to emphasize the narrow terrain on which victimhood was, and is, defined. Furthermore, even on their own terms, the official concern with the needs of crime victims is problematic in that successive governments have been reluctant (it could

be argued, hypocritically reluctant) to fund services for them. Thus, compensation for this group constituted only 1 per cent of expenditure on criminal justice in 2004–5 (Solomon et al., 2007).

8 There was a 39 per cent increase in racially aggravated offences reported to the police in England and Wales between 2003 and 2007. The number of such offences recorded by the police rose from 31,436 to 43,780 during this period (*The Observer*, 27 April 2008).

9 Similar grassroots organizations have emerged in Australia. The 'primary focus' of *Sisters Inside*, for example, 'is the abolition of women's prisons. This value underlies *all* actions of the organization'. To this end, the group has pursued 'two areas of activity; first, legal reform, and second, service provision'. There is close collaboration with women prisoners themselves so that the organization is 'directed by the needs of the women and not the needs of the criminal injustice system' (Kilroy, 2005: 291–292, emphasis added).

10 Pauline Campbell, whose daughter had died in custody at Styal, was involved in organizing 28 peaceful demonstrations. She was arrested at fifteen of the demonstrations and charged five times with public order offences. However, she was never convicted. She was found dead near her daughter's grave in May 2008, providing another poignant example of the collateral damage which deaths in custody engender.

11 A key difference between *Radical Alternatives to Prison* in its earlier manifestation, and its twenty-first century equivalent, is that the group, like many other grassroots organizations, utilizes new technology to disseminate information on its political and strategic position, to organize demonstrations and meetings and to offer a forum for discussion and debate. See www.alternatives2prison.ik.com

12 This quote is taken from interviews I conducted in 1999 as part of a research project, which was funded by the Nuffield Foundation.

BIBLIOGRAPHY

Aitken, I. (1987) 'The little grey cells of a Tory's prison mentality', in *The Guardian*, 2 March: 19.
Aitken, I. (1989) 'Humiliation in the House for Mr Hurd', in *The Guardian*, 13 February: 19.
Ali, T. (2005) *Rough Music*. London: Verso.
Allison, E. (2004) 'Opinion', in *The Guardian*, 22 September: 5.
Allison, E. (2008) 'The head of the prison service must go', in *Society Guardian*, 9 April: 4.
Anderson, D. (2005) *Histories of the Hanged*. London: Weidenfeld and Nicolson.
Anderson, P. and Mann, N. (1997) *Safety First: The Making of New Labour*. London: Granta.
Andrews, K. and Jacobs, J. (1990) *Punishing the Poor*. London: Macmillan.
Ashley, J. (2006) 'The multicultural menace, anti-semitism and me', in *The Guardian*, 16 June: 6–9.
Auge, M. (1995) *Non-places*. London: Verso.
Baker, K. (1993) *The Turbulent Years*. London: Faber and Faber.
Ball, S. and Seldon, A. (1996) *The Heath Government 1970–1974*. Harlow: Longman.
Ballantyne, E. (1985) 'Mr Brittan's short term problem', in *The Guardian*, 6 June: 19.
Ballinger, A. (2000) *Dead Woman Walking*. Aldershot: Ashgate.
Bauman, Z. (1989) *Modernity and the Holocaust*. Cambridge: Polity.
Bauman, Z. (2002) *Society Under Siege*. Cambridge: Polity.
Bauman, Z. (2004) *Wasted Lives*. Cambridge: Polity.
Beckett, F. (2006) 'Managing chaos', in *New Statesman*, 7 August: 49.
Bennett, C. (1998) 'Hurd mentality', in *The Guardian*, 3 October: 21.
Bennett, T. (1986) 'Popular Culture and "the turn to Gramsci"' in Bennett, T., Mercer, C. and Woollacott, J. (eds) *Popular Culture and Social Relations*. Milton Keynes: Open University Press.
Bennett, J. (2007) 'Did things only get better? A Decade of Prisons under Tony Blair and New Labour', in *Prison Service Journal*, 171, May: 3–12.
Berlins, M. (2006) 'A not very happy new years for freedom and the rule of law', in *The Guardian*, 2 January: 12.
Blair, T. (2004a) A New Consensus on Law and Order. Speech, 19 July 2004. Downloaded 24 July 2004 from www.labour.org.uk/news/thecrimespeech
Blair, T. (2004b) PM's speech on crime reduction, 30 March 2004. Downloaded 28 April 2004 from www.number-10.gov.uk/output/Page5603.asp
Blair, T. (2006a) Prime minister's speech on criminal justice reform, 23 June 2006. Downloaded 26 June 2006 from http://society.guardian.co.uk/crimeandpunishment/story/0,,1804484,00.html
Blair, T. (2006b) 'I don't destroy liberties, I protect them', in *The Observer*, 26 February: 29.
Bogdanor, V. (1996) 'The Fall of Heath and the End of the Post-War Settlement' in Ball, S. and Seldon, A. (eds) *The Heath Government*. London: Longman.
Bosworth, M. (no date) 'Prison Activists: Let's Dismantle the Prison Industrial Complex'. Leaflet.
Box, S. (1983) *Power, Crime and Mystification*. London: Tavistock.
Boyle, J. (1984) *The Pain of Confinement*. Edinburgh: Canongate.

Brittan, L. (1983) Home Secretary's Speech to the Howard League, 26 October. London: The Howard League.

Brown, A. and Clare, E. (2005) 'A History of Experience: Exploring Prisoners' Accounts of Incarceration' in Emsley, C. (ed) *The Persistent Prison: Problems, Images and Alternatives*. London: Francis Boutle.

Brown, D. (2005) 'Continuity, Rupture, or Just More of the "Volatile and Contradictory"? Glimpses of New South Wales' penal practice behind and through the discursive' in Pratt, J., Brown, D., Brown, M., Hallsworth, S. and Morrison, W. (eds) *The New Punitiveness*. Cullompton: Willan.

Brown, G. (2005) 'A plan to lighten the regulatory burden on business', in *Financial Times*, 24 May 2005: 2–3.

Brown, M. (2002) 'The Politics of Penal Excess and the Echo of Colonial Penality', in *Punishment and Society*, 4, 4: 403–423.

Brownlee, I. (1998) 'New Labour – New Penology? Punitive Rhetoric and the Limits of Managerialism in Criminal Justice Policy', in *Journal of Law and Society*, 25, 3: 313–335.

Bruce-Gardyne, J. (1984) *Mrs Thatcher's First Administration*. Basingstoke: Macmillan.

Buonfino, A. and Mulgan, G. (2006) 'Goodbye to all that', in *Society Guardian*, 18 January: 1–2.

Burney, E. (2004) Nuisance or crime? The changing uses of anti-social behaviour control', in *Criminal Justice Matters*, 57: 4–5.

Campbell, D (2006) 'A quick fix is a bad law', in *The Guardian*, 15 June: 31.

Carlen, P. (1990) *Alternatives to Women's Imprisonment*. Milton Keynes: Open University Press.

Carlen, P. (2002) 'Carceral clawback', in *Punishment and Society*, 4, 1: 115–121.

Carlen, P. (2004) 'Imprisonment and the Penal Body Politic: The Cancer of Disciplinary Governance. Paper presented to the Cropwood and Prisons Research Centre Conference, The Effects of Imprisonment: An International Symposium, April 14–15, University of Cambridge.

Carlen, P. (2006) Analysing Women's Imprisonment: Abolition and its Enemies. Paper presented to the Howard League for Penal Reform Conference, 'Time to Make a Difference: the abolition of prison for women', 27 June.

Carlen, P and Tombs, J. (2006) 'Reconfigurations of penality: The on-going case of the women's imprisonment and reintegration industries', in *Theoretical Criminology*, 10, 3: 337–360.

Carrabine, E. (2004) *Power, Discourse and Resistance*. Aldershot: Ashgate.

Cavadino, M. and Dignan, J. (2006) *Penal Systems: A Comparative Approach*. London: Sage.

Cavadino, M., Crow, I. and Dignan, J. (1999) *Criminal Justice 2000*. Winchester: Waterside Press.

Christian Aid (2008) *Death and Taxes: The True Toll of Tax Dodging*. London: Christian Aid.

Clark, T. (2006) 'Blair's legacy still hangs in the balance', in *The Guardian*, 27 September: 4.

Coates, D. (1991) *Running the Country*. London: Hodder and Stoughton.

Coggan, G. (1982) 'Whitelaw's Whitewash', in *The Abolitionist*, 11, 2: 3–8.

Coggan, G. and Walker, M. (1982) *Frightened for My Life*. London: Fontana.

Cohen, A., Cole, G. and Bailey, R. (eds) (1976) *Prison Violence*. New York: Lexington.

Cohen, S. (1971) 'Introduction' in Cohen, S. (ed) *Images of Deviance*. Harmondsworth: Penguin.

Cohen, S. (1979) 'Guilt, Justice and Tolerance' in Downes, D. and Rock, P. (eds) *Deviant Interpretations*. Oxford: Martin Robertson.

Cohen, S. (1982) 'Western Crime Control Models in the Third World', in *Research in Law, Deviance and Social Control*, 4: 85–119.

Cohen, S. (1988) *Against Criminology*. New Brunswick: Transaction Books.

Cohen, S. (2001) *States of Denial*. Cambridge: Polity.

Coleman, R. and Sim, J. (2000) "'You'll Never Walk Alone": CCTV surveillance, order and neo-liberal rule in Liverpool city centre', in *British Journal of Sociology*, 51, 4: 623–639.

Coleman, R. and Sim, J. (2005) 'Contemporary Statecraft and the "Punitive Obsession": A Critique of the New Penology Thesis' in Pratt, J., Brown, D., Brown, M., Hallsworth, S. and Morrison, W. (eds) *The New Punitiveness*. Cullompton: Willan.

Coleman, R., Sim, J., Tombs, S. and Whyte, D. (2009) 'State, Power, Crime' in Coleman, R., Sim, J., Tombs, S. and Whyte, D. (eds) *State Power Crime*. London: Sage.

Collins, H. (1998) *Autobiography of a Murderer*. London: Pan.

Commission for Racial Equality (2003) A Formal Investigation by the Commission for Racial Equality into HM Prison Service of England and Wales. Part 2: Racial Equality in Prisons. London: Commission for Racial Equality.

Conservative Central Office (1979) Index of Questions of Policy Nos 1–156, 21 April 1979. Questions of Policy No 19: 1. London: Conservative Central Office.

Conservative Central Office (1982) Extract from a Speech by the Rt. Hon. William Whitelaw MP. 19 February: 1–2. London: Conservative Central Office.

Conservative Party News Service (1983) Extract from the Speech by the Rt. Hon. Leon Brittan QC, MP to the Conservative Party Conference, 11 October. London: The Conservative Party.

Conservative Party Research Department (1983) Politics Today, No. 22, Law and Order, 19 December 1983. London: Conservative Party Central Office.

Cook, R. (2004) ' No one still thinks we're soft on crime', in *The Guardian*, 19 November 2004: 28.

Cordess, C. (2004) 'Foreword' in Jones, D. (ed.) *Working with Dangerous People*. Abingdon: Radcliffe Medical Press.

Coroner's Court Birmingham (1981) Before Dr. Richard Michael Whittington, H. M. Coroner Sitting Before a Jury Inquest on Barry Dennis Prosser Notes of Evidence.

Corrigan, P. and Sayer, D. (1985) *The Great Arch*. Oxford: Blackwell.

Coyle, A. (2005) *Understanding Prisons: Key Issues in Policy and Practice*. Maidenhead: Open University Press.

Crawford, A. (1998) 'Community Safety and the Quest for Security: Holding Back the Dynamics of Social Exclusion', in *Policy Studies*, 19, 3/4: 237–253.

Crawley, E. (2004) *Doing Prison Work: The Public and Private Lives of Prison Officers*. Cullompton: Willan.

Crick, M. (2005) *In Search of Michael Howard*. London: Pocket Books.

Critchley, S. (2007) *Infinitely Demanding: Ethics of Commitment, Politics of Resistance*. London: Verso.

Davis, A. (2003) *Are Prisons Obsolete?* New York: Seven Stories Press.

Davis, D. (2004) Action on drugs and crime. Speech to the Conservative Party Conference, 6th October. Downloaded 13 October 2004 from http://www.conservatives.com/tile.do?def=news.story.page&obj_id=116410&speeches=1.

Dean, M. (2005) 'Opinion', in *The Guardian*, 22 June 2005.

Dean, M. (2006) 'Labour has taken a wrong turn on crime', in *The Guardian*, 14 June: 4.

de Folter, R. J. (1987) 'On the Methodological Foundation of the Abolitionist Approach to the Criminal Justice System. A Comparison of the Ideas of Foucault, Hulsman and Mathiesen' in Blad, J., Mastrigt, H., and Vildniks, N. (eds) *The Criminal Justice System as a Social Problem: An Abolitionist Perspective*. Rotterdam: Erasmus University.

De Giorgi, A. (2007/8) 'Rethinking the political economy of punishment', in *Criminal Justice Matters*, 70: 17–18.

de Reya, M. (2005) Protecting Corporate Britain from Fraud. Research Report. London: Mischon de Reya.

Denham, A. and Garnett, M. (2001) *Keith Joseph*. Chesham: Acumen.

Desai, R. (1994) 'Second-Hand Dealers in Ideas: Think-Tanks and Thatcherite Hegemony', in *New Left Review*, 203, January/February: 27–64.

Dobson, G. (2007) 'Letter', in *The Guardian*, 7 May 2007.

Downes, D. and Morgan, R. (2002) 'The Skeleton in the Cupboard: The Politics of Law and Order at the turn of the Millennium' in Maguire, M., Morgan, R. and Reiner R. (eds) *The Oxford Handbook of Criminology*, 3rd edition. Oxford: Oxford University Press.
Downes, D. and Hansen, K. (2006) *Welfare and Punishment: The Relationship between Welfare Spending and Imprisonment*. London: Crime and Society Foundation.
Dubber, M. D. (2002) *Victims in the War on Crime*. New York: New York University Press.
Dyer, J. (2000) *The Perpetual Prisoner Machine*. Boulder: Westview Press.
Edgar, K. (2003) 'The Criminal Justice Net Widens' in *Prison Report*, 60: 23–24.
Edney, R. (1997) 'Prison Officers and Violence', in *Alternative Law Journal* 22, 6: 289–297.
Edwards, S. (1989) *Policing Domestic Violence*. London: Sage.
Elliott, L. (2003) 'Third-way addicts need a fix', in *The Guardian*, 14 July: 21.
Elliott, L. and Atkinson, D. (1998) *The Age of Insecurity*. London: Verso.
Elliott, L. and Atkinson, D. (2007a) *Fantasy Island*. London: Constable.
Elliott, L. and Atkinson, D. (2007b) 'Talk is cheap', in *The Guardian*, 18 May: 4–7.
Elkins, C (2005) *Britain's Gulag*. London: Jonathan Cape.
Fairclough, N. (2000) *New Labour, New Language?* London: Routledge.
Faulkner, D. (2001) *Crime, State and Citizen*. Winchester: Waterside Press.
Feeley, M. and Simon, J. (1992) 'The New Penology', in *Criminology*, 30, 4: 452–474.
Field, F. (2004) Eleanor Rathbone and the Politics of Citizenship. Eleanor Rathbone Memorial Lecture, University of Liverpool, 9 December.
Finlayson, A. (2003) *Making Sense of New Labour*. London: Lawrence and Wishart.
Fitzgerald, M. (1977) *Prisoners in Revolt*. Harmondsworth: Penguin.
Fitzgerald, M. and Sim, J. (1980) 'Legitimating the Prison Crisis: A Critical Review of the May Inquiry', in *Howard Journal of Penology*, XIX: 73–84.
Fitzgerald, M. and Sim, J. (1982) *British Prisons, 2nd edition*. Oxford: Blackwell.
Fitzgerald, M. (2006) 'End this bad parent stigma', in *The Guardian*, 5 January: 27.
Fitzpatrick, T. (2003) *After the New Social Democracy*. Manchester: Manchester University Press.
Foucault, M. (1979) *Discipline and Punish*. Harmondsworth: Peregrine.
Foucault, M. (1981) 'Question of method: An Interview with Michel Foucault', in *Ideology and Consciousness*, 8: 3–14.
Foucault, M. (1984/2002) 'Interview with Actes' in Faubion, J. (ed) *Michel Foucault: Essential Works of Foucault 1954–1984, Volume 3*, London: Penguin.
Foucault, M. (1988) 'The Catch-all Strategy', in *International Journal of the Sociology of Law*, 16: 159–162 (translated by Neil Duxbury).
Foucault, M. (2004) *Society Must Be Defended*. London: Penguin (translated by David Macey).
Gamble, A. (1988) *The Free Economy and the Strong State*. Basingstoke: Macmillan.
Garland, D. (2001) *The Culture of Control*. Oxford: Oxford University Press.
Garside, R. (2004) *Crime, Persistent Offenders and the Justice Gap*. London: Crime and Society Foundation.
Gearty, C. (2007) 'The Blair Report', in *Index on Censorship*, 36, 2: 49–55.
Gill, P. (2008) 'Intelligence, Terrorism and the State' in Coleman, R., Sim, J., Tombs, S. and Whyte, D. (eds) *State Power Crime*. London: Sage.
Gilmour, I. (1993) *Dancing With Dogma: Britain Under Thatcherism*. London: Pocket Books.
Gilroy, P. (1987) *There Ain't No Black in the Union Jack*. London: Hutchinson.
Gilroy, P. and Sim, J. (1987) 'Law, Order and the State of the Left' in Scraton, P. (ed) *Law, Order and the Authoritarian State*. Milton Keynes: Open University Press.
Glennerster, H. (2003) *Understanding the Finance of Welfare*. Bristol: The Policy Press.
Goldson, B. and Coles, D. (2005) *In the Care of the State?* London: INQUEST.
Gould, P. (1999) *The Unfinished Revolution*. London: Abacus.
Gray, N., Laing, J. and Noaks, L. (2002) 'Risk: the Professional, the Individual, Society and the Law' in Gray, N., Laing, J. and Noaks, L. (eds) *Criminal Justice, Mental Health and the Politics of Risk*. London: Cavendish.

Gray, J. (2005) 'The people and the political class are at one: neither wants to face the future', in *New Statesman* 9 May: 36–37.

Greater London Council (1985) 'Women and Policing in London', in *Policing London*, 18, June/July: 1–6 (Supplement).

Hague, G. and Wilson, C. (1996) *The Silent Pain: Domestic Violence 1945–1970*. Bristol: The Policy Press.

Halcrow, M. (1989) *Keith Joseph: A Single Mind*. Basingstoke: Macmillan.

Hall, S. (1980) *Drifting into a Law and Order Society*. London: The Cobden Trust.

Hall, S. (1988) *The Hard Road to Renewal*. London: Verso.

Hall, S. (2003) 'New Labour's double-shuffle', in *Soundings* 24: 10–24.

Hall, S., Critcher, C., Jefferson, T., Clarke, J. and Roberts, B. (1978) *Policing the Crisis*. Basingstoke: Macmillan.

Haringey Police Research Unit (no date) Cuttings Bulletin from Haringey Police Research Unit. London: Haringey Police Research Unit.

Harvard Business School, (2001) 'Dirty Money: Raymond Baker Explores the Free Market's Demimonde', in Harvard Business School Bulletin, February 2001, Online (downloaded, 12 December 2005).

Hawthorne, J. (1995) 'The Risley Trial', in Jameson, N. and Allison, E. (1995) *Strangeways 1990 A Serious Disturbance*. Larkin: London.

Health and Safety Commission (2006) *Health and Safety Statistics 2005/06*. London: Health and Safety Executive/Statistical Office.

Her Majesty's Chief Inspector of Prisons for England and Wales (2004) *HM Prison Grendon. Report on a Full Announced Visit 1–5 March 2004*. London: Home Office.

Her Majesty's Inspectorate of Prisons for Scotland (1993) *Report on HM Special Unit Barlinnie*. Edinburgh: The Scottish Office.

Hetherington, P. (2004) 'Opinion Extra', in *The Guardian*, 8 September: 9.

HM Inspectorate of Prisons (2005) *HMP Leeds*. London: Her Majesty's Inspectorate of Prisons.

HM Inspectorate of Prisons (2006a) *HMP and YOI Doncaster*. London: Her Majesty's Inspectorate of Prisons.

HM Inspectorate of Prisons (2006b) *Report on an Unannounced Follow-Up Inspection of HMP Pentonville*. London: Her Majesty's Inspectorate of Prisons.

HM Inspectorate of Prisons (2006c) *HMP Risley*. London: Her Majesty's Inspectorate of Prisons.

HM Inspectorate of Prisons (2006d) *HMP Woodhill*. London: Her Majesty's Inspectorate of Prisons.

HM Inspectorate of Prisons (2007a) *HMP Dovegate*. London: Her Majesty's Inspectorate of Prisons.

HM Inspectorate of Prisons (2007b) *Foreign National Prisoners: A Follow-Up Report*. London: Her Majesty's Inspectorate of Prisons.

HM Inspectorate of Prisons (2007c) *HMP Dovegate Therapeutic Community*. London: Her Majesty's Inspectorate of Prisons.

HM Inspectorate of Prisons (2007d) *HMP Grendon*. London: Her Majesty's Inspectorate of Prisons.

Higham, W. (2006) 'Total recall', in *Prison Report*, 70: 14.

Higham, W. and Holmes, E. (2006) 'Indeterminate sentences', in *Inside Time*, 89, November: 22.

Hillyard, P. (1987) 'The Normalization of Special Powers: From Northern Ireland to Britain' in Scraton, P. (ed) *Law, Order and the Authoritarian State*. Milton Keynes: Open University Press.

Hillyard, P. and Tombs, S. (2004) 'Beyond Criminology?' in Hillyard, P., Pantazis, C., Tombs, S. and Gordon, D. (eds) *Beyond Criminology: Taking Harm Seriously*. London: Pluto.

Hirsch, S. and Lazarus-Black, M. (1994) 'Performance and paradox: Exploring Law's Role in Hegemony and Resistance' in Lazarus-Black, M. and Hirsch, S. (eds) *Contested States: Law, Hegemony and Resistance*. New York: Routledge.
Hitchens, C. (2000) 'A Man of Straw', in *The Guardian*, 28 January: 22.
Home Office (1981) *Report on the Work of the Prison Department 1980*. London: HMSO Cmnd 8543.
Home Office (1983) *Report on the Work of the Prison Department 1982*. London: HMSO Cmnd 9306.
Home Office (1986a) *Home Office Statistical Bulletin No 7/86*. London: Home Office.
Home Office (1986b) *Home Office Statistical Bulletin Issue 17/86*. London: Home Office.
Home Office (1986c) *A Fresh Start. What it Means for You*. London: Central Office of Information.
Home Office (1990) *Tackling Crime*. London: Home Office.
Home Office (2001) *Criminal Justice: The Way Ahead Cm 5074*. London: The Stationery Office.
Home Office (2002) *Probation Statistics England and Wales 2000*. London: Home Office.
Home Office (2003) *Prison Statistics England and Wales 2001*. London: Home Office.
Home Office (2004) Probation Statistics England and Wales 2002. London: Home Office.
Home Office (2005) Prison Population Projections 2005–2011. England and Wales Home Office Statistical Bulletin 01/05. London: The Home Office.
Home Office (2006a) Rebalancing the criminal justice system in favour of the law-abiding majority. Cutting crime, reducing reoffending and protecting the public. London: Home Office.
Home Office (2006b) Offender Management Caseload Statistics 2005. Home Office Statistical Bulletin 18/06. London: Home Office.
Home Office (2007) *The Corston Report*. London: Home Office.
Home Office, Scottish Home and Health Department, Welsh Office and Department of Health and Social Security (1980). The Reduction of Pressure on the Prison System. London: HMSO Cmnd 7948
Hope, T. (2002) What's 'What'; and What Does Works Mean? Paper presented at the British Society of Criminology Conference, University of Keele, July.
Hornqvist, M. (2007/8) 'Prison expansion without a labour market orientation?', in *Criminal Justice Matters*, 70: 19–20.
House of Commons Select Committee on Home Affairs (2000) *Fourth Report Blantyre House*. London: HMSO.
House of Lords, House of Commons (2004) *Deaths in Custody. Third Report of Session 2004–5, Volume 1*. London: The Stationery Office.
The Howard Journal (1982) 'Penal Policy File No. 9', in *The Howard Journal*, Vol. XX1: 179–182.
Hudson, B. (1993) *Penal Policy and Social Justice*. Basingstoke: Macmillan.
Hurd, D. (1986) 'The Government's Prison Strategy' in Prison Reform Trust (ed) *Politics and Prisons: Prison Reform Trust Lectures 1985–86*. London: Prison Reform Trust.
Hurd, D. (1998) 'Jack Straw's Battle on Tiptoe', in *Prison Service Journal*, May: 2–3.
Hurd, D. (2004) *Memoirs*. London: Abacus.
Hutchinson, S. (2006) 'Countering catastrophic criminology: reform, punishment and the modern liberal compromise', in *Punishment and Society* 8, 4: 443–467.
Hyde, M. (2007) 'The perfect monument to Blair's defining manias', in *The Guardian*, 17 March: 32.
Ignatieff, M. (1978) *A Just Measure of Pain*. London: MacMillan.
Independent Defence Lawyers (2006). Memorandum to the House of Commons select Committee on Constitutional Affairs. Unpublished.
INQUEST (1990) *INQUEST Annual Report 1989–1990*. London: INQUEST.
INQUEST (2004) *Submission to the Joint Committee on Human Rights-Inquiry into Deaths in Custody*. London: INQUEST.

Inside Time (2006a) 'In the last ten years...', in *Inside Time*, 83: 1. London: Inside Time.
Inside Time (2006b) *Inside Time*, 82. London: Inside Time.
Inside Time (2006c) '£11 billion a year', in *Inside Time*, 80: 1. London: Inside Time.
Inside Time (2006d) 'Prisoner Survey reveals resettlement failings', in *Inside Time*, 85: 1. London: Inside Time.
Jacoby, R. (2005) *Picture Imperfect*. New York: Columbia University Press.
James, E. (2005) 'A long stretch', in *The Guardian*, 26 October: 16–17.
James, O. (1990) 'Crime and the American Mind', in *The Independent*, May: 21.
Jameson, N. and Allison (1995) *Strangeways 1990. A Serious Disturbance*. Larkin: London.
Jenkins, P. (1984) 'A justice trap behind political bars', in *The Guardian*, 22 February: 19.
Jessop, B. (1990) *State Theory*. Cambridge: Polity.
Jewkes, Y. and Johnston, H. (2006) 'Conclusion: Prisons, Public Opinion and the "New Punitiveness"' in Jewkes, Y. and Johnston. H. (eds) *Prison Readings*. Cullompton: Willan.
Johnson, S. D., Bowers, K. J. and Pease, K. (2005) 'Predicting the Future or Summarising the Past? Crime Mapping as Anticipation' in Smith, M. and Tilley, N. (eds) *Crime Science: New Approaches to Preventing and Detecting Crime*. Cullompton: Willan.
Jones, C. and Novak, T. (1999) *Poverty, Welfare and the Disciplinary State*. London: Routledge.
Jones, D. (2004) 'Murder as an Attempt to Manage Self Disgust' in Jones, D. (ed) *Working with Dangerous People*. Abingdon: Radcliffe Medical Press.
Jones, T. and Newburn, T. (2006) 'Three Strikes and You're Out: Exploring Symbol and Substance in American and British Crime Control Politics', in *British Journal of Criminology* 46: 781–802.
Joseph, K. (1974) 'Britain: A Decadent New Utopia', in *The Guardian*, 21 October: 7.
Joseph, K. (1976) *Stranded on the Middle Ground*. London: Centre for Policy Studies.
Kampfner, J. (2004) *Blair's Wars*. London: The Free Press.
Karstedt, S. and Farrall, S. (2007) *The Law-Abiding Majority? The Everyday Crimes of the Middle Classes*. London: Centre for Crime and Justice Studies Briefing 3.
Kavanagh, D. (1987) *Thatcherism and British Politics*. Oxford: Oxford University Press.
Kilroy, D. (2005) 'Sisters Inside: Speaking Out Against Criminal Injustice' in Sudbury, J. (ed) *Global Lockdown*. London: Routledge.
King, R. and McDermott, K. (1995) *The State of Our Prisons*. Oxford: Clarendon.
Kritzman, L (ed) (1988) *Michel Foucault: Politics, Philosophy, Culture*. London: Routledge.
The Labour Party (1997) *New Labour Because Britain Deserves Better*. London: The Labour Party.
Lansley, S. (2006) 'The tax-free lifestyle of Britain's new mega-wealthy is impoverishing us all', in *The Guardian*, 1 April: 30.
Lawson, N. (2005) 'When will Brown move-or a stalking horse emerge?', in *The Guardian*, 27 October: 33.
Levitas, R. (2005) *The Inclusive Society? Social Exclusion and New Labour, 2nd edition*. Basingstoke: Palgrave.
Lewis, D. (1997) *Hidden Agendas*. London: Hamish Hamilton.
Leys, C. (2005) 'The Cynical State' in Panitch, L. and Leys, C. (eds) *The Socialist Register 2006*. London: Merlin.
Liebling, A. (2004) *Prisons and their Moral Performance*. Oxford: Oxford University Press.
Liebling, A. and Price, D. (2001) *The Prison Officer*. Leyhill: Prison Service Journal.
Loader, I. and Sparks, R. (2004) 'For an Historical Sociology of Crime Policy in England and Wales since 1968', in *Critical Review of International Social and Political Philosophy*, 7, 2: 5–32.
Loader, I. (2006) 'Fall of the "Platonic Guardians": Liberalism, Criminology and Political Responses to Crime in England and Wales', in *British Journal of Criminology* 46, 4: 561–586.
Lyon, J. (2006) 'Editorial', in *Prison Report*, 70, Autumn: 3.
MacDonald, D. and Sim, J. (1978) *Scottish Prisons and the Special Unit*. Glasgow: The Scottish Council for Civil Liberties.

Macey, D. (1993) *The Lives of Michel Foucault*. London: Hutchinson.
MacKenzie, J. (1997) 'Glen Parva Therapeutic Community', in *Prison Service Journal*, May: 26.
Mackie, T. and Marsh, D. (1995) 'The Comparative Method' in Marsh, D. and Stoker, G. (eds) *Theory and Methods in Political Science*. Basingstoke: Macmillan.
Marcuse, H. (1972) *One Dimensional Man*. London: Abacus.
Martinson, R. (1974) 'What Works?—Questions and Answers about Prison Reform', in *The Public Interest*, 35: 22–54.
Marx, G. T. (2005) 'Soft Surveillance: Mandatory Voluntarism and the Collection of Personal Data', in *Dissent*, Fall: 36–43.
Mathiesen, T. (1974) *The Politics of Abolition*. London: Martin Robertson.
Mathiesen, T. (1980) *Law, Society and Political Action*. London: Academic Press.
Mathiesen, T. (1986) 'The politics of abolition', in *Contemporary Crises*, 10: 83–94.
Mathiesen, T. (1990) *Prison on Trial*. London: Sage.
Mathiesen, T. (1997) 'The viewer society: Michel Foucault's panopticon revisited', in *Theoretical Criminology*, 1, 2: 215–234.
Mathiesen, T. (2000) 'Towards the 21st Century: Abolition—An Impossible Dream?' in West, W. Gordon and Morris, R. (eds) *The Case for Penal Abolition*. Toronto: Canadian Scholars' Press Inc.
Matthews, R (2003) 'Rethinking Penal Policy: towards a Systems Approach' in Matthews, R. and Young, J. (eds) *The New Politics of Crime and Punishment*. Cullompton: Willan.
Matthews, R. (2005) 'The myth of punitiveness', in *Theoretical Criminology*, 9, 2: 175–201.
Maurutto, P. and Hannah-Moffat, K. (2006) 'Assembling Risk and the Restructuring of Penal Control', in *British Journal of Criminology*, 46, 2: 438–454.
McElligott, G. (2007) 'Negotiating a Coercive Turn: Work Discipline and Prison reform in Ontario', in *Capital and Class*, 91: 31–53.
McEvoy, K., McConnachie, K. and Jamieson, R. (2007) 'Political Imprisonment and the "War on Terror"' in Jewkes, Y. (ed.) *Handbook on Prisons*. Cullompton: Willan.
McFadyean, M. (2006) 'Centres of barbarism', in *The Guardian*, 2 December: 36.
McGraw, E. (2005) 'Jails close to bursting point', in *Inside Time*, 77, November: 1.
McLaughlin, E. and Muncie, J. (1993) 'The Silent Revolution: Market Based Criminal Justice in England', in *Socio-Legal Bulletin*: 4–12.
McMahon, W. (2006) 'The politics of antisocial behaviour', in *Safer Society*, 28: 2–4.
Medlicott, D. (2001) *Surviving the Prison Place*. Aldershot: Ashgate.
Milne, S. (1995) *The Enemy Within*. London: Pan.
Monbiot, G. (2005) 'They bleat about the free market, then hold out their begging bowls', in *The Guardian*, 13 December 2005: 27.
Moore, S. (2007) 'His legacy? We are a society in pieces', in *New Statesman*, 7 May: 40–43.
Morera, E. (1990) *Gramsci's Historicism: A Realist Approach*. London: Routledge.
Morgan, P. (2005) *The Insider*. London: Ebury.
Morgan, R. (2004) 'Resettlement, the Criminal Justice Act 2003 and NOMS: prospects and problems', in *Criminal Justice Matters*, 56: 4–5.
Morrison, W. (2005) 'Rethinking narratives of Penal Change in Global Context' in Pratt, J., Brown, D., Brown, M., Hallsworth, S. and Morrison, W. (eds) *The New Punitiveness*. Cullompton: Willan.
Morrison, W. (2006) *Criminology, Civilisation and the new World Order*. London: Routledge-Cavendish.
Mortimer, P. (2006) 'Lucy in the sky with diamonds', in *Open Mind*, July/August: 12–13.
Moyer, K. (1976) 'Biological Substrates of Violence' in Cohen, A., Cole, G. and Bailey, R. (eds) *Prison Violence*. New York: Lexington.
Murtagh, T. (2007) *The Blantyre House Prisons Affair: Lessons from a Modern-Day Witch Hunt*. Sherfield-on-Loddon: Waterside Press.
Myrick, A. (2004) 'Escape from the Carceral: Writing by American Prisoners 1895–1916', in *Surveillance and Society* 2, 1: 93–109.

NACRO (1986) *A Bleak Year for the Prison System*. London: NACRO.
NACRO (2006) *Safer Society, 28*. London: NACRO.
Narey, M. (2006) 'Blunkett said he didn't care about lives. Prisoners should be "machine-gunned"', in *The Times*, 17 October: 21.
Nathan, S. (2007) 'Privatisation Factfile 50', in *Prison Report*, 71, Spring: 15–18.
National Association of Probation Officers (2004) Anti Social Behaviour Orders—Analysis of the First Six Years. London: National Association of Probation Officers.
New Law Journal (1983) 'Editorial', in *New Law Journal*, 8 April: 314.
New Statesman (2003) 'Leader: Who are the real yobs?', in *New Statesman*, 20 October: 6–7.
Nichol, D. (2006) Speech by Professor Sir Duncan Nichol—Chairman of the Parole Board, 14 December. London: Centre for Crime and Justice Studies, King's College London.
No More Prison (2006) *Manifesto*. No Place of Publication: No Publisher.
Oborne, P. (2005) *The Rise of Political Lying*. London: The Free Press.
O'Halloran, T. (1995) 'Control and Restraint' in Jameson, N. and Allison, E. (eds) *Strangeways 1990: A Serious Disturbance*. Larkin: London.
Oleson, J. C. (2002) 'The Punitive Coma', in *California Law Review*, 90: 829–901.
O'Malley, P. (1996) Criminology and the New Liberalism. Second Annual Lecture in Honour of the Centre for Criminology, University of Toronto's Founding Director John Ll. J. Edwards, November 13.
O'Neill, R. (2006) 'Total suck up', in *Hazards*, 93, January–March: 6–7.
Open Mind (2005) 'Army of new psychologists and therapists to treat depression', in *Open Mind*, 136, November/December: 5.
Osborne, G. (2006) 'Scientific Experimentation on Canadian Inmates, 1955 to 1975', in *The Howard Journal*, 45, 3: 284–306.
O'Shaughnessy, H. (2000) *Pinochet: The Politics of Torture*. London: Latin America Bureau.
Pallister, D. (2007) 'Account for the cash', in *The Guardian*, 15 March: 38.
Panitch, L. and Leys, C. (2005) 'Preface', in *Socialist Register 2006*. London: Merlin.
Parenti, C. (1999) *Lockdown America*. London: Verso.
Paxton, R. (2006) 'A certain type of character', in *Inside Time*, 90: 19.
Peck, J. (2003) 'Geography and public policy: mapping the penal state', in *Progress in Human Geography*, 27, 2: 222–232.
Pemberton, S. (2004) 'A Theory of Moral Indifference: Understanding the Production of Harm in Capitalist Society' in Hillyard, P., Pantazis, C., Tombs, S. and Gordon, D. (eds) *Beyond Criminology*. London: Pluto.
Pemberton, S. (2005) 'Deaths in Police Custody: The Acceptable Consequences of a "Law and Order" Society?', in *Outlines*, 7, 2: 23–42.
Pilger, J. (1998) No Title, in *New Statesman*, 3 April: 23.
Piven, Frances Fox. (2004) 'The Politics of Policy Science' in Shapiro, I., Smith, R. and Masoud, T. (eds) *Problems and Methods in the Study of Politics*. Cambridge: Cambridge University Press.
Playfair, G. (1971) *The Punitive Obsession*. London: Victor Gollancz.
Police, (1982) 'Over 150,000 citizens respond to Federation call', in *Police*, April: 4.
Pollard, S. (2005) *David Blunkett*. London: Hodder and Stoughton.
Poole, S. (2006a) *Unspeak*. London: Little Brown.
Poole, S. (2006b) 'War of the words', in *The Guardian*, 18 February 2006: 23–24.
Porter, H. (2001) 'Dr Jekyll, Mr Straw', in *The Guardian*, 1 February: 19.
Porter, H. (2006a) 'We don't live in a police state yet, but we're heading there', in *The Observer*, 23 January: 25.
Porter, H. (2006b) 'Only a constitution can save us from this abuse of power', in *The Observer*, 2 April: 23.
Pratt, J. (2000) 'The Return of the Wheelbarrow Men', in *British Journal of Criminology*, 40: 127–145.
Pratt, J., Brown, D., Brown, M., Hallsworth, S., and Morrison, W. (eds) (2005) *The New Punitiveness*. Cullompton: Willan.

Price, L. (2006) 'Rupert Murdoch is effectively a member of Blair's cabinet', in *The Guardian*, 1 July: 32.

Prison Reform Trust (1986) *House of Commons Home Affairs Committee: Inquiry into the State and Use of Prisons; Memorandum by the Prison Reform Trust*. London: Prison Reform Trust.

Prison Reform Trust (1999) 'Privatization Factfile 27', in *Prison Report*, 48: 13–16.

Prison Reform Trust (2003) 'More money, more prisons', in *Prison Report*, 60: 4.

Prison Reform Trust (2006a) *Bromley Briefings Prison Factfile April*. London: Prison Reform Trust.

Prison Reform Trust (2006b) 'Inside Criminal Justice', in *Prison Report*, 69: 4–6.

Prison Reform Trust (2006c) *Bromley Briefings Prison Factfile*. London: Prison Reform Trust.

Prison Reform Trust (2007) *Bromley Briefings Prison Factfile May*. London: Prison Reform Trust.

Prison Review (1999) 'Jack Straw, the Home Secretary', in *Prison Review*, Summer: 3.

Reeves, R. (2005) 'Words matter in politics', in *New Statesman*, 24 January: 29–31.

Richards, S. (1998) 'Interview: Michael Howard', in *New Statesman*, 19 June: 16–17.

Richards, S. (2005) 'Blair has a new role: leader of the people against parts of his party and parliament', in *The Independent*, 11 November: 47.

Riddell, M. (2003) 'And don't do it again, Charles', in *The Observer*, 13 April: 26.

Riddell, M. (2007) 'In this muddy field, teenage lives are being turned round', in *The Observer*, 3 June: 31.

Riddell, P. (1985) *The Thatcher Government*. Oxford: Blackwell.

Ridley, N. (1991) *My Style of Government*. London: Macmillan.

Rigakos, G. and Hadden, R. (2001) 'Crime, capitalism and the "risk society": Towards the same old modernity?', in *Theoretical Criminology*, 5, 1: 61–83.

Roberts, Y. (2006) 'The politics of boredom', in *The Guardian*, 28 July: 32.

Rose, D. (2005) '"At the end of the day, all of us sitting here are monsters, whether we're armed robbers, child molesters, or killers—we're monsters"', in *The Observer Magazine*, 20 November: 20–28.

Rose, D. (2007) 'My sister was killed while the police did nothing', in *The Observer*, 11 March: 10–11.

Rutherford, A. (1982) 'The Home Office is geared up for expansion of the prison population throughout the 1980s', in *The Listener*, 21 October: 2–4.

Rutherford, A. (1992) 'Abolition and the Politics of Bad Conscience' in Duff, A., Marshall, S., Dobash, R.E. and Dobash, R.P. (eds) *Penal Theory and Practice: Tradition and Innovation in Criminal Justice*. Manchester: Manchester University Press.

Ryan, M. (1978) *The Acceptable Pressure Group*. Farnborough: Teakfield.

Ryan, M. (1996) *Lobbying from Below*. London: UCL Press.

Ryan, M. (1999) 'Penal Policy Making Towards the Millennium: Elites and Populists; New Labour and the New Criminology', in *International Journal of the Sociology of Law*, 27: 1–22.

Ryan, M. and Sim, J. (1984) 'Decoding Leon Brittan' *The Abolitionist*, 16: 3–7.

Ryan, M. and Sim, J. (1995) 'The Penal System in England and Wales: Round Up the Usual Suspects' in Ruggiero, V., Ryan, M. and Sim, J. (eds) *Western European Penal Systems*. London: Sage.

Ryan, M. and Sim, J. (1998) 'Power, Punishment and Prisons in England and Wales 1975–1996' in Weiss, R. and South, N. (eds) *Comparing Prison Systems*. Amsterdam: Gordon and Breech.

Ryan, M. and Sim, J. (2007) 'Campaigning For and Campaigning Against Prisons: Excavating and Re-affirming the Case for Prison Abolition' in Jewkes, Y. (ed) *Handbook on Prisons*. Cullompton: Willan.

Ryan, M. and Ward, T. (1989) *Privatisation and the Penal System*. Milton Keynes: Open University Press.

Sandler, M. and Coles D. (2008) *Dying on the Inside: Examining Women's Deaths in Prison*. London: INQUEST.

Scammell, M. (1994) 'The Phenomenon of Political Marketing: The Thatcher Contribution' *Contemporary Record*, 8, 1: 23–43.

Schlesinger, P. and Tumber, H. (1995) *Reporting Crime*. Oxford: Clarendon.

Schoch, R. (2006) 'Do you sincerely want to be happy? Then stop all this pleasure seeking', in *The Independent on Sunday*, 16 April: 34–35.

Scott, D. (2006) Ghosts Beyond Our Realm: A Neo-Abolitionist Analysis of Prisoner Human Rights and Prison Officer Occupational Culture. Unpublished PhD, University of Central Lancashire.

Scott, D. (2007) 'The Changing Face of the English Prison: A Critical Review of the aims of imprisonment' in Jewkes, Y. (ed) *Handbook on Prisons*. Cullompton: Willan.

Scottish Prison Service (1994) *Small Units in the Scottish Prison Service: The Report of the Working Party on the Barlinnie Special Unit*. Edinburgh: Scottish Prison Service.

Scraton, P. (1987) 'Unreasonable Force: Policing, Punishment and Marginalisation' in Scraton, P. (ed) *Law, Order and the Authoritarian State*. Milton Keynes: Open University Press.

Seldon, A. (2004) *Blair*. London: The Free Press.

Shaw, S. (2007) 'Deaths following release from custody', in *On the Case*, 23, November: 1.

Sikka, P. (2006) 'The corporate scams that aid terrorist money launderers', in *The Guardian*, 23 February: 32.

Sim, J. (1982) 'Scarman: The Police Counter Attack' in Eve, M. and Musson, D. (eds) *The Socialist Register*. London: Merlin.

Sim, J. (1983) 'Law and Order', in *Critical Social Policy*, 8: 16–20.

Sim, J. (1986) 'Watching the Prison Wheels Grind: The 1984 Report of Her Majesty's Chief Inspector of Prisons', in *The Abolitionist*, 21: 6–9.

Sim, J. (1987) 'Working for the Clampdown: Prisons and Politics in England and Wales' in Scraton, P. (ed) *Law, Order and the Authoritarian State*. Milton Keynes: Open University Press.

Sim, J. (1990) *Medical Power in Prisons*. Milton Keynes: Open University Press.

Sim, J. (1994a) 'The Abolitionist Approach: A British Perspective' in Duff, A., Marshall, S., Dobash, R. E. and Dobash, R. P. (eds) *Penal Theory and Practice: Tradition and Innovation in Criminal Justice*. Manchester: Manchester University Press.

Sim, J. (1994b) 'Reforming the Penal Wasteland? A Critical Review of the Woolf Report' in Jenkins, M. and Player, E. (eds) *Prisons After Woolf*. London: Routledge.

Sim, J. (1994c) 'Tougher than the Rest? Men in Prison' in Newburn, T. and Stanko, E. (eds) *Just Boys Doing Business?* London: Routledge.

Sim, J. (1995) Anaesthetizing Criminological Dissent: Power, Reform and Research in the 1990s. Paper presented to the conference on The Social and Political Aspects of Crime and the Reform of the Criminal Justice System, University of Edinburgh, May.

Sim, J. (2000a) 'Against the Punitive Wind: Stuart Hall, the State and the Lessons of the Great Moving Right Show' in Gilroy, P., Grossberg, L. and McRobbie, A. (eds) *Without Guarantees: In Honour of Stuart Hall*. London: Verso.

Sim, J. (2000b) '"One Thousand Days of Degradation": New Labour and Old Compromises at the Turn of the Century', in *Social Justice*, 27, 2: 168–192.

Sim, J. (2000c) 'Confronting the "Vileness of the Reptile, Bourgeois, Newspaper Hacks"': Media Interventions and Critical Academics. Paper presented at the Conference of the European Group for the Study of Deviance and Social Control (British Section), University of Bangor, April.

Sim, J. (2002) 'The Future of Prison Health Care: A Critical Analysis', in *Critical Social Policy*, 22, 2: 300–323.

Sim, J. (2004a) 'Thinking About Imprisonment' in Muncie, J. and Wilson, D. (eds) *Student Handbook of Criminal Justice and Criminology*. London: Cavendish.

Sim, J. (2004b) 'The Victimised State and the Mystification of Social Harm' in Hillyard, P., Pantazis, C., Tombs, S. and Gordon, D. (eds) *Beyond Criminology*. London: Pluto.

Sim, J. (2004c) 'Militarism, Criminal Justice and the Hybrid Prison in England and Wales: A Response to Julia Sudbury', in *Social Justice* 31, 1–2: 39–50.
Sim J. (2005) 'At the Centre of the New Professional Gaze: Women, Medicine and Confinement' in Chan, W., Chunn, D. E. and Menzies, R. (eds) *Women, Madness and the Law*. London: GlassHouse Press.
Sim, J. (2006a) 'Abolitionism' in McLaughlin, E. and Muncie, J. (eds) *The Sage Dictionary of Criminology, 2nd edition*. London: Sage.
Sim, J. (2006b) 'Protecting who from what?' in Garside, R. and McMahon, W. (eds) *Does Criminal Justice Work?* London: Crime and Society Foundation.
Sim, J. (2008a) '"An Inconvenient Criminological Truth": Pain, Punishment and Prison Officers' in Bennett, J., Crewe, B. and Wahidin, A. (eds) *Prison Staff*. Cullompton: Willan.
Sim, J. (2008b) 'Pain and Punishment: The Real and the Imaginary in Penal Institutions' in Carlen, P. (ed) *Imaginary Penalties*. Cullompton: Willan.
Sim, J. and Thomas, P. (1983) 'The Prevention of Terrorism Act: Normalising the Politics of Repression', in *Journal of Law and Society*, 10, 1: 71–84.
Sim, J., Scraton, P. and Gordon, P. (1987) 'Introduction: Crime, the State and Critical Analysis' in Scraton, P. (ed) *Law, Order and the Authoritarian State*. Milton Keynes: Open University Press.
Simon, J. (2007) *Governing through Crime*. Oxford: Oxford University Press.
Smart Justice (2006) *Crime Victims Say Jail Doesn't Work*. London: Smart Justice.
Smith, R. (2004) *A Few Kind Words and a Loaded Gun*. London: Viking.
Solomon, E. (2006) 'History repeating itself', in *Inside Time*, 89, November: 18.
Solomon, E. (2007a) 'Casting a wider net', in *Inside Time*, January: 15.
Solomon, E. (2007b) 'Fragile progress', in *Inside Time*, March: 22.
Solomon, E., Eades, C., Garside, R. and Rutherford, M. (2007) *Ten Years of Criminal Justice Under Labour An Independent Audit*. London: Centre for Crime and Justice Studies.
Soothill, K. (2005) 'Capturing Criminology' in Peelo, M. and Soothill, K. (eds) *Questioning Crime and Criminology*. Cullompton: Willan.
Sparks, R. (1996) 'Penal "Austerity": The Doctrine of Less Eligibility Reborn?' in Matthews, R. and Francis, P. (eds) *Prisons 2000*. Basingstoke: Macmillan.
Spensky, M. (1992) 'Producers of Legitimacy: Homes for Unmarried Mothers in the 1950s' in Smart, C. (ed) *Regulating Womanhood*. London: Routledge.
Stanko, E. (1985) *Intimate Intrusions*. London: Unwin Hyman.
State Research (1982) 'Crisis in the prisons', in *State Research* 5, 29: 100–103.
Statewatch (2000) 'Bill to Introduce Far-Reaching Surveillance', in *Statewatch*, 10, 1: 25–27.
Steele, J. (2002) *The Bird That Never Flew*. Mainstream: Edinburgh.
Sudbury, J. (2004) 'A World without Prisons: Resisting Militarism, Globalized Punishment and Empire', in *Social Justice*, 31, 1–2: 9–30.
Sumner, C. (1982) 'Crime, Justice and Underdevelopment: Beyond Modernisation Theory' in Sumner, C. (ed) *Crime, Justice and Underdevelopment*. London: Heinemann.
Sutton, J. (2004) 'The Political Economy of Imprisonment in Affluent Western Democracies, 1960–1990', in *American Sociological Review*, 69, 2: 170–189.
Tax Justice Network (2005) Briefing Paper: The Price of Offshore. No Place of Publication: Tax Justice Network/UK.
Tebbit, N. (2006) 'You ask the questions…', in *The Independent*, 7 August: 24–25.
Tetlock, P. (2005) *Expert Political Judgment*. Princeton: Princeton University Press.
Thatcher, M. (1977) *Let Our Children Grow Tall*. London: Centre for Policy Studies.
Thatcher, M. (1978) Beware of Labour's Trap. Text of a Speech by the Right Honourable Margaret Thatcher MP. Address to the Conservative Local Government Conference, 4 February. London: Conservative Party Central Office.
Thatcher, M. (1993) *The Downing Street Years*. New York: Harper Collins.
Thatcher, M. (1995) *The Path to Power*. New York: Harper Collins.

Tolmaer, I. (2006) 'Prison officers—keepers or carers?', in *Inside Time*, 79: 3.
Tombs, J. (2003) 'Justify Prison not the Alternatives', in *Prison Report*, 60: 8–9.
Tombs, S. and Whyte, D. (eds) (2003) *Unmasking the Crimes of the Powerful*. New York: Peter Lang.
Tombs, S. and Whyte, D. (2007) *Safety Crimes*. Cullompton: Willan.
Tombs, S. and Whyte, D. (2008) *A Crisis of Enforcement: The Decriminalisation of Death and Injury at Work*. London: Centre for Crime and Justice Studies.
Tory Reform Group (1983) *Imprisonment in the 80's*. London: Tory Reform Group.
Towl, G. (2002) 'Psychological services in HM Prison Service and the National Probation Service: working towards an effective partnership', in *The British Journal of Forensic Practice*, 4, 3: 3–10.
Toynbee, P. (1999) 'Straw shakes his iron fist at prison reform', in *The Guardian*, 23 June: 16.
Toynbee, P. (2005) 'How could Cherie Blair do this without blushing?', in *The Guardian*, 8 June: 24.
Toynbee, P. (2006a) 'Emoting over hoodies is no substitute for a policy', in *The Guardian*, 11 July: 27.
Toynbee, P. (2006b) 'The Byers plan deliberately ignores obscene inequality', in *The Guardian*, 22 August: 27.
Toynbee, P. and Walker, D. (2001) *Did Things Get Better? An Audit of Labour's Successes and Failures*. Harmondsworth: Penguin.
Vagg, J. (1994) *Prison Systems: A Comparative Study of Accountability in England, France, Germany and the Netherlands*. Oxford: Clarendon.
van Swaaningen, R. (1997) *Critical Criminology: Visions from Europe*. London: Sage.
Wacquant, L. (1999) 'How Penal Common Sense Comes to Europeans: Notes on the transatlantic diffusion of the neoliberal state', in *European Societies*, 1, 3: 319–352.
Wacquant, L. (2001) 'The Advent of the Penal State is Not a Destiny', in *Social Justice*, 28, 3: 81–87.
Wacquant, L. (2005) 'The "Scholarly Myths" of the New Law and Order Doxa' in Panitch, L. and Leys, C. (eds) *The Socialist Register 2006*. London: Merlin.
Wall, T. (2004) 'Police state UK', in *New Statesman*, 22 November: 12–13.
Walters, R. (2003) *Deviant Knowledge*. Cullompton: Willan.
Warren, D. (1982) *The Key to My Cell*. London: New Park Publications.
Warrington, M. (2000) "I Must Get Out": The Geographies of Domestic Violence. Paper presented at the RGS-IBG Annual Conference 2000, University of Sussex.
Wheen, F. (2000) 'The Coward's Way Out', in *The Guardian*, January 19: 5.
Wheen, F. (2004) How Mumbo Jumbo Conquered the World London: Fourth Estate.
Whitelaw, W. (1989) *The Whitelaw Memoirs*. London: Aurum Press.
Whyte, D. (2007/8) 'Gordon Brown's Charter for Corporate Criminals', in *Criminal Justice Matters*, 70: 31–2.
Wilcox, P. (2006) 'Communities, care and domestic violence', in *Critical Social Policy*, 89: 722–747.
Williams, H. (2006) *Britain's Power Elites*. London: Constable.
Williams, R. (2007) Criminal Justice-Building Responsibility – The Prison Reform Trust Annual Lecture, available on www.prisonreformtrust.org.uk/subsectionasp?id=758, downloaded 30 March 2007.
Wilson, D. (2006) 'The prison trick', in *The Guardian*, 17 June: 25–26.
Women's Resource Centre (2006) *The Crisis in Rape Crisis*. London: Women's Resource Centre.
Woolf, Lord Justice (1991) Prison Disturbances, April 1990. London: HMSO, Cm. 1456.
Woolf, Lord Justice (2007) Oral Evidence to the Home Affairs Committee on Towards Effective Sentencing, Uncorrected Transcript, 17 April 2007 (downloaded 8 May 2007).

Worsthorne, P. (1971) *The Socialist Myth*. London: Cassell.

Wrong, M. (2006) No title, in *New Statesman*, 17 April: 27.

Wyatt, W. (1998) *The Journals of Woodrow Wyatt, Volume One*. Basingstoke: Macmillan.

Young, H. (1985) 'The ill-gotten gains from law and disorder', in *The Guardian*, 5 November: 19.

Young, H. (1989) *One of Us*. Basingstoke: Macmillan.

Young, H. (2000) 'The strange fruits of a thousand days in office', in *The Guardian*, 27 January: 20.

Young, H. (2004) *Supping with the Devils*. London: Atlantic.

Young, J. (1981) 'Thinking seriously about crime: some models of criminology', in Fitzgerald, M., McLennan, G. and Pawson, J. (compilers) *Crime and Society*. London: Routledge.

Zedner, L. (2002) 'Dangers of Dystopia in Penal Theory', in *Oxford Journal of Legal Studies*, 22, 2: 341–366.

WEBSITES

www.criticalresistance.org (downloaded, 29 July 2005)

www.theherald.co.uk/news (downloaded, 9 January 2006)

http://www.labour.org.uk (downloaded, 10 January 2006)

http://www.tuc.org/h_and_s (downloaded by Steve Tombs, 28 February 2006)

http:news.bbc.co.uk/1/hi/Scotland/Glasgow_and_west/5060956.stm (downloaded, 8 June 2006)

http://news.bbc.co.uk/1/hi/uk_politics/5091720.stm (downloaded, 19 June 2006)

www.corporateaccountability.org (downloaded 27 July 2006)

www.number-10.gov.uk/output/Page10023.asp. (downloaded 2 April 2007)

www.napo2.org.uk 'Fourfold increase in recalls to prison' (downloaded 4 April 2007).

http://news.bbc.co.uk/1/hi/uk/6528425.stm (downloaded 5 April 2007).

http://news.bbc.co.uk/1/hi/england/6524495.stm (downloaded 5 April 2007).

www.dailymail.co.uk/pages/live/articles/news/newscomment.html?in_article_id (downloaded 6 April 2007).

www.medicaljustice.org.uk (downloaded 17 August 2007).

www.alternatives2prison.ik.com

TELEVISION PROGRAMMES

'When Did You Last Beat Your Wife?' Dispatches, Channel 4, broadcast 19 March 2007.

INDEX